Jean Rhys
THE WEST INDIAN NOVELS

Jean Rhys
THE WEST INDIAN NOVELS

TERESA F. O'CONNOR

NEW YORK UNIVERSITY PRESS
NEW YORK AND LONDON

LIBRARY OF CONGRESS CATALOGING-IN-PUBLICATION DATA

O'Connor, Teresa F., 1943–
Jean Rhys: the West Indian novels.
Bibliography: p.
Includes index.
1. Rhys, Jean. 2. West Indies in literature. 3. Rhys,
Jean. Voyage in the dark. 4. Rhys, Jean. Wide Sargasso
Sea. 5. Novelists, English—20th century—Biography.
I. Title.
PR6035.H96Z83 1986 823'.912 86–8542
ISBN 0–8147–6164–X

Book design by Ken Venezio

To my parents,
James P. O'Connor and
Gladys Kersey O'Connor
and in memory of my brothers,
Jimmy and Jack.

Contents

Acknowledgments

There are so many people without whose help I could not have completed this work.

Josephine Hendin's readings of this book, at all stages of its preparation, taught me more than I could ever say here. Her suggestions and insights, her kind criticism and encouragement were invaluable to me.

Early in this study M. L. Rosenthal supported my work on Jean Rhys who was, at that time, virtually unknown in the United States. He was helpful in suggesting approaches and for supporting me in my belief in the value of such a study.

Jean Rhys's friends and colleagues answered my queries and letters with an openness and a goodwill that made the research on this book a continuing pleasure. I am particularly grateful to Diana Athill for her permission to quote from her letters which contain so many insightful comments about Jean Rhys and her work. David Plante generously answered my questions and suggested avenues that I had not considered. To Francis Wyndham I am indebted for his permission to photocopy manuscripts in the McFarlin Library at the University of Tulsa as well as permission to quote from Jean Rhys's Black Exercise Book and a letter of his to me.

I could not have completed this study in its present form without the unusually generous help of the staff of the McFarlin Library at the University of Tulsa and for permission to quote from their manuscripts in the Jean Rhys Collection. In particular Caroline Swinson, Curator of Art and Literary Manuscripts, continued to provide assistance and insights that made me feel reluctant to end this work. I cannot thank her enough.

I am also grateful to André Deutsch for permission to quote from "The Day They Burned the Books" in *Tigers Are Better Looking,* published in the United States by W. W. Norton; to David Higham Associates for permission to quote from Stella Bowen's *Drawn from Life*; to Wallace and Sheil Agency as agents for the Estate of Jean Rhys for their kind permission to quote from *Voyage in the Dark, Wide Sargasso Sea* and "Overtures and Beginners" in *Sleep It Off, Lady*.

Other scholars of Jean Rhys have been as kind and generous as her friends. In particular, Martien Kappers den-Hollander has shared with me her own work and answered what must at times have been tedious queries. To Paul Delaney I am thankful for lending his copy of *Barred* to a stranger and for sharing his unpublished work.

Of course I could not have worked without the help of my friends and colleagues who continued to give me sound advice, good counsel, encouragement and so many acts of personal kindness, especially Bill Bernhardt, David Falk, Joan Hartman, Stephen Khinoy, Melvin Maiman, Maureen McHugh, Rose Ortiz, and Judith Stelboum.

For help in understanding my own intentions about this study, and for encouragement when it was most needed, I am continually thankful to Magda Denes and Lenora DeSio. I do not think I could have written it without them.

For critical readings of the final manuscripts I am particularly grateful to the generosity of Bhaskar Menon and Charles Riley and, for suggestions at earlier stages of its preparation, Carol Flynn, Joan Hartman and Ilsa Lind.

The University of Texas at Austin kindly provided me with photocopies of Jean Rhys's letters to Evelyn Scott and happily, the College of Staten Island of the City University of New York, through a Fellowship Leave, allowed me the time to complete this work.

To my husband, Hirotsugu Aoki and my son Owen, my thanks for more than I can say here. To Masako Kuzutani, my appreciation for being such a good friend to us and for being there when we needed her.

And to Jean Rhys herself, I owe much. She was generous and helpful to me when I first began this study.

Jean Rhys
THE WEST INDIAN NOVELS

Introduction

In her early twenties, Jean Rhys, living alone in England and far from her West Indian home, began a journal in which she wrote of a recent and devastating love affair. She wrote obsessively until she completed her account and then packed her notebooks away for almost two decades. That journal eventually became the basis for her third published novel, *Voyage in the Dark* (1934).

Between 1924 and 1939, Rhys wrote and published three other novels, the genesis of each bearing a relation to that of *Voyage in the Dark*—the necessary outpouring of autobiographical pain relieved only by the act of writing. That Rhys was also a painstaking editor and reworked her compositions endlessly is a well-known fact. But the impulse for her writing, she always claimed to be the exorcism of unhappiness. In a private and unpublished exercise book Rhys, recalling her childhood and the intense moments of feeling she experienced, writes:

It was so intolerable this longing this sadness I got from the shapes of the mountains, the sound of the rain the moment just after sunset that one day I spoke of it to my mother and she at once gave me a large dose of castor oil.

One day I discovered however that I could work off the worst of it by writing poems and was happier.[1]

This brief entry indicates Rhys's literary preoccupations: the very direct connection of place to feeling, the impossibility of expressing that feeling otherwise than in writing and the mixture of sadness and pain caused by the perception and experience even of beauty. That original impulse toward expression for Rhys, even in her last novel, remained rooted in the West Indies in which she was born and spent her youth, specifically the island of Dominica. That the West Indies always posed a problem in understanding for Rhys, that they remained an enigmatic and tainted

Paradise, is also clear in the conclusion to her journal entry. She says: "There is an atmosphere of pain and violence about the West Indies. Perhaps it wasn't astonishing that I was tuned in to it." (fol. 14) While England later became the embodiment of hell for Rhys, unlike Dante's Paolo, who says there is no greater pain than to recall a happy time in the midst of misery, her memories of the past in the West Indies and her compulsive summoning up of them, both in her private and published writing, provided a mixed blessing: the pain that Paolo alludes to, mixed with the pleasure of escaping the present time and place.

Place is what informs Rhys's novels and what distinguishes them each from the other. In her writing, place is most concretely represented by three countries: Dominica, England and France—the first representing an Eden-like state of grace, at least on first recollection, the second a cold and neurasthenic hell, and the third a limbo capable of at least providing distraction from the self.

Though Rhys's early novels were well received and published both in England and America, after 1939 she did not write or publish another book until 1966, when her last novel, *Wide Sargasso Sea,* an invention of a biography (an autobiography really) of Rochester's mad West Indian wife in *Jane Eyre,* appeared. In that book Rhys draws again from the facts and experiences of her own life and weaves them into a fabric that also draws on the fictional autobiography of Jane Eyre.

Until the publication of *Wide Sargasso Sea,* Rhys's novels and her first book of short stories, *The Left Bank* (1927) were long out of print, although a small group of admirers continued to read and praise her carefully crafted and spare prose. Many thought her dead. Had it not been for the diligent search for her by the British actress Selma Vaz Dias, who wanted to adapt the 1939 novel, *Good Morning, Midnight* for a radio play, Rhys might never have written her last novel. *Wide Sargasso Sea* won the W. H. Smith Literary Prize upon its publication and brought Rhys much-delayed fame at the age of 76.

In writing *Wide Sargasso Sea,* almost half a century after the initial composition of *Voyage in the Dark,* Jean Rhys returned again to the themes and concerns of her first writing: the relationship between colonial and colonizer, black and white, child and parent, woman and man and, weaving them together, the very intricate connections they have in her work to sex and to money. Underlying all of Rhys's fiction, sustained in its tone and its atmosphere, is a pervasive note of loss and of death coupled to a paralysis of the spirit that makes action impossible. In *Voyage in the Dark* and *Wide Sargasso Sea,* Rhys explores the sources and causes of that dread and of that inertia.

While *Voyage in the Dark* was Rhys's fourth novel published, its position in terms of her development as a writer—the establishment of major themes and concerns, the "recording" of her own life and its transmutation into literature, even the decision to consider herself a writer at all—is closer to that of a first novel.

The novels that lie between the composition of *Voyage in the Dark* and *Wide Sargasso Sea,* what I term her Continental novels, are most concerned with the peripatetic life of heroines who seem variants of the same woman as she ages. Her personality, her obsessions and frailties, even much of her history remain constant. Rhys's first published novel, *Quartet* (1928), about the young Marya Zelli, is virtually a roman à clef: already living in France, Rhys wrote of the breakup of her first marriage following her affair with Ford Madox Ford after her husband was imprisoned by the French authorities. Rhys's second novel, *After Leaving Mr. Mac-Kenzie* (1930) follows Julia Martin as she moves, bereft of family, friends and lovers, between Paris and London. Her fourth novel, *Good Morning, Midnight* (1939)—like its predecessor *Voyage in the Dark,* a first-person narration—examines the life of Sasha Jansen, a woman similar to Marya Zelli and Julia Martin who, now older, attempts to hold on to her sanity and a sense of worth and power as she haunts the places of Paris she knew in her youth.

Rhys's Continental novels have much in common with the West Indian ones: the passive and masochistic heroine without home, mother or apparent center, the sparseness of the prose, and the bleakness of the emotional landscape. The themes and concerns treated in the West Indian novels are present too, though at times submerged and subterranean. But in her first and last compositions, Rhys seeks a center for her heroines, a center that is clearly attached to Rhys's own literal home in the West Indies, the island of Dominica.

Jean Rhys is an intensely personal writer. More directly than most, she has used her own emotional and biographical history as the source and stuff of her writing. She has said: "There's very little invention in my books,"[2] and "I don't know other people. I never have known other people. I have only ever written about myself."[3] She wrote about what she knew best, her own life. That Rhys apparently had little curiosity about others, including the lives and histories of her three husbands, is a fact she often acknowledged. The lives both of Rhys and her self-reflecting heroines turn forever inward, revolving about a center and source that is connected to her being a woman and a colonial; in Rhys, the two ultimately become synonymous.

That Rhys used her self as the model for all her heroines, and her own experiences as the basis of the material for their lives, many critics have noted. None, however, has examined in detail the very intricate relationship between her life and her work and the way in which her private and unpublished journals became a constant source for her fiction. Indeed, parts of *Voyage in the Dark, Good Morning, Midnight* and *Wide Sargasso Sea,* as well as her more public autobiography, *Smile Please,* and several short stories ("Goodbye Marcus, Goodbye Rose;" "The Day They Burned the Books") appear verbatim in an exercise book of hers, henceforth referred to as the Black Exercise Book, in the Jean Rhys Collection of the McFarlin Library at the University of Tulsa.[4]

In the Black Exercise Book, Rhys writes at length about her early life in Dominica and describes episodes between her and her mother, father and other members of the household, most notably her despised nurse Meta. Rhys also describes in detail, though the handwriting degenerates enough to act as a mask to the material, a highly disturbing psycho-sexual involvement with an elderly British gentleman, Mr. Howard, who visited Dominica with his wife. The need to write about this episode, an episode which she believed was essential in the formation of her character, is one of the reasons she wrote in the book at all. The episode is scarcely fictionalized in the short story "Goodbye Marcus, Goodbye Rose."[5]

The Black Exercise Book was sold to Tulsa by Rhys in 1976, along with what remaining papers and manuscripts she still possessed. The book is most difficult to follow. For the most part Rhys kept the journal in pencil and apparently often wrote in it while she was drunk. Most of the inclusions are fragmentary, almost incoherent and with virtually no punctuation; it is not quite clear at times whether certain inclusions are notes for fiction or whether Rhys was writing about fact—in some cases probably a combination of the two.[6]

Although Jean Rhys was an autobiographical writer, she was strongly aware of the process by which she turned autobiography into fiction, a problem she struggled with in reverse in her old age as she tried to write her autobiography. In the interview in the *Paris Review* in 1979, she discussed the relationship between life and literature: "The things you remember have no form. When you write about them, you have to give them a beginning, a middle, and an end. To give life shape—that is what a writer does. That is what is so difficult." (p. 225) In that same interview, Rhys tried to explain the problems in writing her autobiography, in trying *not* to write fiction. She said:

Reality is what I remember. You can push onto reality what you feel. Just as I felt that I disliked England so much. It was my feeling which made me dislike it. Now I make a lot of the nice part of the Indies, and I've sort of more or less forgotten the other part, like going to the dentist who only came to the island every now and again. I'm trying to write the beauty of it and how I saw it. And how I did see it as a child. That's what I've been toiling at. It's such a battle. (p. 230)

Certainly there is an overlap in the process of writing fiction and auto-biography. The dilemma Rhys describes in writing nonfiction suggests that overlap and the problems involved in writing the kind of fiction that she did.

Rhys's initial impulse for writing apparently took the form of a need to write out events and feelings as if all were accidental. Writing meant ordering her experience and rendering it meaningful. In writing, as in nothing else, the past could be retrieved and redeemed. Even when Rhys recognized herself as "a writer," she perceived herself at once as an "instrument" and as an artist pursuing her craft. Both aspects of herself as writer could be triggered by "returning" to the West Indies.

In a rather disjointed section of the Black Exercise Book, in what may be two separate entries, Rhys writes about these aspects of her craft. At the end of her description of the Mr. Howard episode she says:

I have written this for a very definite reason two definite reasons.

I've been working for a year at a book about Paris [most probably *Good Morning, Midnight*]. The wish to write it was so irresistable (I hadn't been able to write a word for three years) that I thought I could do it quickly. But it wouldn't come right and I've been nearly crazy with it. I have been drinking heavily. Well I've been drinking for the last six years but lately I'm drunk mostly all the time. I could still go on fairly clear headedly writing but the book began to obsess me the words sentences repeating themselves over and over again in my head till I thought I should go mad. I have really worked hard at this book and forced myself to it.

Well I woke up two days ago with the thing wiped clean out. It had slipped away from me. I hope not too soon. Instead of that I was back in the West Indies living my life as a child over again.

I began to write it and found the relief of just for once writing as I wished straight from my heart without being forced to torture the thing into the form of a novel was very—this that and the other—great. And that I drank less. (fol. 35)

In some sense Rhys saw her relationship to writing as parallel to her relationships with men, her lovers to whom she must give herself up "unreservedly" and without control; she was a willing and unwilling "instrument" who nevertheless, once "relieved" of the need to compose, was enough of a writer to return to her work and rewrite and recompose until she had, as she said, given it "shape." About having finally written out the Mr. Howard experience, Rhys concludes:

It has relieved me to write. I wish I could get it clearer, this motif of pain that has gone through all my life. Whenever I've tried to escape it has reached out and brought me back.

Now I don't try any longer. I felt in Paris that I was being possessed by something and to have given myself up to it this time utterly unreservedly—as utterly as in Mr. Howard's story I had to give myself up to my imaginary lover. Not for hope of heaven not for fear but—Was that what I've been always meant to learn? (fol. 36)

In the Black Exercise Book Rhys laments that she has ruined herself with alcohol, that she "will never succeed in England" and that she shall never be able to "make a little money for" her daughter (fol. 37). But then, recalling her relationship to her art, she says: "Then I think that after all I've done it. I've given myself up to something which is greater than I am. I have tried to be a good instrument. Then I'm not unhappy— I am even rather happy perhaps." (fol. 37)

Although Jean Rhys left Dominica in 1907 at the age of 17, the island and its inhabitants figure strongly in her first and last compositions, marking that in Rhys's work culture, character and place are inseparable. The past constantly intrudes on the present. In *Voyage in the Dark,* a personal history shaped by a childhood in the West Indies continually recurs for Anna Morgan. In *Wide Sargasso Sea,* a cultural history is mutated by the individual personalities of the characters. But in both works the formation of what we might term a colonial sensibility and psychology is a deep and early experience crystallized perhaps by change, by time passing, and by exile. One should note that Rhys's family's intention for her, and her own intentions, had not been immigration. But even though her father died shortly after her leaving Dominica, her sojourn away from "home" became permanent, interrupted only by a brief and apparently disappointing return visit in 1936. All of Rhys's siblings, in fact, left the island, a migration that David Plante, Rhys's friend and sometime amanuensis, attributes to the colonial mentality of the family, their sense that the entire empire was at their disposal.[7]

It might also be true that Rhys's lifelong obsession with her first and perhaps only home was due, in part, to the early and difficult age at which she left Dominica. Neither child nor woman, she left with many conflicts yet unresolved. If we look at the particulars of Rhys's youth in Dominica we see even there early elements that engendered her own sense of being an "outsider" and outcast—a feeling that permeates all of her work and which continued in her peripatetic life in England and the Continent. Her alienation in her childhood and adolescence was a result of a combination of factors which include the nature of the island of Dominica, the West Indian colonial experience, her relationship to her family, especially her mother, and the already mentioned sexual trauma of the episode with Mr. Howard.

Rhys's entire oeuvre is an attempt to create or locate a wholeness, to fit the pieces together, the problem with which the young Anna Morgan struggles in *Voyage in the Dark;* to separate myth from reality, while paradoxically regenerating and recreating myth; and to synthesize what was essentially an alienated and outcast position—perhaps an impossible task in life and a difficult one in literature.

Rhys often claimed that *Voyage in the Dark* was her favorite novel. Certainly it is her most clearly autobiographical in that it explores, in terms that mirror her own life, the facts of Anna Morgan's youth, spent on an island which is clearly Dominica. That Rhys continued to identify with Anna Morgan seems apparent even in her lying about her own age—

her alteration of the date from 1890 to 1894, making her the same age as Anna Morgan.

Most sources still give Jean Rhys's year of birth as 1894. However, Diana Athill, in her foreword to *Smile Please,* suggests an 1890 date. She writes that the confusion about Rhys's age was because Jean Rhys "disliked revealing it." Athill states that "an old passport" contains the date 1890, and adds that a cousin of Rhys's told her that "as children they often used to comment on Rhys being " 'ten years older than the century.' "[8] In answer to an inquiry made to the Perse School in Cambridge, Rhys's first school in England, the headmistress verified that Rhys attended the school for one term beginning September 1907.[9] They have no record of her birth date and all records in Roseau, Dominica were destroyed by fire. The Royal Academy of Dramatic Art, which Rhys attended after leaving the Perse School, records that Jean Rhys entered on 16 January 1909 (Athill gives the date 1908) and remained there for two terms, until July 23, 1909. Registered under the name Gwendolyn Williams, her age at time of entry was given as 18.[10] (Rhys, née Ella Gwendolen Rees Williams, used many names before settling on Jean Rhys.) The RADA records corroborate the 1890 birthdate and also indicate that there was, contrary to what all sources indicate, a time after leaving the Perse School when Rhys was not in school at all. Jean Rhys's daughter has also stated that, based on old passports in her possession, the 1890 birthdate is correct.[11]

It is uncertain when Rhys might have begun lying about her age. Perhaps it was when she became involved with her first husband, Jean Lenglet, who was one year her junior. That she firmly adopted the new birthdate and internalized it as true seems apparent by an entry in the Black Exercise Book in which she recalls a suicide from her youth in Dominica: "Ella Parson shot herself by the walls in the garden of Belle Ouve on the 9th of July 1894. my birthday" (fol. 43).[12]

While Athill is correct that Rhys disliked telling her age, I think that the fallacy goes deeper than that. Rhys not only gave her own life to her heroines, she also took her heroines to be herself. For example, in interviews Rhys often interchanged references to her heroines with "she" and "I." It is this very confounding that perhaps gives truth to her heroines' voices, especially the first-person narrations of Anna Morgan, Sasha Jansen, and Antoinette Cosway. Rhys, herself caught between places and cultures, classes and races, never able to identify clearly with one or another, gives the same marginality to her heroines, so that they reflect the unique experience of dislocation of the white Creole woman, even when not identified as such.

While Jean Rhys later became peripherally involved with American and British expatriates in France during the 1920s and 1930s, none was perhaps so lost as she. She remained an outsider even to that band of outsiders. It is this dislocation that Rhys explores in her fiction and the source of which she locates in her two West Indian novels, a source which is identified with the distinct experience of her own life.

The critical reputation of Jean Rhys is substantial, although the biographical sources of her work have not been fully probed. Francis Wyndham, who was among those who had read and admired Rhys's earlier works and who later was instrumental in bringing her to public attention, attributes her long literary absence before *Wide Sargasso Sea,* in the years that her books were out of print, to the fact that "they were ahead of their age, both in spirit and in style."[13] Later, in a widely heralded article in the *New York Times Book Review,* after Rhys had begun to win public attention, A. Alvarez referred to her as "the greatest living British novelist."[14] In her last years, Rhys figured in many interviews and short articles, many of them unnervingly repetitive. The first book on Jean Rhys, by Louis James, appeared in 1978;[15] it is a short, impressionistic work in which he unqualifiedly reads Rhys's work as simple autobiography. It is at times unreliable and confusing, in part because when detailing her biography he quotes from her fiction, without noting that it is fiction. James, for the most part, ignores the subtle ways in which Rhys both used her own history and transmuted it.

In 1979, shortly after Rhys's death, Thomas Staley published a critical study of Jean Rhys.[16] It remains the most comprehensive treatment of Rhys and her work, though Staley is prone to oversimplifying the relationship of her work to her biography. That is, he tends to hypothesize the colonial experience Rhys *might* have had and deduce generalizations about what should have been true, minimizing her specific experiences, the personal influences on her, and her idiosyncratic examination of the colonial theme.

Thus far, no published work has dealt in depth with Rhys's *need,* to reinvoke the myth of her own beginnings: her colonial upbringing in a land that is for her at once female- and black-identified, a place for which she yearns and which is at best indifferent to her. Nor has any critic discussed the "negative motherliness" Rhys attaches to the island: the unsatisfying mothering she received as a child and her own identification, often unconscious, of the island and her mother. This identification of the island with her mother is both mythical and literal, since Rhys's father, born in Wales, was not Creole. It is primarily because of this unresolved relationship with her mother that I think Rhys returned again and again, in her youth and in her old age, to the myth of Dominica. That this maternal indifference and failure coincided with the failure of colonialism in developing a clearly defined and centered people, that the mother country too failed to give sustenance and definition to its child colonies, is an identification Rhys makes. It is inherent in her own life and in her work and is an insight that unites the experiences of the child, the woman and the colonial in one voice.

Part One

The Voyage Out:
A Provincial Writer's Journey

Dominica: The Failure
of Home

A range of rugged mountains runs the length of Dominica, its peaks often covered in thick rain clouds and its lush and wild vegetation bright and green. Though Dominica is the largest of the five Windward Isles, lying on the intersection of the parallels 15 degrees north and 61 degrees west, between the better-known islands of Guadeloupe and Martinique, it has remained rather untouched. The early reason for Dominica's relative isolation is attributable to the fierceness of the Carib Indians who inhabited it and to the inaccessibility of its rough terrain. Even now, in part because of its black volcanic beaches, it is still off the usual tourist path. One recent guide book refers to it as "like an Eden." Dominicans say that the island contains 365 rivers and streams, one for each day of the year. Many of the rivers of the island are unnavigable and because of the terrain, much of the island was for a long time without roads or easy passes, so that later colonial traffic from one part of the island to the other was by sea rather than land.

The island, discovered by Columbus on his second voyage in 1493, was sighted on a Sunday, hence its name. Joseph Sturge and Thomas Harvey, reporting on their visit to Dominica in 1837, retell an old story of Columbus's report of the island: "When asked by the King of Spain for a description of it, he is said to have crushed a sheet of paper in his hand and presented it as a representation of the extreme irregularity of its surface. It would be difficult, perhaps, to describe it better."[1] This same image for her own lost, but unnamed, island occurs to Anna Morgan in a revery in *Voyage in the Dark*: "Lying between 15°10′ and 15°40′N. and 61°14′ and 61°30′W. 'A goodly island and something highland, but all overgrown with woods,' that book said. And all crumpled into hills and mountains as you would crumple a piece of paper in your hand—rounded green hills and sharply-cut mountains."[2] Interestingly, Anna credits a book for the first description but assumes invention of the second, an often-used image for Dominica.

In 1888, a few years prior to Rhys's birth, an Englishman, James Froude, visited the West Indies, including the island of Dominica, and wrote a book about his trip. That book, *The British in the West Indies,* was much disputed after its appearance because of its negative depiction of the blacks there. The book is actually named by Rhys in a story, "The Day They Burned the Books."[3] Froude's description of the sight of Dominica, which is not essentially different from earlier travelers', will serve to show what the island looked like during Rhys's youth. He says:

The mountains of Dominica are full in sight from Martinique. The channel which separates them is but thirty miles across, and the view of Dominica as you approach it is extremely grand. Grenada, St. Vincent, St. Lucia, Martinique are all volcanic, with lofty peaks and ridges; but Dominica was at the centre of the force which lifted the Antilles out of the ocean, and the features which are common to all are there in a magnified form. The mountains range from four to five thousand feet in height. Mount Diablot, the highest of them, rises to between five and six thousand feet. The mountains being the tallest in all the group, the rains are also the most violent, and the ravines torn out by the torrents are the wildest and most magnificent. The volcanic forces are still active there. There are sulphur springs and boiling water fountains, and in a central crater there is a boiling lake. There are strange creatures there besides: great snakes—harmless, but ugly to look at; the diablot—from which the mountain takes its name—a great bird, black as charcoal, half raven, half parrot, which nests in the holes in the ground as puffins do, spends all the day in them, and flies down to the sea at night to fish for its food.[4]

This landscape, even this sense of mystery, figures in both *Voyage in the Dark* and *Wide Sargasso Sea.*

Of the town of Roseau, where Rhys was born and raised, Froude writes:

The situation of Roseau is exceedingly beautiful. The sea is, if possible, a deeper azure even than at St. Lucia; the air more transparent; the forests of a lovelier green than I ever saw in any other country. Even the rain, which falls in such abundance, falls often out of a clear sky as if not to interrupt the sunshine, and a rainbow almost perpetually hangs its arch over the island. (p. 142)

This sense of Dominica's vivid terrain and its specialness figure strongly in *Voyage in the Dark* and *Wide Sargasso Sea.*

Racially, culturally and historically, Dominica is an island of mixtures. Long ignored by the Spanish who were the original claimants of the island, it was later much disputed over by the French and the British. Its first European settlers were French, who brought black slaves with them and lived on peaceable terms with the Carib Indians who inhabited the island. In the lore of Dominica and the Caribbean, the Caribs, from whom the entire area derives its name, play an important part.

The Caribs, a fierce tribe of cannibalistic warriors, had driven the more peaceful Arawaks from most parts of the Caribbean prior to the Spanish invasion of the New World. They were known to be so fierce that the British and French had made several early treaties in which they agreed to leave Dominica in their hands. These Indians, who some believe to have originated in South America, had made their major strongholds on the islands of Dominica and several others in the Windward group. While the Spanish had largely ignored the islands occupied by the Caribs, the British and French began fighting with them until they had control of all the Windward Islands except Dominica, which was so heavily forested and steep that the Indians were able to maintain a stronghold there for some time. Their resistance to the European invaders was perhaps the most prolonged and passionate of all of the Indian groups. When they were finally overcome by the French and English, they were granted a small reservation on the island of Dominica. Although the Caribs on other islands have all but disappeared through extermination and intermarriage with the blacks, there is still a small group on Dominica that in Rhys's time, and now, occupied a small quarter there.

Rhys makes scant reference to the Caribs, as compared with her near obsession with the blacks. But some of her heroines identify with their expulsion and virtual extermination. In *Voyage in the Dark,* Anna Morgan identifies the Caribs with her own deathwish and with her particular form of passive resistance. In one of Rhys's finest short stories, "Temps Perdi," the narrator views the Caribs as a forgotten and adulterated group, subject to the scorn and brutalization of the English colonizers and tourists.[5]

Although the French were unable to hold onto Dominica after 1805, their influence on the island has remained strong (including its pronunciation, Do-min-í-ca). While English is its official language, the language spoken by the majority even now is a French patois. The main religion is still Roman Catholicism and many of the place names—for example, the names of the mountains that figure in *Voyage in the Dark,* the town of Roseau, the names of the rivers, the flora and fauna—remain French in origin. Froude, an Englishman desiring more Englishness and English control in the British West Indies, said of the Dominica of Rhys's youth:

The population . . . was only 30,000; of these 30,000 only a hundred were English. The remaining whites, and those in scanty numbers, were French and Catholics.

The European element in Roseau, small as it is at best, is more French than English. The priests, the sisterhoods, are French or French-speaking. A French patois is the language of the blacks. They are almost to a man Catholics, and to the French they look as their natural leaders. England has done nothing, absolutely nothing, to introduce her own civilisation; and thus Dominica is English only in name. . . . Not a black in the whole island would draw a trigger in defence of English authority, and, except the Crown officials, not half a dozen Europeans. . . .

The only really powerful Europeans are the Catholic bishop and the priests and sisterhoods. They are looked up to with genuine respect. (pp. 143–46)

Rhys, as a child, was exposed to this strong French influence, and while she never formally studied French, she did understand the patois. In a letter to me she writes:

I was not really bilingual, but in Dominica the people used to speak a French 'patois', and so of course I heard it all my childhood, also a lot of the nuns at the convent I went to were French so I was used to the sound of the language, but I can't say that I was fluent.

I certainly did not read French Literature as a child.[6]

Certainly, in the culture of Dominica there is a mixture of things French and things English, but the French has remained dominant. A white Creole and colonial of English and Welsh origins like Rhys most probably would have felt some confusion about which group to identify with, especially if we consider the very strong effect that her attendance at a Catholic convent school had upon her—an effect that she describes in her autobiography and in the Black Exercise Book.

In *Smile Please,* in the chapter Rhys calls "The Religious Fit," she describes some of the conflict she felt about Catholicism and Anglicanism and her rather intense involvement with Catholicism after she began attending the convent school. Rhys describes preferring the Catholic catechism to the Anglican which she says "was much more forthright" (p. 78). Later, when her mother and father left for a six-month or year's trip (Rhys is uncertain of the amount of time) to England, she was boarded at the convent. She writes in *Smile Please*:

It had all along been understood that I was not to be pressured into Catholicism, and I wasn't. But there was a disadvantage to this: I was never allowed to go into the chapel, nor was I taken to Mass. However, twice I went to the service they called Benediction.

The Roseau cathedral was much larger than the Anglican church and I'd always heard it was a hideous place, worse than the Anglican which was bad enough. But when I went into it I thought it beautiful. Instead of the black people sitting in a different part of the church, they were all mixed up with the white and this pleased me very much. I thought it right. Of course, very few of the white people were Catholics but there were some Irish families on the island and the occasional tourist.

I was fascinated by the service, the movements of the priest, the sound of Latin, the smell of incense. It wasn't long before I decided firmly that I would become a Catholic and not only a Catholic but a nun. (pp. 78–79)

Clearly Rhys was not only attracted to the Catholic ritual and mystery but also identified that religion with the blacks, about whom she maintained ambivalent feelings all her life. And she also identifies Catholicism as un-English, an aspect that would immediately attract her. In the Black Exercise Book she describes this religious phase of her life as "the happiest time of my life." (fol. 19) In both *Smile Please* and the Black Exercise Book, Rhys describes her family's unspoken dismay at her behavior during this period and concludes in the Black Exercise Book with a typically anti-English statement about her religious upbringing. She says, "I haven't escaped much but at least I escaped the horrible effects of a British religious upbringing" (fol. 20). And while she describes the religious period as one of the happiest, in an ironic aside in the Black Exercise Book, Rhys reveals her own ambivalence, an ambivalence shared by her heroines, about her desire for "happiness." She says:

Quite suddenly this perfect bliss [of religion] departed. One morning I woke up doubting, by next day the whole thing was like a dream.

The sky receded, the sun was again God. Terror came back into my world.
And also life. I was glad—I'd missed it. (fols. 20–21)

This Catholic and French influence works its way into Rhys's novels
and short stories and into the allegiances—or perhaps the lack of them—
she felt during her own life. The white colonials in Dominica, while from
different European backgrounds, seem to have maintained social contact
with each other, although certainly for Rhys and her family, England
remained the "mother country." But there was always a strong French
influence on Rhys which perhaps contributed to the dichotomies she
draws in her later fiction between France and England, between the
French and the English and, with perhaps more complications, between
all whites and blacks. This confusion is in part the subject of Rhys's short
story, "The Day They Burned the Books" which is set on a small West
Indian island. Eddie, whose mother is "a decent, respectable, nicely educated coloured woman" and whose father is an Englishman who "de-
tested the moon and everything else about the Caribbean," is the friend,
the narrator remembers,

who first infected me with doubts about 'home', meaning England. He would be
so quiet when others who had never seen it—none of us had ever seen it—were
talking about its delights, gesticulating freely as we talked—London, the beautiful,
rosy-cheeked ladies, the theatres, the shops, the fog, the blazing coal fires in
winter, the exotic food (whitebait eaten to the sound of violins), strawberries and
cream—the word 'strawberries' always spoken with a guttural and throaty sound
which we imagined to be the proper English pronunciation.

'I don't like strawberries,' Eddie said on one occasion.

'You *don't like* strawberries?'

'No, and I don't like daffodils either. Dad's always going on about them. He
says they lick the flowers here into a cocked hat and I bet that's a lie.'

We were all too shocked to say, 'You don't know a thing about it.' We were so
shocked that nobody spoke to him for the rest of the day. But I for one admired
him. I also was tired of learning and reciting poems in praise of daffodils, and
my relations with the few 'real' English boys and girls I had met were awkward.
I had discovered that if I called myself English they would snub me haughtily:
'You're not English; you're a horrid colonial.' 'Well, I don't much want to be
English,' I would say. 'It's much more fun to be French or Spanish or something

and to the position of the blacks. Even in a book written as late as *Wide Sargasso Sea,* these influences are apparent. In her autobiography Rhys writes:

> I knew more of my mother for she was born in Dominica on what was then Geneva estate, and Geneva estate was part of my life. . . .

> Geneva was an old place, old for Dominica. I tried to write about Geneva and the Geneva garden in *Wide Sargasso Sea.* (p. 33)

Rhys's mother was Creole, a white West Indian. The white Creole in the West Indies inhabits a peculiar place in part because there is often the well-grounded supposition that the Creole may have "mixed blood," a perhaps disorienting possibility in a land where racial prejudice and exploitation have long existed. But even ignoring this aspect, white Creoles in the West Indies occupied an anomalous position. Unlike the absentee colonials, they were not natives of the "motherland" and yet, according to Kenneth Ramchand and other writers on the West Indian colonial, "like all later West Indians they thought of England as home."[8] The attitude that England was "an educational and cultural focus came to be institutionalized in a derivative and unrealistic system of peculiar education imported from England" (p. 37). This particular conflict—of the colonial's relationship to the "motherland"—arises in much of Rhys's work, both in her heroines' attitudes toward England and the English attitude toward her heroines. In fact, the problem goes so deeply into her work that it surfaces even when the heroines are not of West Indian origin. There is inevitably a clash between Rhys's woman and the English, not just the bourgeois and the establishment but virtually all English people, and especially English women.

But concomitantly, many white West Indians, while ostensibly yearning for "home" or England, had also become used to and fond of their island homes and had developed a different style of living there. They were accustomed to the warm climate, to the lush vegetation and to the relaxed, more languid life. Some, as Rhys claimed for herself, loved the colonial land; yet, to deepen the conflict, many never felt as much a "part of the place" as the blacks and, in the case of Dominica, the Caribs, so that they were not completely a part of the island and at the same time they no longer belonged to England. As Ramchand says, they "evolved a way of life that was not quite European" (p. 32).

Unlike Rhys's mother, her father was a new emigrant to Dominica. Rhys Williams was the son of a Welsh clergyman who, like the Rochester of *Jane Eye* and Rhys's sequel, *Wide Sargasso Sea,* ran off to sea as a youth; he was also a less favored younger son. In her autobiography Rhys devotes a chapter to her father, about whose past she says she learned primarily from his sister Clarice, who serves as the model for Anna's stepmother Hester in *Voyage in the Dark.* Of her father's sea escape she writes in *Smile Please,* "I only heard him speak once of the sailing voyage on which he was so unhappy, and I remembered it. The captain seems to have been a very brutal man who said, 'I'll teach you to think you're a gentleman.' However, as my father didn't like his father he was even more unhappy at home" (p. 67). Later, Rhys describes spying her father standing in front of a photograph "of an old man with a clerical collar in the sitting-room in Roseau" (p. 67). Her father was "shaking his fist and cursing" (p. 68). She says: "My mother's version of this was: 'The old man grudged every penny spent on Willie. Everything must go to the eldest son, his favourite' " (p. 68). While Rhys had a somewhat distant relationship with her father, she seems to have adored him and to have identified with him. Certainly she must have learned from him something about denial of parental, and other, authority, and about running away. In *Smile Please* she says: "I probably romanticised my father, perhaps because I saw very little of him" (p. 71).

In the Black Exercise Book, Rhys is much more specific and personal about her relationship with both her father and her mother and the relationship appears to have been a complex one. Of the two of them she says:

The curious thing was that I was afraid of my father who never touched me.

My mother who beat me ["whipped me severely" is inserted above the line] I was fond of but somewhere in my heart I despised her. (fol. 12)

Further on, talking again about her father, Rhys describes one of her few encounters with him. She writes:

He was very kind though with a tendency to shout, gave me pocket and occasional half crowns. One day I took some tea up [to] his room and clumsily spill[ed] a lot of it on the bed. I was frightened to speak. I could only stand there as if I expected the roof to fall on me.

He was very surprised and rather hurt I think. I saw it in his eyes. Good God the poor little devil's frightened of me. He put his arm round me, kissed me, stroked my hair, was very gentle.

What's the matter, aren't you well? You haven't got one of your headaches have you? What is it? Tell me.

How could I tell him that I was being beaten too often and much too severely, teased too much, thrust back on myself and given a kink that would last for the rest of my life. I didn't know myself. (fols. 23–24)

While Rhys says that she feared her father she clearly experienced some affection, tenderness and intimacy with him. In speaking of her mother (and mothers), Rhys never once portrays a scene, either in her fiction or nonfiction, of warmth or gentleness between mothers and daughters or between her own mother and herself.

Anna Morgan also identifies with her father and he with her. It may be that Rhys's identification with Rhys Williams, who was not even English, increased her hostility and confusion about the British. If the father in *Voyage in the Dark* is based on Rhys's own—and that seems to be the case as they are both from Wales, have similar appearances and share a similar character and personality—then we can see Anna/Rhys learning about the English and about mixed feeling for them *from* him. In *Voyage in the Dark,* Anna recalls a scene with her father in which he comforts her and then says: " 'I believe you're going to be like me, you poor little devil' " (p. 59). She follows this recollection immediately with another in which her father, involved in an argument about local politics, says: " 'I've met some Englishmen . . . . who were monkeys too' " (p. 59).

Rhys, though afraid of her father, may have adored him. Her relationship with her mother seems to have been far more negative. While she perhaps identified with her father, especially in terms of his renegade proclivities, even a style of being the "romantic outsider," it appears that her mother may have coldly relegated the young Ella to that outsider position, distant from herself and the family. It seems likely that much of the young Rhys's behavior and perhaps her behavior and concerns all her life was in part a response to this negative relationship with her mother.

Rhys treats her mother more kindly in her autobiography than in the Black Exercise Book. The pictures of her mother in the Black Exercise book are of a cold, punitive, even cruel woman who is unable to protect or comfort her daughter. Nor is she able to understand or sympathize with the pain the young Ella often felt. In a section of the Black Exercise Book, Rhys describes vividly a childhood nightmare and her screams for her mother to come and protect her. This dream appears almost verbatim 30 years later in *Wide Sargasso Sea* and in its context in the Black Exercise Book also appears related to the Mr. Howard involvement. Rhys concludes the presentation of the nightmare thus:

My nightgown is wet with sweat. The bedclothes are on the floor. I stare at the ticking on the mattress, the sick fear is still there. I can't stop shivering and weeping. The door opens and my mother comes in. She has a lamp in her hand. Her two long plaits hang down, her face looks dark and mysterious. . . . She sits on the bed and puts her arms round me. I'm little again. Now everything is forgotten.

Oh stay on. Hold me. Protect me. Save me. Don't ever let me go. Stay.

'What's the matter with you? Have you got a stomach ache?'

'No. No.'

She feels my forehead. 'What is it? Did you have a nightmare?'

'Yes. Keep your arms round me. Don't let me go. Stay to save me. Yes. I dreamt I was in hell,' I say.

She says 'Haven't I told you over and over and over again that there is no such place—that it's all imagination.'

Hold me. don't let me go. Save me. But she takes her arms away from me. She said, 'Really you mustn't go on like this. You're making Audrey cry.' She left me and went over to Audrey. She said, 'Aren't you ashamed of yourself waking your little sister up?'

'Yes' I said because when she took her arms away I knew that no one would save me and that I must do it. (fols. 42–43)

While it is difficult to ascertain in this section exactly what elements are part of the dream—whether the entire narration constitutes the dream or not—what is clear is that the young Rhys felt no emotional support or comfort from her mother.

In a further section of the Black Exercise Book, in the long and detailed account of her adolescent involvement with Mr. Howard, it is clear that Rhys, in part, held her mother responsible. In fact, the dream from which she describes awakening above appears to be connected to the sexual stories Mr. Howard told her. The young Rhys feared telling her mother about the man's physical advances toward her and of the sadomasochistic erotic tales he told her of what their "life together" would be like. It seems that when she tried to hint to her mother or to try to avoid outings with Mr. Howard, it was her mother who insisted she accompany him. Rhys writes: "I never even thought of telling my mother, I had that dose of castor oil" (fol. 31). Later, she writes that she felt her mother must have suspected something because her manner to Mr. Howard became colder and she discouraged her daughter from accompanying him. But by then, as Rhys writes it, she "was completely under his spell" (fol. 33).

I would hazard a guess that the introduction of Mr. Howard into the young Rhys's world and the lack of help or understanding that she got from the adults surrounding her was perhaps a major cause of her unfortunate relationship to men throughout her life. That relationship figures in most of Rhys's books and involves a female masochism and dependency. The woman is hopelessly absorbed with an older man, often married or unavailable, who, for a time, buys her presents, gives her money and indulges her like a child, just as Mr. Howard took the adolescent Ella Williams on rides in the country and bought her chocolates. Though he encouraged her to talk about herself, he inevitably concluded with a "serial story" (fol. 31) of her own sexual submission and humiliation.

This is not to say that other elements in her life, preceding her involvement with Mr. Howard, did not make Rhys particularly vulnerable to his advances and to the peculiar form of his "mental seduction." Rhys herself, in the Black Exercise Book, suggests that the beatings she received as a child, in fact, made her "used to the idea" (fol. 32) of submission and even goes so far as to ruminate that "he might have made it a lot worse, this rare and curious story" (fol. 32). Furthermore, like her young heroines in the short stories based on the Mr. Howard episode, she accepts a large degree of the responsibility and guilt for the involvement. In the Black Exercise Book she writes: "Oh I agree I only struggled feebly. What he had seen in me was there all right" (fol. 31). But certainly the "affair" with Mr. Howard crystallized the nascent confusions about sex, money, men, women, submission and passive rebellion and their interconnections, that fused into a permanent and oft-repeated pattern throughout Rhys's adult life. In fact, in the Black Exercise Book, Rhys describes how years later she went into Sylvia Beach's bookshop to find some book that might describe or analyze an experience such as the one she had had, an experience which she writes "was the thing that framed me, made me as I am" (fol. 22).

Early in her autobiography Rhys indicates her own outcast position vis-à-vis her family. She points this out in language that intimates both her lifelong sense that this was her fate and that this singular fate contributes to her sense of specialness, though she also concludes her assumption with a characteristic note of self-hate. She asks, "Why was I singled out to be the only fair one, to be called Gwendolen which means 'white' in Welsh I was told? . . . From my head to my black stockings which fell untidily round my ankles, I hated myself" (p. 20). While both the socio-cultural situation of Dominica and the familial situation contributed to the young Rhys's alienation, Rhys also seems to have taken pride in her position, as if perhaps, it came to be part of her definition of self and her identity.

In the opening pages of her autobiography Rhys describes herself in the convent school she attended as "one of the untidiest girls in the convent" (p. 20) and as an outcast (p. 21). Once, approached by another child who too was very sloppy and who "perhaps thought," Rhys tells us, "that outcasts should stick together," the young Ella Williams rejected this child's overtures of friendship. Rhys writes: "I preferred being an outcast by myself" (p. 21). This element of pride over her outcast position is, along with its inherent loneliness, a strong motif in Rhys's life and in the lives of her heroines. However, Rhys also states that she did try to tidy herself before her mother saw her because she "was afraid of her" (p. 21). Rhys's characters often have a similar response to matriarchal women or to matrons who represent the bourgeois English establishment—a mixture of defiance and fear—a guarantee of the continuation of an alien position.

There also appears to be an added dimension to this relationship to British women, an aspect that suggests a pattern in which Rhys, even as a young girl, figured as the apex of a sexual "triangle." For example, in the Black Exercise Book, when Rhys describes at length and in great detail her psycho-sexual seduction by Mr. Howard, she is particularly disturbed by Mrs. Howard's response to her, to her cold treatment of the young Rhys and Mrs. Howard's words to her. Mrs. Howard says: " 'You are a

wicked girl . . . you have made me unhappy and you will be punished' "
(fol. 34). And in *Smile Please* Rhys describes herself as a young girl giving
reading and writing lessons to a man nearby, the lessons finally being
interrupted by the wife's jealousy. Both situations suggest the later situation developed in *Quartet,* Rhys's first novel. There are to be sure, also
overtones of this "triangle" situation in her relationship to her own parents, her father having been apparently, the figure toward whom she
looked for love and understanding.

Most of Rhys's heroines, whether in her West Indian or her Continental
novels, are singularly motherless; they live without nurture or sustenance,
though they seek both endlessly, and hopelessly, often from men. In *After
Leaving Mr. MacKenzie* and especially in *Wide Sargasso Sea* the heroines'
negative and almost masochistic relationships with their mothers are explored in painful detail. In *After Leaving Mr. MacKenzie,* Julia Martin,
worn-out and lonely, is denied access to her dying mother by her sister.
Rhys has said this sister, a rueful woman who is antipathetic toward Julia,
is based on her own sister.[9] Julia Martin's recollections of her mother
during childhood are remarkably similar to Rhys's. In *After Leaving
Mr. MacKenzie,* Rhys writes:

> Julia sat there remembering that when she was a very young child she had loved
> her mother. Her mother had been the warm centre of the world. You loved to
> watch her brushing her long hair; and when you missed the caresses and the
> warmth you groped for them. . . . And then her mother—entirely wrapped up
> in the new baby—had said things like, 'Don't be a cry-baby. You're too old to go
> on like that. You're a great big girl of six.' And from being the warm centre of
> the world her mother had gradually become a dark, austere, rather plump woman,
> who, because she was worried, slapped you for no reason that you knew. So that
> there were times when you were afraid of her; other times when you disliked her.
>
> Then you stopped being afraid or disliking. You simply became indifferent and
> tolerant and rather sentimental, because after all she was your mother.[10]

In *Smile Please,* written fifty years later, Rhys, recalling her mother
and the time after the birth of her youngest sibling, a sister seven years
younger, writes:

> Even after the new baby was born there must have been an interval before she
> seemed to find me a nuisance and I grew to dread her. Another interval and she
> was middle-aged and plump and uninterested in me.

Yes, she drifted away from me and when I tried to interest her she was indifferent. (pp. 42–43)

In *Wide Sargasso Sea,* Antoinette's mother too is cold and rejecting, preferring Antoinette's younger brother, Pierre. Antoinette describes this in an episode from her childhood, a rejected attempt by the young girl simply to touch her mother. Antoinette recalls:

A frown came between her black eyebrows. . . . I hated this frown and once I touched her forehead trying to smooth it. But she pushed me away, not roughly but calmly, coldly, without a word, as if she had decided once and for all that I was useless to her. She wanted to sit with Pierre or walk where she pleased without being pestered, she wanted peace and quiet. I was old enough to look after myself. 'Oh, let me alone,' she would say, 'let me alone,' and after I knew that she talked aloud to herself I was a little afraid of her.[11]

In her autobiography and her private writings, Rhys never specifies the eventual fate of her mother. Though it seems likely that her mother came to England after her father's death and that she died in England, Rhys has never written about her aside from her childhood reminiscences. Her mother is thoroughly and permanently ensconced in the island of Dominica and in some sense permanently alive.

Rhys's breach with her mother and most of her siblings seems to have been lifelong and Rhys's intimates of her later years whom I have queried about her family are also uncertain as to the details. Diana Athill, Rhys's longtime friend and editor, writes in a letter to me that she knew no more about the facts of Jean Rhys's mother's life than I, but she does discuss the alienation that existed between Rhys and her mother and sister. She says that Rhys's sister, who had married in England, was never mentioned by Jean Rhys and that apparently they remained unreconciled until the sister's death. In fact, Athill says that Rhys's older brother, who lived in Devon, "was the only member of her family who Jean ever saw or referred to." Rhys's later letters certainly indicate that in her old age, this brother, Edward (Col. Rees Williams), was of great help to her. In a 1953 letter to Selma Vaz Dias, Rhys closes with a slightly humorous remark about her family. She writes: "My family are completely horrible. They all say I have written feelthy books and deserve my present lot, and much more. Quite detestable people. I've *one* nice brother [Edward] but he is poor. *What* luck don't you think?" (JRL, p. 109). Of Rhys's mother and sister,

Athill writes, "At some very early stage she must have felt that her mother and sister absolutely rejected her in a way that was impossible to forgive. They probably did, too!"

Athill also states that Rhys probably expected rejection by her mother, perhaps invited it and concludes that "the alienation went back very early, and I suppose that the one way to make it bearable was to make it complete." Although it was difficult to get Rhys to talk about her mother, Athill remembers, "just once, when the person we were talking abut was really her father: [Rhys said,] 'I loved my father. I hated my mother, but I loved my father.' "

In her letter, written to me before the publication of the Wyndham and Melly edition of Jean Rhys's letters, Athill says that Wyndham considers "the shock of her betrayal by her first lover as the thing that did her in (as far as feeling comfortable in life was concerned, and being able to cope)." But, Athill adds: "Personally I'm sure it had happened long before that—it was her mother who did it. (And, of course, her own nature combining in its particular way with the experiences it underwent.)"[12]

In his introduction to Rhys's letters Wyndham does, as Diana Athill wrote, attribute to her first affair the prime cause for Rhys's subsequent and life-long alienation. He writes:

More mysteriously, ever since the end of her first love affair she had also been cursed by a kind of spiritual sickness—a feeling of belonging nowhere, of being ill at ease and out of place in her surroundings wherever these happened to be, a stranger in an indifferent, even hostile world. She may have wanted to think that this crippling sense of alienation was merely that of a native West Indian exiled in a cold foreign land, but in fact she believed that the whole earth had become inhospitable to her after the shock of that humdrum betrayal. (JRL, pp. 10–11)

Wyndham's analysis of the cause of Rhys's "feeling of belonging nowhere" certainly differs from her public posture of, more simply, the exile in a hostile land. But, the Black Exercise Book and even the omissions and suggestions I point to in *Smile Please,* as well as Rhys's two West Indian novels, present the picture of a young girl who, even in her native home and with her family, felt all of the feelings—both about herself and the world—that Francis Wyndham presents above. Certainly her abandonment by her first lover, as well as the death of her father and her early dislocation from Dominica, contributed to Rhys's alienation. But that sense of being outside began before any of these events occurred.

David Plante has posited an additional cause for Rhys's estrangement from her family. He thinks that: "as colonials, they [the family] imagined all of the empire was open to them, one brother going off to India and to Africa, another sister leaving for St. Lucia . . . even her own father coming all that way to settle." Rather than a sense of strong estrangement, Plante feels that the family, as colonials, "drifted away from one another" because of "the curious family situation of British colonials."[13] In *Difficult Women,* he writes of Rhys's relationship with her family:

. . . She talked calmly about herself and, for the first time, about her family: . . . Her eldest brother went to India. The other brother, who had many illegitimate half-caste children in Dominica before he left . . . finally died in England, falling down a flight of stairs somewhere. Her elder sister, when young, went to stay with an aunt and uncle in the Bahamas . . . and stayed. . . . Jean stayed in England and "sort of drifted away" from her family. Her younger sister came to England with her mother. Jean had hardly seen either of them. She wasn't in England when her mother died. Her sister, whom she never saw in later life, had died a few years before. (pp. 43–44)

Rhys's antipathetic and at times ambivalent relationship with her mother, I believe, is linked to another motif in Rhys's work: the desire of her outcast West Indian heroines to be black. Other reasons for this of course would include a need to confirm their outcast position by identifying with a group clearly "outside" but which nevertheless constituted a strongly bonded unit. In *Smile Please,* Rhys writes of the blacks: "They were . . . more a part of the place than we were" (p. 50). But Rhys herself has suggested another reason for this strong desire to be black. She says that her mother "loved babies, any babies. Once I heard her say that black babies were prettier than white ones" (p. 42). Rhys then asks, "Was this the reason why I prayed so ardently to be black, and would run to the looking-glass in the morning to see if the miracle had happened? And though it never had, I tried again. Dear God, let me be black" (p. 42). Apparently, even Rhys herself, in her later years, recognized the degree to which she yearned for her mother's love. In most interviews, and in her West Indian fiction, Rhys invariably links this desire to be black with an envy of their mores and culture, and in the Black Exercise Book, perhaps with a racial guilt. The above explanation in *Smile Please* is the only time Rhys examines a deeper reason for her envy of the blacks and links it to her own self-doubt engendered by her mother. The insight suggests the total lack of self-acceptance she endured as a child and her early incorporation of her mother's rejecting voice, a voice that haunts all of Rhys's fiction, from the condemnations and jibes of the British matrons and landladies and the Paris concierges, to the looks and imagined insults of waiters, waitresses, taxi drivers, even strangers who pass in the street.

Further on in *Smile Please,* Rhys tells us that her mother "seemed to find me a nuisance and I grew to dread her. Another interval and she was middleaged and plump and uninterested in me" (p. 42). She says that her relationship with her mother became more and more distant "until at last she was almost a stranger. . . ." (p. 46). I think there is a connection between her relationship to her mother and to her feeling about the blacks of Dominica and, of course, to all women. These relationships inform almost all of Rhys's work. It is a queerly turned relationship, mixed with love, hate, envy, fear and guilt.

Often Rhys, both in *Smile Please* and in her fiction, attributes to some black women more overt examples of aggression and hostility toward her than she receives from white women. And yet, elsewhere there are "motherly" black women: Francine in *Voyage in the Dark,* Christophine in *Wide Sargasso Sea,* Frances in *Smile Please* and Victoria in the Black Exercise Book. And there are a few black women, such as Selina Davis in the story "Let Them Call It Jazz,"[14] who appear as much victimized as Rhys's white heroines. And, of course, there are the many instances in which the heroines, and Rhys, state their explicit yearning to be black. Rhys's and Anna Morgan's yearning for their island home is also mixed with this same unacknowledged love and hate.

One of the first black figures Rhys introduces in *Smile Please* and in the Black Exercise Book is her nurse Meta, whose cruelty to her as a child Rhys describes, and adds, "I never dreamed of complaining to my mother about all this, and I doubt if it would have been any good if I had. . . . But in any case it was too late, the damage had been done. Meta had shown me a world of fear and distrust, and I am still in that world" (p. 32).

At a further point in her autobiography, Rhys describes an attempt to befriend a beautiful "coloured" girl at the convent in which white girls, Rhys tells us, "were very much in the minority" (p. 49). The girl turned to her with a look that the child Rhys recognized as hatred. She concludes: "I never tried to be friendly with any of the coloured girls again" (p. 49). Perhaps these two incidents provide again a microscopic example of the way in which Rhys's alienation from her family, and from her mother especially, compounded with her alienation and rejection by the "real people" of the island—the blacks—put her into a situation where there was no place that she could belong, no place and no way that she could attain mother love, sustenance, warmth and nurturing, the themes that inform most, if not perhaps all, of Rhys's fiction. In *Wide Sargasso Sea,* Antoinette tells her unloving husband Rochester that a black girl was singing a song for her to hear. She tells him:

"It was a song about a white cockroach. That's me. That's what they call all of us who were here before their own people in Africa sold them to the slave traders. And I've heard English women call us white niggers. So between you I often wonder who I am and where is my country and where do I belong and why was I ever born at all." (p. 519)

Rhys's mixed feelings about blacks remained evident throughout her entire life. The Fall 1979 issue of the *Paris Review* contains both an interview with Rhys which was one of her last, and a "Remembrance" of her by David Plante, who had worked with her on transcribing her autobiography.[15] To the interviewer's question: "Have you written of your relations with the black people in Dominica?" Rhys replies:

That's very complicated because at the start I hated my nurse. A horrid woman. It was she who told me awful stories of zombies and *sucriants,* the vampires; she frightened me totally. I was a bit wary of the black people. I've tried to write about how I gradually became even a bit envious. They were so strong. They could walk great distances, it seemed to me, without getting tired, and carry those heavy loads on their heads. They went to the dances every night. They wore turbans. They had lovely dresses with a belt to tuck the trains through that were lined with paper and rustled when they moved. (p. 230)

When asked if she had young friends who were black she says, "No, it was more divided then. There were a lot of colored girls at the convent I went to. I didn't always like them—but I was kind of used to them" (p. 231).

In his "Remembrance," David Plante recalls conversations with Rhys. In a talk about the blacks in Dominica, she says, " 'I want to tell the truth, too, about Dominica. No it's not true we treated the black people badly. We didn't, we didn't. Now they say we did. No, no' " (p. 245). She then describes her memory of:

"a black man in Dominica walking through the yard. My father and I were on the back steps of the house. My father made me give loaves of French bread . . . and sixpence to poor black men who came to us. No women ever came. I recall this black man walking away from us, the loaf under his arm, and his dignity. His dignity and his unconquerable mind." (p. 245)

Further on, she speaks about England and the loss of good and great people and again she refers to that man in the yard, " 'I'll never, never forget the dignity of that black man walking through the yard with his sixpence and the loaf of bread under his arm. And it's all gone, all gone. They've destroyed it themselves' " (p. 246). Plante reports that Rhys began crying and suddenly shouted:

"I hate. I hate. Do they understand? No. Does anyone understand? I hate. I hate them. We didn't treat them badly. We didn't. I hate them. . . . And yet, I was kissed once by a Nigerian, in a café in Paris, and I understood, a little. I understand why they are attractive. It goes very deep. They danced, danced in the sunlight, and how I envied them." (pp. 247–248)

Plante has indicated that in many of their conversations, if not all, Rhys was often drunk, and Plante, a novelist himself, might have been, in part, dramatizing these conversations with literature in mind. But I cite this rather long passage because the story of the black man who walks away with the bread occurs in a longer form in Rhys's autobiography; later she makes a connection between him and her mother. She describes a moment in which she saw her mother alone, just before leaving Dominica. Her mother had not been well and Rhys says:

She looked lonely, patient, and resigned. Also obstinate, 'you haven't seen what I've seen, haven't heard what I've heard'. From across the room I knew she was like someone else I remembered. I couldn't think who it was, at first. She was like the old man walking out of the gate with a loaf of bread under his arm, patient, dignified. (p. 45)

Clearly Rhys identifies her mother with the blacks of the island, a connection that links the black and the white Creole and underlies the experience of all Creoles and yet in Rhys's peculiar relation to both groups, excludes her. In the conversation with Plante we see the convoluted and mixed feelings that she had about the black Creole—love, hate, envy and fear. Rhys sometimes intimated that she might have "black blood" and of course it would come from her mother's side.

Thomas Staley, one of the few who have written on Rhys with much detail concerning her early life in Dominica, bases his information, in part, on interviews with Rhys and others. His book was published before *Smile Please* but nevertheless contains information not included in it. Staley says of Rhys:

Her later encounters with exploitation in England and Europe, combined with the domestic and passive role expected of white women in Dominica, were sources of constant tension within her. Although she would eventually recall her years on the island with some nostalgia, she would nevertheless recognise that in both worlds masculine aggression was a common denominator, however different the form it would take. This is not to say that her anxieties were created solely by a male-female conflict, but rather that she recognized very early the conflicting and unstable role of women and how little their natures were understood by men.[16]

Staley is correct in pointing to Rhys's understanding, as depicted in her novels, of the power relationship that exists between men and women, but the basic nature of her own conflict had much more to do with her own rejecting and "indifferent" mother than with masculine aggression. In fact, Rhys, in her fiction and her private journals makes almost no reference to male aggression in the West Indies. Rather, it is most often a function of English men in England or as recent and temporary inter- lopers in the West Indies (e.g., Mason and Rochester in *Wide Sargasso Sea*, even perhaps Mr. Howard in the Black Exercise Book).

Staley continues:

The passivity and turbulence, the racial mixture, the cultural contrasts between colonial and native life, all of these she absorbed with their inherent conflicts. . . . Her journals . . . record with fidelity how these experiences as a child re- mained a deep part of her essential being. Even amid her happy moments as a child in Dominica, she saw beneath the lazy, surface calm the continued domi- nation of the black and the subordinate, reductive role that women had in this culture—the boredom and the feeling of uselessness. Boredom and domination and their effects become important themes in her fiction. (p. 4)

While what Staley says here is not incorrect, the focus on the particular relation between Dominica and Rhys's work is off center. His analysis is far more political and simple (i.e., the racial and sexual conditions of life generally in Dominica) than Rhys's own autobiography, her journals and the fiction itself indicate. Certainly boredom and domination figure in Rhys's work as themes but they are symptoms and results of a deeper malaise: the dislocation and alienation that comes from having neither a true home, metaphorically and literally, or a loving mother, which for many may be the equivalent—and no way of fabricating either. It was Rhys's mother's indifference to her which forced Rhys to become indifferent in return. It is her heroines' statelessness, homelessness and lack of familial and deep ties that lead to their malaise. Of course, that they are women deepens their inability to repair the damage done to them.

Staley also adds:

Her sense of displacement and cultural rift created a curious racial identity with blacks. . . . Her own attitude towards blacks as revealed in her work is complex and not easily categorised. . . . but her close relationship with blacks as a child and her own experiences in England enabled her to understand and identify with the plight of the black immigrant who enters the alien world of white England. . . . This initial empathy created a deep sympathy for those who were outcasts or, . . . 'the underdog.' (p. 5)

Staley is dealing here with disparate, though overlapping, elements and it seems to me that his generalizing leads to some inaccuracy. Rhys, neither in her fiction (except for the story "Let Them Call It Jazz") nor in her autobiography or interviews reveals any particular empathy for blacks—either in Dominica or in England. While it is true that her relationship to blacks, both in her life and fiction, is not easily categorized there does not seem to be a "racial identity." It would seem more likely that Rhys's very complicated relationship to blacks, which I described earlier, led her to assign them a partly symbolic function in her work. And they are not always—in fact rarely—"the underdogs." Certainly Christophine in *Wide Sargasso Sea* and Francine in *Voyage in the Dark* are powerful and often intimidating women, unlike the white heroines, Antoinette and Anna. And Rhys makes almost no, if any, allusion to the inescapable prejudice and exploitation that must have occurred in the history of blacks in the West Indies. In fact, in *Wide Sargasso Sea,* in part set in the West Indies, the blacks are a menace. Even Rochester's antipathy toward Christophine seems to be more personal and ideological than racial. Staley's analysis is too simplistic for the portrait of blacks that Rhys offers in her fiction, her interviews and her autobiography. Furthermore, Staley depicts Rhys's relationship to blacks as "close." Rhys, in her interviews and autobiography, has suggested that she has viewed blacks at close hand but that her relationships with blacks, in fact, were not close.

There is however perhaps one passage in the Black Exercise Book in which Rhys talks about blacks almost in a political way and which, on first reading, appears to come close to Staley's point of view.

In the first passage in which she talks about blacks, her usual conflict is apparent. She says:

I was curious about black people. They stimulated me and I felt akin to them. It added to my sadness that I couldn't help but realise that they didn't really like or trust white people. White cockroaches they called us behind our backs. (Cockroach again.) One could hardly blame them. I would feel sick with shame at some of the stories I heard of the slave days told casually even jocularly. The ferocious punishments the salt kept ready to rub into the wounds etc etc. I became an ardent socialist and champion of the down-trodden, argued, insisted of giving my opinion, was generally insufferable. Yet all the time knowing that there was another side to it. Sometimes being proud of my great grandfather, the estate, the good old days, etc. . . . Sometimes I'd look at his picture and think with pride, He was goodlooking anyway. Perhaps he wasn't entirely ignoble. Having absolute power over a people needn't make a man a brute. Might make him noble in a way. No—no use. My great Grandfather and his beautiful Spanish wife. Spanish? I wonder.

I thought a lot about them. But the end of my thought was always revolt, a sick revolt and I longed to be identified once and for all with the others' side which of course was impossible. I couldn't change the colour of my skin. (fols. 14–15)

But even in this passage Rhys concludes, not with the "outcast" or "underdog" position of the black but with her own sense of exclusion, alienation and perhaps even envy. But another passage in the Black Exercise Book in which Rhys appears to be talking about her relationship to blacks occurs within the context of a longer discussion of her relationship to her parents. In fact, her description of her "concern" for and attitude toward the blacks, on closer analysis, bears a strong connection to an (unconscious) description of one form of her own rebellion against her parents, particularly her mother. In the passage, Rhys first describes a confrontation with her mother, the conclusion of which results in her mother's saying to her: " 'You'll never learn to be like other people' " (fol. 22). Rhys then writes:

There you are, there it was. I'd always suspected it. I saw the long road of isolation and loneliness stretching in front of me as far as the eye could see and further and collapsed, cried heartbrokenly as my worst enemy could wish.

I see now that she was trying to drive [out] something she saw in me, that was alien, that would devour me. She was trying to drive it out at all costs. However after this she ceased her efforts. (fols. 22–23)

It is in the paragraph immediately following the above that Rhys describes her position at that time as a defender of the blacks, as if it were an aspect of either a rebellion against her mother or as a way of finding some group with which to temporarily identify in the face of her mother's rejection of her or as a way to win the attention of her family. This of course is not to deny that Rhys, both as an adult and as a child, felt concern, sympathy and guilt about the treatment of blacks. However, her concern for them seems clearly not to have been a considered or political response to injustice but rather, immediately tied to her peculiar relationship to her parents. About her "attitude to black people" Rhys writes in this section of the Black Exercise Book: "I met anyone who sympathised with my feelings in this matter. I was always told that I was (a) showing off (b) mad or (c) a liar, (d) all three. I had no answer except: Don't care what you think don't care what you say. But I never [could] stand much teasing and the end of my Liberty speeches was usually that I wept and they shouted Cry baby cry" (fol. 23). Rhys immediately turns from this very personalized and solipsistic description of her attitude toward blacks to a continuation of her discussion of her relation with her parents. The next line begins: "The curious thing about this relationship with my parents . . ." (fol. 23) as if the discussion of her attitude toward blacks is an example or part of her parental relationship.

Staley's analysis makes little or no mention of the complex relationship Rhys had with her mother which, aside from being bound up with her attitude about blacks and being black, seems to have contributed more to her eventual sense of herself as an outcast and hence her particular understanding of the outcast's position in society.

Smile Please, Rhys's unfinished autobiography, put together for the most part when she was in her eighties, reveals both overtly and inadvertently perhaps, the essential corrosion underlying her relationship to her family, in particular her mother, and even to the land which she claimed she loved and to which she constantly returned in her writing. Rhys uses, in the autobiography, a similar technique of compression or oblique qualification, which she had used earlier in *Voyage in the Dark,* to suggest the tension and lack of resolution in these areas of her past. For example, in an early section of *Smile Please,* she describes in vivid and nostalgic language the musical evenings that were held in her parents' house. It is part of a section in the autobiography in which she describes some of the pleasures the family shared in Dominica. She says: "As I grew up, life didn't seem monotonous or dull to me. Even apart from books, life was often exciting" (p. 64). She adds, ironically, "It was not, of course, anything like as wonderful as England would be . . ." (p. 64). Describing the sounds of the music that she hears from her child's place on the staircase she says:

Beyond was the room where the music came from. 'Night has a thousand eyes', someone sang, and suddenly I don't want to listen anymore but go up to my bedroom and undress quickly.

'Night has a thousand eyes', yes, everything has eyes. Spiders have eyes, a good many eyes it seems if you look at a spider through a microscope. Moths have eyes, beetles have eyes, so have centipedes I suppose. Detestable flying cockroaches have eyes. [Rhys, like her mother, was terrified of cockroaches.] (p. 65)

Here Rhys rehearses the terrors that underly even the warmest memory of her childhood in Dominica.

In another recollection Rhys, inadvertently perhaps, suggests the relationship in her unconscious between the island and her mother. In a section in which she describes a religious phase in her life, spurred by her exposure to Catholicism at the convent school, Rhys, at the end, recollects the second estate her father owned. She calls it Morgan's Rest in *Smile Please*—Anna's surname in *Voyage in the Dark*. Rhys writes:

Not a beautiful place, just a pretty place. . . .

It was there, not in wild beautiful Bona Visa [her father's other estate], that I began to feel I loved the land and to know that I would never forget it. There I would go for long walks alone. It's strange growing up in a very beautiful place and seeing that it is beautiful. It was alive, I was sure of it. Behind the bright colours the softness, the hills like clouds and the clouds like fantastic hills. *There was something austere, sad, lost, all these things. I wanted to identify myself with it, to lose myself in it. (But it turned its head away, indifferent, and that broke my heart.)* (p. 81; emphasis added)[17]

At times Rhys herself, especially in the Black Exercise Book, seems peculiarly unaware of her own conflict about her childhood in Dominica. For example, she describes a confrontation between her mother and herself in which her mother apparently is about to beat her. Rhys mentions beatings a great deal in the Black Exercise Book and they seem to have been harsh and most often administered by her mother. The young girl cries to her mother, " 'God curse you if you touch me I'll kill you' " (fol. 11). To this, her mother replies: " 'Ah you're growing up are you, Well I can't do anything now' " and Rhys writes that "after that she never beat me again" (fol. 11). She then adds, perhaps in a half-hearted justification of her mother:

She must [have] seen something alien in me which would make me unhappy and she was trying to root it out at all costs—

I can't imagine any place where a child could be happier. (fol. 11)

Interestingly, this observation of Rhys's, that she can't imagine a place where a child could be happier, occurs at least three times in the Black Exercise Book and inevitably it is linked, apparently unconsciously, with pain—as if Rhys cannot reconcile her own past memories of unhappiness with her *idea* of what her life was like or should have or could have been like. For example, in another section of the Black Exercise Book, Rhys writes, as if surprised, "I keep on talking about pain darkness etc. but really I can't imagine a place where a child could be more happy than Dominica" (fol. 16). This particular inclusion, apparently a summing up in favor of her childhood, is immediately followed by the line, almost a nonsequitur: "No poisonous snakes"—as if their absence were the proof of paradise.

The third time this assertion of the idyllic quality of a childhood in Dominica occurs in the Black Exercise Book is perhaps the most interesting in terms of the way in which Rhys, again apparently unconsciously, undercuts her assertion. Rhys discusses the "black moods" that she used to have as a young girl, moods in which she felt "doomed," apparently a message reinforced by her mother. She writes at the conclusion of this discussion, "But sometimes weeks months would go by smoothly and happily no black moods nothing going wrong. And indeed I can't think of any place in the world where a child could be happier." (fol. 24) What is most interesting about this third protest is that it is immediately followed by the introduction to her account of the awful and traumatic "affair" with the elderly Mr. Howard—who became perhaps, for the adolescent Ella Williams, in Freudian terms, the human embodiment of a "poisonous snake."

The island of Dominica figures as a strong symbol for Rhys both in her fiction and in her own myth of herself and her past. As an island symbol it maintained for her its insularity, cut off and separated from all that followed in Rhys's own life, safely contained and relegated to the other side of the ocean—like all her memories of her mother. Though Rhys compulsively returned to the memories of her island, often for solace and comfort, she also chose to exile and separate herself from it. That the island she associated with her mother both attracted and repelled Rhys was something she could never wholly come to terms with, just as she never directly came to terms with her mother even in later years.

While the surface of Rhys's writing about Dominica offers a vision of Eden, the depths of her work suggest that it, and childhood perhaps, contain unknowable and unfathomable dangers. In a passage that suggests this dichotomy in *Smile Please* Rhys writes, "Wondering what my life would be like now that God and the Devil were far away. And the sea, sometimes so calm and blue and beautiful but underneath the calm— what? Things like sharks and barracudas are bad enough but who knows, not the wisest fisherman nor the most experienced sailor, what lives in the Cuba deep" (p. 87).

Rhys's heroines are sometimes terrifyingly clear about the danger, death, the violence and threat and the anomie lurking beneath the surfaces of "civilized" society. It may be that Rhys, as she grew older, recognized that same threat lying beneath the idyllic surface of her remembered island home. While the myth remained compelling, it is that insight, I believe, that forges the essential difference between *Voyage in the Dark* and *Wide Sargasso Sea*.

2

England: The Disappointment of the Motherland

When she was 17 Jean Rhys left for England with her paternal aunt Clarice, who had been visiting Dominica. This aunt does not seem to have been sympathetic or especially warm to her young charge. Or, at least this is the way Rhys perceived her, though in later years she writes of her aunt in a scarcely disguised story, "Overtures and Beginners Please":

She was a nice woman, I see that now. It was kind of her to take charge of me to please her favorite brother. But she wasn't exactly demonstrative. Even pecks on the cheek were very rare. And I craved for affection and reassurance. By far my nicest Cambridge memory was of the day an undergraduate on a bicycle knocked me flat as I was crossing the road. I wasn't hurt but he picked me up so carefully and apologized so profusely that I thought about him for a long time.[1]

After their arrival in London, Rhys's aunt showed her young niece the sights of the city, all of which Rhys records later, both in *Voyage in the Dark* and *Smile Please,* as intimidating and hateful. Of St. Paul's, she says, it was "too cold, too Protestant" (SP, p. 100) and of herself, she remembers: "I kept going to sleep" (SP, p. 169). In a journal, kept in the 1940s and included in *Smile Please,* Rhys, remembering her first impressions of England, wrote, "I never once thought this is beautiful, this is grand, this is what I hoped for, longed for." (p. 169)

As soon as Rhys arrived in London she began what was to be a mode of living that persisted almost her entire life—the taking of lodging in temporary, and often inhospitable, quarters. In England her life was spent living in constantly changing boarding houses and bed-sitting rooms. Later, on the Continent, she lived the same life in small hotels. Rhys never seemed able, after leaving Dominica, to establish a real home, or find quarters that were to her liking, even up to the time of her death, though, in the 1940s diary, writing of her current rooms she says: "The place I live in is terribly important to me, it always has been . . ." (SP, p. 165). Even in letters written in her old age, Rhys often expressed the half-hearted hope that she might find an acceptable and permanent place in which to live.

In September, 1907, Rhys began at the Perse School for Girls in Cambridge. In *Smile Please,* she says that she left the school after one term because she had written to her father that she wanted to be an actress and he "true to his promise" had written back, " 'That is what you must do' " (p. 101). She then enrolled at the Academy of Dramatic Art in London (later the Royal Academy of Dramatic Art).

The story "Overtures and Beginners," published three years before *Smile Please,* also details this period in her life. In fact, it is hardly a "story," which is true for many of the selections in *Sleep It Off, Lady.* Even the names remain unchanged. In *Difficult Women,* writing about his work with Jean Rhys on her autobiography, David Plante recalls, "She often had me check to make sure a passage she thought of using in her autobiography hadn't already been used in one of her novels or short stories. I did my best, but I too couldn't always remember" (p. 51).

"Overtures and Beginners," however, is more detailed than the autobiography about aspects of this time in her life and is particularly revealing about the impulsive way in which she says she decided to study acting. The narrator says that she received a letter from a classmate telling her she was a " 'born actress' " (p. 73) and "suddenly, like an illumination, I knew exactly what I wanted to do" (p. 74). She says that the next day she wrote to her father and told him that she "longed to be an actress and wanted to go to the Academy of Dramatic Art in Gower Street" (p. 74).

In both *Smile Please* and "Overtures and Beginners," Rhys also talks about the death of her father which occurred at the time she was studying at the Academy. The last paragraph of this section in the autobiography concludes briefly:

During vacation from the Academy I went to Harrogate to visit an uncle. It was there that I heard of my father's death. My mother wrote that she could not afford to keep me at the Academy and that I must return to Dominica. I was determined not to do that, and in any case I was sure that they didn't want me back. My aunt and I met in London to buy hot-climate clothes, and when she was doing her own shopping I went to a theatrical agent in the Strand, called Blackmore, and got a job in the chorus of a musical comedy called *Our Miss Gibbs*. (pp. 104–105)

Though the description of the same time in "Overtures and Beginners" may be slightly fictionalized, it seems to reveal more of the emotional truth that the young Ella Williams must have felt. She writes:

I spent the vacation with relatives in Yorkshire and one morning early my uncle woke me with a cablegram of the news of my father's sudden death. I was quite calm and he seemed surprised, but the truth was that I hadn't taken it in, I didn't believe him.

Harrogate was full of music that late summer. Concertinas, harpists, barrel organs, singers. One afternoon in an unfamiliar street, listening to a man singing 'It may be for years and it may be forever', I burst into tears and once started I couldn't stop.

Soon I was packed off to responsible Aunt Clare in Wales. 'You cry without reticence," she told me that day after I arrived. 'And you watch me without reticence,' I thought. . . .

She had heard from my mother who wished me to return home at once. I said that I didn't want to go, 'not yet.' But you'll have to. 'I won't. . . .' [Rhys's ellipses]

. . . At last we went up to London to do some shopping for hot weather clothes and one afternoon when she was visiting friends I went to Blackmore's agency in the Strand and after some palaver was engaged as one of the chorus of a touring musical comedy.

. . . Then Aunt Clare said that it was unfair to expect her to deal with me, that she'd write to my mother. 'Perhaps we'll be rehearsing before she answers,' I said hopefully. But when my mother's letter arrived it was very vague. She didn't approve, neither did she altogether disapprove. It seemed as if what with her grief for my father and her worry about money she was relieved that I'd be earning my own living in England (pp. 75–76)

From the additional information that Rhys gives in the "story," which otherwise almost exactly parallels the autobiography, including place names and the names of characters, it seems that a word from her mother could have brought the young Ella back to Dominica, that her mother's own indifference, her "vagueness" helped launch Rhys in her pursuit of a career which rather quickly became painful and unsuccessful. The two passages are also interesting in terms of seeing how Rhys, through the addition of a few details, especially the kind of detail involved in the inclusion of music in the second paragraph, transmutes history or auto-biography into fiction. In much, perhaps all of Rhys's fiction, the intro-duction of "popular" musical melodies or lyrics is a trigger to experiencing (often unexpected) feeling and internal revelation.

In *Smile Please* Rhys describes the one-and-a-half to two years that she spent in *Our Miss Gibbs,* touring small northern towns in the winter and seaside resorts in the summer. She says:

There was, however, a dreadful gap after the winter tour finished and before the summer tour started. It was impossible to save enough to tide you over this gap, so most of the girls lived at home for those two or three months. The few who, like myself, *had no home* tried to get a job in what were known as music-hall sketches. . . . (p. 106; emphasis added)

Certainly Rhys had relatives in England and Wales, perhaps even siblings, but apparently by this time she was confirmed in her perpetual state of homeless outsider, abandoned by family and friends, a statelessness clearly engendered first and foremost at home.

Rhys made the decision to become an actress impulsively; it turned out to be a profession for which she was unsuited and which she came to dislike. In *Smile Please* she summarizes the experience thus:

Going from room to room in this cold dark country, England, I never knew what it was that spurred me on and gave me an absolute certainty that there would be something else for me before long. Now I think the 'something else' was something small and limited. I realise that I was no good on the stage, forgot my lines, didn't thirst for the theatre as some of the girls did, yet I was so sure. (pp. 111–112)

Though Rhys declares that acting was her choice, like many of her her-oines she also insists, in at least one interview, that it was her "fate" to stay in England and to be an actress, denying in some sense her own responsibility for the homeless and alienating life of the chorus girl, a career that necessarily involves a tangential life outside a conventional mode.

Elizabeth Vreeland, interviewing Rhys for the *Paris Review,* raised the question of choice with Rhys, something other interviewers have rarely done and none persistently. In an answer that significantly alters both the sequence of events and her motivations for staying in England as she presents them in her autobiography, Rhys says:

I left school early because I wanted to become an actress. While I was studying at the Royal Academy of Dramatic Arts in London, my father died in the West Indies. My mother wrote me that she couldn't afford to keep me at school. But I didn't want to go back to Dominica. I knew I'd miss my father too much. So I joined the chorus of a show on tour around England. (p. 222)

When asked how her family in Dominica reacted, Rhys replied: "There wasn't much they could do about it. Anyway I believe in fate" (p. 222). When the interviewer asserted to Rhys that she could have returned, and "did have the choice," Rhys replied:

I suppose so. But I wanted to be an actress. I was a very bad actress, but that's what I wanted to be. I do believe that life's all laid out for one. One's choices don't matter much. It is really a matter of being adapted. If you can adapt, you're all right. But it's not always easy if you're born not-adapted, a bit of a rebel; then it's difficult to force yourself to adapt. One is born either to go with or to go against. (p. 222)

In the short story "Tigers Are Better Looking," one of the women gives voice to this rather Darwinian explanation of Rhys's for human survival. About women who "get on" she says, " 'No, it isn't being pretty and it isn't being sophisticated. It's being—adapted, that's what it is. And it isn't any good *wanting* to be adapted, you've got to be born adapted.' "[2]

Thomas Staley, describing this period in Rhys's life, offers yet another explanation for her remaining in England and working in a profession for which she was apparently unsuited. He says:

Her father died shortly after her arrival in England, and her mother came to England in bad health. Her father had left little money, and Jean found herself suddenly completely on her own. Jean's mother was not happy that she had left school and gone to study at the RADA, but she was too ill to raise much protest, and Jean was determined to pursue a career on the stage. (pp. 5–6)

Staley's information is based on interviews with Rhys and others and if it is true that her mother came to England and in bad health, it is a striking omission from Rhys's autobiography.

Jean Rhys's involvement with the stage petered out as she began her first love affair. This affair, especially its demise and the distraught state in which it left Rhys, eventually provided the initial impetus for her to write the journal upon which *Voyage in the Dark* is based. The affair also began a pattern which remained with Rhys for much of her life, a pattern which included fruitless dependence on men, especially for intermittent financial support.

Rhys talks about this first affair in her autobiography. While she never describes the man in detail she points to two of his important attributes. "He had money. I had none" (SP, p. 114); and "He lived in Berkeley Square, and I got used to the warmth, the fires all over the house, the space, the comfort" (SP, pp. 114–115). Rhys insists that he was a "very kind man" and the evidence she presents throughout *Smile Please* indicates that he was at least rather paternal and protective toward her, even years after the affair ended. In fact, her summation of him is remarkably similar to her final remarks about Mr. Howard, though both men may be considered culpable of sexual exploitation of a young girl.

From what Rhys writes in her autobiography and in the fictionalization of the affair in *Voyage in the Dark,* Rhys was intimidated by her first lover's social position, his wealth and the accoutrements and servants that accompanied his class. The description of the affair in *Smile Please* has strong parallels to the affair Marya has in Rhys's first novel *Quartet* and to Julia Martin's affair with Mr. MacKenzie. Rhys writes in *Smile Please* that when she first met him she "rather disliked him" (p. 114) but that as she came to "worship him" (p. 114) she devoted most of her time to "looking out of the window for the messenger boy, because he always sent his letters by messenger" (p. 113). Eventually her lover broke the relationship, alloting a small monthly sum to her. Rhys describes her hurt and anger when she was notified of the allotment by his lawyers. But, like most of the women in her books, she saw no alternative but to take the money. In *Smile Please* she writes:

It seems to me now that the whole business of money and sex is mixed up with something very primitive and deep. When you take money directly from someone you love it becomes not money but a symbol. The bond is now there. The bond has been established. I am sure the woman's deep-down feeling is 'I belong to this man, I want to belong to him completely'. It is at once humiliating and exciting. (p. 121)

Toward the end of this affair, Rhys had an abortion, which provided the material for the vivid denouement of *Voyage in the Dark;* at the end of that relationship, Rhys describes herself as being in a state of deep depression, unable to care for or about herself. She worked at jobs as a movie extra in the nascent British film industry, apparently engaged in a more literal kind of prostitution and, as usual, moved from one set of shabby quarters to the next. It was one of these places that prompted her, she says in *Smile Please,* to buy some quills to place "in a glass, to cheer up my table." She adds, "Then I noticed some black exercise books on the counter. . . . I bought several of those, I didn't know why, just because I liked the look of them" (pp. 128–129). She says that after supper that evening,

. . . it happened. My fingers tingled, and the palms of my hands. I pulled a chair up to the table, opened an exercise book, and wrote *This is my Diary.* But it wasn't a diary. I remembered everything that had happened to me in the last year and a half. I remembered what he'd said, what I'd felt. I wrote on until late into the night, till I was so tired that I couldn't go on, and I fell into bed and slept.

Next morning I remembered at once, and my only thought was to go on with the writing. (p. 130)

She concludes the description of her first writing with these words:

I filled three exercise books and half another, then I wrote: 'Oh, God, I'm only twenty and I'll have to go on living and living and living.' [What Anna Morgan says in *Voyage in the Dark* when she is 19.] I knew then that it was finished and there was no more to say. I put the exercise books at the bottom of my suitcase and piled my underclothes on them. After that whenever I moved I took the exercise books but I never looked at them again for many years. (p. 130)

In the *Paris Review* interview Rhys refers to these notebooks and says: "I hadn't really written a book; it was more or less a jumble of facts" (p. 223). Rhys has always described *Voyage in the Dark* as her favorite book and has said in the *Paris Review* the reason was "because it came easiest" (p. 223).

In 1914, at the start of World War I, Rhys was 24. During the war she worked at odd theater jobs and then at a canteen for soldiers. At a boarding house she met Jean Lenglet, a Dutchman who was staying in London on a diplomatic passport. Lenglet, who was apparently involved in some intelligence work, asked Rhys to marry him after the war. When he proposed that they live in Paris, Rhys writes: "It came to me in a flash that here it was, what I had been waiting for, for so long. Now I could see escape" (SP, pp. 138–139).

When Jean Rhys finally joined Lenglet in Holland in 1919, she had spent more than a decade, from the age of 17 to 29, in England. These years, instrumental in forming many of her attitudes toward women, men, sex and money, in diminishing her own sense of worth and in crystallizing her antipathy toward England and the English, were permeated by loneliness, hopelessness, transcience and isolation. In her 1940s diary she wrote: "Ten years were wasted before I got away" (SP, p. 169). Certainly her first affair in England increased her despair and dependence. It was only upon leaving England that she terminated the support checks that had continually been sent by her ex-lover.

The crossing of the ocean to England was a terrifying and irreversible wrenching for Rhys, a crossing which figures in *Wide Sargasso Sea, Voyage in the Dark* and in her autobiography and is marked in all three by a sudden change in the weather. "It began to grow cold. The sky was grey, not blue" (SP, p. 97). Jean Rhys's first view of England, its landscape and topography, its climate and industry, presented an immediate antithesis to home. That antithetical place very quickly became identified with many other negative elements, some personal, some clearly indigenous to England. Certainly upon arriving in England, the young Ella Williams had been disappointed; but in the 1940s diary she claims that she did not begin "to hate London, to hate England" (SP, p. 172), until her first affair. She eventually imbued England with *all* that was hateful to her.

Most probably the components of her initial life in England—the antipathy between herself and her aunt; the death of her father, unwitnessed and unconfirmed by the young girl and the sudden loss of income accompanying it; the inhospitability of her living conditions; the disappointment and grim life of the chorus; the bitter love affair with an older man who in his final abandonment of her echoed the recent loss of her father; and the apparent final breach with her mother—all of these crystallized the nascent attitudes the young Ella Williams already had regarding women, men and money and their complicated relationship to love, parenting and sex. It is at this time that Rhys began a lifelong identification of England with human cruelty, exploitation, coldness, sterility, death and separation and her own feelings of failure, disaffection and alienation.

The disappointments represented by England led to a perpetuation of the myth of home, and an overwhelming sense of loss represented most by the death of her father and the abandonment by her lover, a dualism that informs the entire first half of *Voyage in the Dark*. These two events and the final breach with her mother seem to have signified and validated the permanence of her homelessness and her statelessness, though as we've seen, these feelings were already developing in Dominica.

The sea that Ella Williams crossed marked a literal and symbolic separation, the loss of part of her self. For both Jean Rhys and her young autobiographical heroine, Anna Morgan, one of the last memories of home is of her father, a memory mixed with fondness, identification, anticipation and the destruction of what was fragile in the young girl, symbolized in both cases by the crushing of her coral brooch. In *Smile Please*, Rhys writes, in part one supposes, ironically:

[My father] came with my aunt and myself as far as Bridgetown, Barbados, where we caught the ocean boat. When we said goodbye, he hugged me tightly but I said: 'Goodbye, goodbye' very cheerfully, for already I was on my way to England. Down in the cabin which I shared with my aunt I saw that the little coral brooch which I was wearing had been crushed. I had been very fond of it; now I took it off and put it away without any particular feeling. Already all my childhood, the West Indies, my father and mother had been left behind; I was forgetting them. They were the past. (pp. 93–94)

And in *Voyage in the Dark*, Anna Morgan says, "And that time when I was crying about nothing and I thought he'd be wild, but he hugged me up and he didn't say anything. I had on a coral brooch and it got crushed. 'I believe you're going to be like me, you poor little devil'" (p. 59).

In Rhys's developing symbology, England provided the antithesis to "home," an anti-home. If Dominica was light, England was dark; if Dominica was warm, England was cold; if in Dominica the male seduction was "mental" and paid for with chocolates, in England it approached prostitution; if Dominica was dominated by the rejecting figure of Rhys's mother, England proffered an endless line of hostile landladies; and if Rhys's island suggested the expansiveness of the soul, England offered finite enclosure, infinitely.

Women. But Plante's version also points to Rhys's feelings of guilt. Plante reports Rhys's words to him:

'I came back to the hotel room with it, from the hospital. It slept in a cot in a corner. One day the *sage femme* came from the hospital to look at it. She said, 'I think your child has to go back to the hospital.' I said, 'You think so?' She took it away. I got a *bleu* a little while later to say it was dying and did I want it baptized? I asked Jean. He said, 'No, never, I won't have a child of mine baptized.' I became upset. He went out and bought some champagne; we drank the champagne and I felt better. The next morning I got another *bleu* saying my son had died. I wondered if it died while we were drinking champagne. . . .

I must have done something wrong. I was never a good mother.' (p. 18)

At about this time, in March 1920, Jean Lenglet obtained a post with the Interallied Commission in Vienna. Rhys later joined Lenglet there. Her first published story, "Vienne," deals with the time in Vienna, a period in her life when she appears to have had some money and a brief sense of pleasure in life. In the story, of course written in hindsight after the entire Vienna escapade fell apart, the memory, as in most of Rhys's work, is tinged with a fatalistic sense of its necessary end. At some point Lenglet had become involved in some illegal trafficking of money and they had to flee. This flight provides the last section of "Vienne." Rhys has described in several interviews her ignorance of what her husband was doing, " 'Maybe it was ego, maybe selfishness . . . but I never asked my husband where the money was coming from.' "⁵ In the novel *Quartet,* the first 18 pages of which incorporate some of Rhys's early history with Lenglet, Marya also is unaware—perhaps chooses to remain unaware— of where her husband gets his sudden sums of money, although she suspects that it is something illegal. The history of her marriage to Lenglet reoccurs in several of Jean Rhys's works: it forms the basis for flashbacks in *Good Morning, Midnight, Quartet,* and the story "Vienne."

Rhys gave birth to a daughter, Maryvonne, in Brussels in 1922. According to David Plante, she also returned to England twice during this period, at least once to borrow money from " 'the only person who, as usual, would give it' " (PR, p. 259). This was almost certainly the man with whom she had had her first love affair and to whom she refers even in her last interviews. Meanwhile, Rhys's daughter remained in care in a clinic in

Brussels while Rhys and Lenglet tried to seek some source of money. Rhys never once mentions her daughter in the autobiography, nor does she seem to surface in Rhys's fiction. However, her relationship to her daughter, as revealed in her letters, appears to have been a deep and affectionate one. The section of the letters devoted to their later correspondence reveals not only Rhys's essential difficulty in mothering or nurturing, but also her very strong feeling of love toward her daughter.

It was about this time that Rhys became involved with the idea of publishing—not her own work but translations of Lenglet's. She also met Ford Madox Ford, who was to have a strong influence on her and her work. In *Smile Please,* Rhys describes it this way: "I thought one day that if Jean [Lenglet] wrote three articles I would translate them and sell them to some English paper or magazine" (p. 153). Rhys says that she eventually took the translated articles to a Mrs. Adam, the wife of the British correspondent for the *Times* in Paris whom she'd met earlier in London. Mrs. Adam explained that the articles were not appropriate for the *Times* and asked Rhys if she had written anything herself. Rhys writes: "I thought of the exercise books that I'd carried round without having looked at them for years" (p. 154). She reluctantly dropped off the books, having explained to Mrs. Adam that " 'I've got a sort of thing I wrote years ago—a diary or rather I wrote it in diary form' " (p. 155). Mrs. Adam wrote to her saying she liked what she'd read. When Rhys met with her again she asked if she might type them up and send them, as Rhys reports in *Smile Please,*

to a man called Mr. Ford Madox Ford, who published a small magazine, *The Transatlantic Review.* She said that Ford Madox Ford had been the brilliant editor of the *English Review,* a London magazine, and that he was famous for spotting and helping young authors. 'You don't mind if I change parts of it in the typing, do you?' she said. 'It's perhaps a bit naive here and there.' I said, no, I didn't mind at all what she did.

. . . However, when she showed me the typed manuscript which she'd called *Triple Sec* I didn't really like it. She had divided it up into several parts, the name of a man heading each part. It was sent to Ford. I kept the notebooks, and started looking at them again one day several years later. I became interested in them and they were the foundation for *Voyage in the Dark.* (pp. 155–156)

Rhys's account of this beginning, in terms of its chronology, of what she actually did show Mrs. Adam, and how she met Ford, differs markedly in several sources. It may be that Rhys, at that time, showed some of Lenglet's work as her own or that she showed work which was the product of their collaborative effort.

In the *Paris Review,* when asked "the story of the publication of *The Left Bank,*" Rhys answered, " 'It's an odd story. My first husband was a poet, half-French half-Dutch. He had been on the Disarmament Commission in Vienna after the first World War. . . . someone in his office became interested in my writing and showed my stories to Ford Madox Ford' " (p. 225). In 1925 Ford did publish a story by Rhys ("Vienne") in the *Transatlantic Review.* A note accompanying the story says: "From a novel called *Triple Sec.*"[6] Later, in her first published book, *The Left Bank* (which appeared with an introduction by Ford), this story is the last selection and is about twice the length of the *Transatlantic Review* piece.

Stella Bowen, Ford's common-law wife at the time of Rhys's involvement with him, writes of Rhys in her own autobiography, *Drawn from Life.* She refers to a manuscript that Rhys had and writes, "The girl was a really tragic person. She had written an unpublishably sordid novel of great sensitiveness and persuasiveness. . . . When we met her she possessed nothing but a cardboard suit-case and the astonishing manuscript."[7] It would seem that Bowen's reference is to the notebooks that Rhys said she always carried with her. It appears that Ford had been shown them and that Bowen at least was unfamiliar with any other writing that Rhys might have done or possessed.

Thomas Staley's account differs from the above. He says that Rhys and Mrs. Adam had met a few times, the initial visit coming about as Rhys describes in *Smile Please*:

Mrs. Adam asked Jean if she had done any writing herself, and Jean shyly mentioned that she had written a few slight sketches. Pearl Adam took them and tried to make them into a fictional narrative which she called 'Triple Sec'. The project was doomed from the beginning because Mrs. Adam tended to romanticise the stories from Jean's material, and neither was satisfied. (p. 10)

In a chapter note Staley adds:

There is some confusion about the material which Rhys gave Mrs. Adam. In an interview she insists that it was not what was to become *The Left Bank* stories. Elgin Mellown in his essay . . . suggests that the stories were later published under *The Left Bank* title. Some of them may have been radically changed later and included in the volume, but several of the stories, because of their subject matter, were written after Rhys met Ford, and therefore, could not have been given to Mrs. Adam. In any event, the stories or sketches, at least in the form given to Mrs. Adam, have not survived. (p. 132)

In the essay to which Staley refers in this note, Elgin W. Mellown says:

In 1922 or 1923, . . . Mrs. George Adam . . . brought her stories and sketches to the attention of Ford Madox Ford. . . . In the last issue of the *Transatlantic Review,* he published under the title 'Vienne' a few sections of a novel called *Triple Sec* which she was then writing. . . . He also wrote a lengthy preface to Rhys's first book, a collection of short stories entitled *The Left Bank.*[8]

Mellown's article was published in 1972, when very little biographical information was available on Rhys. In a preliminary footnote Mellown includes in the sources of his biographical information Francis Wyndham's introduction to *Wide Sargasso Sea* and an interview by Marcelle Bernstein in the *London Observer.*[9] Mellown's article also makes reference to Bowen's autobiography for references to the ménage à trois formed by Rhys, Bowen and Ford.

Marcelle Bernstein's article, cited by Mellown, says that Rhys showed Mrs. Adam English translations of some articles by Lenglet and that Mrs. Adam asked her for more of her writing, eventually sending it to Ford Madox Ford who published them [sic] in a magazine. Mellown reiterates Bernstein's version, making no suggestion that the stories shown to Mrs. Adam were among the stories which later appeared in *The Left Bank.*

Given Rhys's insistence to Staley and given the later account in her autobiography, coupled with Bowen's recollection of the manuscript, it would appear that, along with other material, Rhys showed Mrs. Adam the exercise books. She may also have shown her the story or sketches that appeared under the title "Vienne." Many of the sections of "Vienne" appear under the subtitle of a man's name, similar to what Rhys describes Mrs. Adam having done in the typescript she made.

In 1975, when very little information about Rhys was in print, I asked her in a letter whether *Voyage in the Dark* was written sometime before its publication or before any of the work published previous to it. I also asked her if the manuscript Stella Bowen refers to in *Drawn from Life* was ever published. I thought that perhaps Stella Bowen was referring to the manuscript for *Voyage in the Dark*. Rhys's answer to my inquiry is still another version of her publishing history and quite different from her later account in *Smile Please*. She says in her letter:

I never wrote or showed Mr. Ford any long novel publishable or otherwise.

I did show him some short stories. He published one in the 'Transatlantic' and advised me about writing very generously.

Something else that I'd written when a very young girl may have been shown him by *someone else*. [Rhys's emphasis] Not by me. Nor was it a novel.[10]

This unique version of the story seems to be the most specific about two kinds of work having been shown to Ford. It would appear that Rhys may have shown Ford some short stories and sketches after his interest had been whetted by Mrs. Adam's showing him the exercise books and perhaps the story "Vienne."

In at least two other interviews Rhys says that Ford was shown the diaries. The *Arts Guardian* reports, "Unasked, Mrs. Adam typed out the diary, knocked it into shape with a connecting narrative, and presented the manuscript to Ford, then editor of the "Transatlantic," who was bowled over, . . . The diary was later to form the basis of Miss Rhys's favourite novel, *Voyage in the Dark*.[11] The *New York Times* writes, "Ford saw her diaries, urged her to write for publication and offered her advice, encouragement and the cash she needed even more urgently after her marriage broke up."[12]

Rhys's longtime friend and publisher, Diana Athill, also believes that Rhys gave the diaries to Mrs. Adam. In a letter to me Athill writes:

I don't personally have any doubt that the ms she gave to Mrs. Adam was the first, 'diary-like' attempt at Voyage, and nothing else. She told me the story so often . . . how it made her feel quite sick to take it out of the suitcase, and how she stuffed it through the letter-box and hurried away, thinking 'There's still a chance that the concierge will lose it, or something' (because the thought of Mrs. Adam reading it was so nerve-racking). But I have never thought it figured that she sat down as soon as she met Ford, and began to write stories.[13]

Rhys's contact with Mrs. Adam is interesting too in that it reflects a writing partnership between Rhys and Lenglet that only recently has been uncovered in any detail. Martien Kappers-den Hollander traces the relationships between some of Rhys's work and some of Lenglet's published pieces. Prior to Kappers-den Hollander's work it was rather well known that Lenglet's novel, *Barred,* published under his pen name Edouard de Nève,[14] was a rendering of the story of *Quartet,* which was based on Rhys's relationship with Ford, his common-law wife Stella Bowen and Lenglet. *Barred* presents essentially the same story as told from the husband's point of view. It was published in 1932, four years after *Quartet,* as *In de Strik* (*In the Snare*) and was translated into French and English, the English edition appearing in the same year as the French (*Sous les verrous*) in 1933.

Barred, written in the first person, relates the entire episode from the point of view of the husband, who is sent to jail. While de Nève's writing lacks the intimacy and subtle inclusion of psychological detail and mood of Rhys's writing and while the novel tends toward a sociopolitical didacticism, it is at times a strangely moving piece of writing, in part because of the concern and love the narrator feels for the wife who has betrayed him. More importantly, it allows us a view of Rhys/Marya not clearly revealed in *Quartet*—how, for example, the wife's passivity, or at least de Nève's perception of it, in part contributes to the husband's inability to present his defense before the law: His wife fails even to try to get him evidence he needs to defend himself.

What is also interesting about the English version of the novel is the dedicatory letter to "Jean" that de Nève includes, in which one senses a continuing love and closeness between the by-then estranged couple. That the feeling may have been reciprocal may be borne out too by a flashback in the much later novel *Good Morning, Midnight* and which also appears in the Black Exercise Book, in which Sasha recalls her ex-husband Ennio (clearly based on de Nève) and says: "I knew that I loved him, and that it was for always."[15] Rhys's letters to her daughter and at least one to Francis Wyndham also attest to the affection she continued to have for Lenglet. In a letter to her daughter, on learning of Lenglet's serious illness, she writes: "You know of all the things I *might* say I will risk saying this: If I had never met John [Lenglet] there would have been no books, no "aliveness" and above all, no you. I can't imagine what my life would have been at all at all—Useless and boring—" (15 Feb. 1960; JRL, p. 182).

The English translation of *Barred* in fact was done by Jean Rhys although, as Martien Kappers-den Hollander has pointed out, Rhys must have used the French version, *Sous les verrous,* as she did not know Dutch. In the foreword to *Smile Please,* Diana Athill reports of this translation that Rhys "thought it 'only fair' that her husband's fictionalised version of events should be available as well as hers, and she took a good deal of trouble to find a publisher for her translation of it. She also said that she had given way to the temptation to cut a few—a very few—sentences about herself which struck her as 'too unfair' " (p. 15). However, in an unpublished paper, Paul Delaney has examined the relationship between *Sous les verrous* and *Barred* and found quite a few other changes. And Martien Kappers-den Hollander has examined *Barred, Sous les verrous,* and the Dutch version *In de Strik.*[16]

According to Kappers-den Hollander, Lenglet and Rhys often collaborated on works even after their separation. She cites stories of his, published long after he and Rhys had separated, which are clear, word-for-word borrowings from published and not yet published works of Rhys's. Kappers-den Hollander reports that he also translated in 1935 into Dutch an "authorized" version of *Voyage in the Dark* in which the narrative is changed to the third person. Furthermore, in 1969, another translation in Dutch appeared, this time by Lenglet's second wife, Henriette van Eyck. (Lenglet, who died in 1961, and van Eyck, who died in 1980, were divorced.) Kappers-den Hollander also quotes their daughter Maryvonne's recollection of their collaboration:

'That fragments and episodes should be verbally almost identical is not astonishing. After the Ford episode their literary collaboration was considerable. . . . The financial situation of both was quite miserable. Jean Rhys was very generous and more than once wrote short pieces that Ed. de Nève would then publish under his own name. On the other hand, Ed. de Nève supplied her with themes during the "Hudnut" period.' [The time when Rhys wrote "fairy tales" for adults for women's magazines.] (p. 34)

Even in Rhys's last collection of short stories, Rhys herself points out and Kappers-den Hollander mentions that the story "Le Chevalier of the Place Blanche" is "a much-adapted translation of one written by Edouard de Nève."[17]

Diana Athill has also commented on this literary collaboration and on Rhys's thoughts about including "The Chevalier of the Place Blanche" in

Sleep It Off, Lady. She writes in a letter to me that "Jean made heavy weather about including 'The Chevalier' with her stories, asking me repeatedly whether I thought it all right to use it considering that it was really Lenglet's story, although she had done quite a lot to it."[18]

In 1923 Jean Lenglet was arrested in France. He was imprisoned and eventually extradited to Holland. In the meantime, Rhys had become involved in a ménage à trois with Ford and his common-law wife, the painter Stella Bowen. The relationship with Ford had a tremendous effect on Rhys both in terms of herself as a writer and in terms of her personal life. Yet aside from the meeting with Mrs. Adam, Rhys never mentions Ford in *Smile Please.*

After Lenglet was arrested, Ford and Bowen wrote to Rhys, asking her to have dinner with them. As in the novel *Quartet,* they asked her to come and live with them, offering to take care of her—which it would appear they did do, at least financially. During that time Ford introduced her to many of the literati in Paris—Stein, Hemingway and once Joyce. But in general, Rhys remained on the periphery. In fact, one gets very little sense that at this time Rhys actually considered herself a writer, although she always seemed to have been clear about what was needed and necessary in her work.

The relationship between Rhys and Bowen appears to have been, understandably, an unpleasant one and according to David Plante, Rhys found her "a down to earth, business-like snob, grimly determined to get on" (PR, p. 260). Bowen, on the other hand, seems to have had a hard time managing financial affairs, which were always difficult for herself and Ford. She also seems to have been coerced into "cooperating" with Ford's love affairs. She reports on the Rhys-Ford affair, which she says ultimately "cut the fundamental tie" between them, in *Drawn from Life,* though she never names Rhys. While Bowen's account betrays a long-held grudge against "Ford's girl," as she refers to Rhys, she also reveals a bitter understanding of the conditions of Rhys's life and the difficulty of not having money. She writes:

It showed me a side of life of which I had had no previous knowledge. The girl was really a tragic person. . . . Her gift for prose and her personal attractiveness were not enough to ensure her any reasonable life, for on the other side of the balance were bad health, destitution, shattered nerves, an undesirable hus-

band, lack of nationality, and a complete absence of any desire for independence. . . .

She lived with us for many weeks whilst we tried to set her on her feet. Ford
gave her invaluable help with her writing, and I tried to help her with her clothes.
I was singularly slow in discovering that she and Ford were in love. We finally
got her a job to "ghost" a book for someone on the Riviera.

She had a needle-quick intelligence and a good sort of emotional honesty, but
she was a doomed soul, violent and demoralised. She had neither the wish nor
the capacity to tackle practical difficulties. . . .

She took the lid off the world that she knew, and showed us an underworld of
darkness and disorder, where officialdom, the bourgeoisie and the police were the
eternal enemies and the fugitive the only hero. All the virtues, in her view, were
summed up in 'being a sport,' which meant being willing to take risks and show
gallantry and share one's last crust; more attractive qualities, no doubt, than
patience or honesty or fortitude. She regarded the law as the instrument of the
'haves' against the 'have nots' and was well acquainted with every rung of that
long and dismal ladder by which the respectable citizen descends towards degradation.

It was not her fault that she knew these things, and the cynicism they engendered had an unanswerable logic in it. It taught me that the only really unbridgeable gulf in human society is between the financially solvent and the destitute.
You can't have self-respect without money. You can't even have the luxury of a
personality. To expect people who are destitute to be governed by any considerations whatever except money considerations is just hypocrisy. If they show any
generous instincts as well, it is more than society has any right to expect. . . .

Life with Ford had always felt to me pretty insecure. Yet here I was cast for
the rôle of the fortunate wife who held all the cards, and the girl for that of the
poor, brave and desperate beggar who was doomed to be let down by the bour-
geoise. . . . I simply hated my rôle! (pp. 166–167)

One can sympathize with Bowen's resentment at being placed in the
position of someone with power and comfort when she herself was probably hurt, and struggling to support their household. Furthermore, Bow-
en's reminiscences were published in 1941, several years after Rhys had
already published four novels, the first of which, *Quartet,* was an account
of the affair with Ford in which Stella (Lois) is cast in a most unsympathetic light. Bowen neglects to mention the pressure both she and Ford
may have put on Rhys to participate in the affair—Rhys treats this aspect

in *Quartet*—and she neglects to mention that "Ford's girl" eventually became a writer whose works were well received.

What is interesting in Bowen's description, aside from the biographical information it gives us about Rhys at this time, is that her account might easily be a description of any one of the heroines of Rhys's first four novels. David Plante, in *Difficult Women,* makes an interesting observation about Rhys and the relationship of her life to her novels. In discussing the death of her infant son, Rhys appeared to be surprised that Plante had any idea of the story. He says, "I wondered if she thought I might have had some access to the story of her life which she didn't know about—and of course I did: her novels. She did not, however, think that in reading her novels one knew anything about her life" (p. 18). In fact, in interviews, Rhys often treats incidents from the past in a far more cavalier manner than she does in her writing. The writing seems to delve more deeply into the "emotional truth" (e.g., her descriptions of the deaths of her father and her son).

Rhys always felt very bitter about the treatment afforded her in *Drawn from Life,* though she said that she'd never read it, and the treatment she received in Mizener's biography of Ford in which selections about Rhys from Bowen's memoir appear. In a letter to me Rhys says:

> I have never read Stella Bowen's 'Drawn from Life' but some quotations from it appeared in a life of Ford which I did read.
>
> Much of what she said about me was untrue, yet it was all quoted as proved fact.
>
> I was angry about it but I was advised to be dignified and silent. However it seems that 'Drawn from Life' even when totally untrue is still believed or half believed. I really don't know what to do about it.
>
> Nothing I suppose!
>
> It all happened long ago & nearly everyone concerned is dead.
>
> But old lies have long shadows too![19]

More than fifty years after her affair with Ford and more than thirty after the publication of *Drawn From Life,* Rhys was still surprisingly disturbed by the episode, so much so that she concludes the letter above with the

statement: "What an immense letter! But it has relieved me to write it."
Perhaps Rhys's concern about Bowen's account was linked to her sense
of herself as a writer. In the *Paris Review* interview, when asked about
the writing of *Voyage in the Dark,* Rhys described the story of its genesis
and then added: "Someone described the result as unpublishably sordid
but with great sensitiveness and persuasiveness so I went on to other
things!" (p. 225). This is the precise wording of Stella Bowen's description of Rhys's "incredible manuscript" in *Drawn From Life.*

In 1925 Rhys went to the south of France to work with Mrs. Huenot
who wanted help in writing a book on furniture (the "ghost job" Bowen
refers to). According to David Plante, Ford had arranged for the job by
sending two pieces he had written but claiming they'd been written by
Rhys. Later, Ford sent a rude letter to Mrs. Huenot accusing her of
paying Rhys too little. Rhys was dismissed and Ford found her a room
in Paris. This was 1925. She traveled back to Paris with Mrs. Huenot,
and Ford met her at the station. Plante says that Rhys never fully understood why Ford sent the letter. He notes that: "All of this Jean left out
of the novel *Quartet* because it did not fit into the novel's shape" (PR,
p. 263). In fact, in *Quartet,* Marya, who is sent to the south of France
by her lover Heidler (Ford), finally returns to Paris because her husband
has been released from prison and writes to her that he will be going to
Paris; he encloses money for her return. This portion of the novel, toward
its end, signals "a faint stirring of hope."[20] In fact, according to David
Plante, Rhys did return again to the south of France after Ford had
brought her back and this time was helped to leave by her husband in a
similar way that Marya is helped in *Quartet.* Rhys's omission of the first
return to Paris is a suitable example of the way she used and changed her
own biography to fit the shape of her fiction.

Whatever may have been the repercussions of Rhys's love affair with
Ford, it is certain that not only did he encourage Rhys by teaching her
about writing, he actually helped launch her career. In 1927, although
their affair was coming to a painful conclusion, he arranged for the publication of her first book of short stories, *The Left Bank and Other Stories,*
which contained the long piece "Vienne," already published by Ford in
shorter form in the *Transatlantic Review.* The collection also contained
an introduction by Ford of 21 pages, the first 16 of which never once
mention Rhys or her work. Ford, at this time, says Samuel Putnam in
his memoirs of Paris, "was on a veritable spree of preface- and blurb-

writing and, as it seemed to happen most of his discoveries were women."[21]

In his preface to *The Left Bank,* Ford rambles on about his memories of France, Paris and the Left Bank of his youth. Finally he asks, "what . . . is the lot of those who must wait till their Thought is the accepted Thought of tomorrow?"—meaning the artists, writers, painters and sculptors who inhabit the Left Bank. He says:

> To some extent the answer will be found in Miss Rhys's book for which I have not so much been asked, as I have asked to be allowed the privilege of supplying this Preface. . . .

> Coming from the Antilles, with a terrifying insight and a terrific—an almost lurid!—passion for stating the case of the underdog, she has let her pen loose on the Left Banks of the Old World—on its gaols, its studios, its salons, its cafés, its criminals, its midinettes—with a bias of admiration for its midinettes and of sympathy for its law-breakers. It is a note, a sympathy of which we do not have too much in Occidental literature with its perennial bias towards satisfaction with things as they are. But it is a note that needs sounding—that badly needs sounding, since the real activities of the world are seldom carried much forward by the accepted, or even by the Hautes Bourgeoisies![22]

Despite Ford's inflated and patronizing prose, he pinpoints here one of the characteristics of Rhys's work: her sympathy and assumption of the point of view of the alien and outcast character, the "loser."

Ford continues, saying that when he "lately edited a periodical," he was "immensely struck" by Rhys's stories "of which I published as many as I could" (p. 24). Since he only published one of her stories, either Rhys only had one to publish or Ford craftily suggests that her publishing background was wider than it actually was. Ford also commends Rhys's "singular instinct for form . . . , an instinct for form being possessed by singularly few writers of English and by almost no English women writers" (pp. 24–25). Ford also wrote that he tried to induce Rhys to:

> introduce some sort of topography of that region [the Left Bank], bit by bit, into her sketches—in the cunning way in which it would have been done by Flaubert or Maupassant. . . . With cold deliberation, once her attention was called to the matter, she eliminated even such two or three words of descriptive matter as had crept into her work. Her business was with passion, hardship, emotions: the locality in which these things are endured is immaterial. (pp. 25–26)

Unless Ford was fabricating, his preface points to the fact that Rhys was already very clear about what she wanted her work to be like. Certainly this particular lack of "topography," as Ford calls it, or local color continued throughout Rhys's work—except perhaps in parts of *Wide Sargasso Sea* and *Voyage in the Dark* where the land and the landscape of Dominica are vital to an understanding of both Anna and Antoinette.

When *The Left Bank* was published, the affair between Rhys and Ford had apparently already come to an end. In fact, if we put both Staley's and Plante's accounts together, it would appear that the second time Rhys returned to the south of France, the affair was already over. Plante says:

Ford and Stella lent her money to return to the south of France. . . .

Jean felt depressed, in a rage. She felt that all Ford had said about her writing, his concern for it, was false. That was what hurt most: she had imagined she had been a bit in love with Ford, but she wasn't, and she didn't think he was ever in love with her, but only in her writing, and he was, finally, false to that, because she couldn't believe he could behave as he had and still be sincere about her work. (PR, p. 263)

It was at this time that Rhys's husband sent her money to return to Paris; he then offered to take her to Amsterdam, although he was never to forgive her for the episode with Ford. (Plante gives the year as 1925.) Martien Kappers-den Hollander suggests that the Lenglets separated in 1924, prior to going together to Amsterdam. According to David Plante, in 1925 Jean Lenglet made the offer to go to Amsterdam and Rhys decided to accompany him. They left Paris almost immediately, leaving their daughter Maryvonne at a place in Paris that the Richelot family had found for her. Meanwhile, Ford had gotten Rhys a job translating Francis Carco's novel *Perversity,* which was published in Chicago by Covici in 1928.[23] According to both Staley and Plante, Rhys was aided in the translation by her husband.

Perversity contains one novella and one pseudo-journalistic "story." Carco's stories deal with the "underworld" of petty thieves, prostitutes and pimps; his characters, unlike Rhys's, often fall into stereotypes while the plots are melodramatic and cliched. There is none of the directness and emotional honesty in *Perversity* that characterizes the best of Rhys. Perhaps the melodramatic conclusion of *Perversity* shares something in kind with the end of *Quartet* but other than that, Carco's novel shares little with Rhys's, except for some of the subject matter and that only peripherally and superficially. Rhys's translation is also quite uncomfortable and awkward in parts and, unlike *Barred,* does not seem strongly influenced by her own style.

When *Perversity* was published, Ford was credited with the translation; in fact, his name shares the place of honor with Carco on the cover of the book. According to Arthur Mizener in *The Saddest Story,* this was absolutely not Ford's intention but was a fortuitous mistake for the publisher. In a letter to Isabel Patterson written in 1928, Ford credits Rhys with the translation and says, "I could not have done it myself half so well if at all because translating is not one of my gifts and I do not know the particular Parisian argot that Mr. Carco employs."[24] Rhys also mentions the translation of *Perversity* in a 1966 letter to Francis Wyndham in which she says that she knew "Ford did his best to put things right." She also expresses her own dissatisfaction with the translation, saying that "it had to be done in a hurry and there was a good deal of slang" (JRL, p. 295).

Although Rhys joined her husband in Amsterdam, the affair with Ford had signalled the end of her marriage. He could not forgive Rhys's involvement with Ford and felt it as a great betrayal. If we accept *Barred* as Lenglet's rendition of the period, his bitterness and hurt remained for some time. According to Thomas Staley, at this time "Jean and de Nève did not live as husband and wife" (p. 14). At some point de Nève returned to Paris to get their daughter; when the couple split up completely, he assumed primary care of her. Meanwhile, in Amsterdam, Rhys was working on the Carco translation and also on her first novel, *Quartet,* which she finished there. According to Staley, Jonathan Cape, which had first published *The Left Bank,* refused to publish *Quartet* because they knew that it was very close to the events of Ford's life and they feared libel. The book was eventually published by Chatto and Windus under the title *Postures* in 1928. In America, Rhys's preferred title of *Quartet* was used. Staley says: "Jean later wrote that she never really understood why Chatto insisted on changing the title." In a letter to me Rhys wrote, "I wrote a novel 'Quartet' which was the original title but the publishers feared libel and asked me to change it, I was so fed up with the whole thing I called it 'Postures' which has no meaning whatsoever!!"[25] There seems to be no definitive account of the years that followed the affair with Ford. Although that affair did signal the essential end of the marriage between Lenglet and Rhys, they remained in close contact with each other, in part for financial reasons, for their daughter, and perhaps because of their "literary collaboration." Some of the confusion appears to arise from differing accounts that Rhys herself may have given. While that may have been a result of her advanced age and perhaps inaccurate memory, Rhys also, while surprisingly "open" in her novels about her own life, seems to have cloaked a considerable number of the facts of her life in mystery.

It was about this time that Rhys and Lenglet split up for good and Rhys met the man who became her second husband, Leslie Tilden Smith. Staley and Plante differ in their accounts of this period. It would seem from some additional information that Plante includes that his version is most accurate. In addition, his account accords, in part, with other information given by Martien Kappers-den Hollander. Staley says:

She and de Nève finally broke off altogether, were eventually divorced, and Jean returned to England. Shortly after her arrival she met Leslie Tilden Smith, who was then a literary agent and had been a reader with several publishers. . . . Leslie and Jean became very close and by 1929 they began living together. They were later married and remained together until Leslie died on 2 October, 1945. (p. 15)

Plante states that when *Quartet* was finished,

Jean went to London to try to sell it, though she hated it. She was ill. Her husband persuaded her to go. Through Ford, Jean had an agent in London, Leslie ———. He had written Ford asking him if Ford wanted an agent, and Ford had replied that he himself didn't, but he knew of a writer who could use an agent, Jean. Leslie ——— gave the book to Edward Garnett, a kind comfortable man, an influential publisher's reader. He said that Cape, who had published *Left Bank,* didn't want to publish *Quartet* because of libel, but Chatto would. . . . Jean and Leslie had a fifty-fifty affair. The book was sold in America, from which Jean got enough money to go to Paris, alone. (PR, p. 264)

Plante goes on to say that by 1932, "Jean's husband was very distant. When he found out about Leslie, he asked for a divorce. He asked, too, for possession of their daughter. He wrote Jean a nice letter: they couldn't go on as they were, he wanted their daughter to be educated in Holland, but she could visit on holidays. Jean agreed" (p. 265). Diana Athill, who knew Rhys longer and possibly more intimately than Plante or Staley, includes in her introduction to *Smile Please* a brief chronology. She states

that Rhys met Leslie Tilden Smith in 1927 and was divorced from Jean
Lenglet and married Smith in 1932. Martien Kappers-den Hollander,
whose work concentrates more on Lenglet, says that the Lenglets separated in 1924, agreeing to share responsibility for their daughter. According to Kappers-den Hollander, Lenglet spent some time in 1924 to 1925
as a private tutor. She adds:

> After a while this quiet life became too much for him and he left her in the care
> of friends and relatives. He travelled to New York and Tokyo, then back to
> France, where he became a correspondent for *Le Petit Parisien,* until he suffered
> some kind of breakdown. After his return to Holland Lenglet met Henriëtte van
> Eyck and in 1932 he finally agreed to divorce his first wife.
>
> In the same year Jean Rhys married Leslie Tilden Smith, whom she had met
> in England in 1927, and Jean Lenglet . . . married Henriëtte van Eyck. Their
> daughter, by mutual consent, stayed in Holland for her schooling, both parents
> providing for her. She would spend her holidays with her mother in England.
> When Henriëtte van Eyck went to London to marry Jean Lenglet, she travelled
> together with his daughter, who was on her way to one of these vacations. In fact,
> the contact between her parents and their respective spouses was so good that
> they would occasionally meet, in London as well as in Amsterdam. (p. 31)

Staley gives an account of Leslie Tilden Smith's background and of the
years Rhys spent with him. Tilden Smith, who had himself been married
and separated, had three children before World War I and Staley bases
some of his information on their reports. According to Staley, during the
years 1929 to 1932, Rhys "made several visits back to Paris mainly to
work on *After Leaving Mr. MacKenzie*" (p. 15). Staley reports that the
years they spent together "were anything but idyllic" because of financial
and drinking problems (p. 16).

In her letters to Evelyn Scott, which are now in the Humanities Research Center at the University of Texas at Austin and were written
during her marriage to Tilden Smith, Rhys indicates that they continued
to move from lodging to lodging, that they rarely had enough money and
that she was unable to control her drinking. In addition, Rhys seems to
have been in a fragile state, both mentally and physically.[26]

In the Black Exercise Book, also kept during her marriage to Tilden
Smith, Rhys complains about her drinking, what it has done to her physically, socially and even mentally and adds that she's been drinking heavily
for years. Alcohol continued to be a problem for Rhys up until her death;

she apparently at times tried to stop drinking. In a 1933 letter to Evelyn Scott she says that she hasn't had "a drop for a month" but that she is looking forward to the "kick" that will result from her resumption of alcohol (JRL, p. 22).

In 1936, after inheriting some money on the death of Tilden Smith's father, the couple made a trip to the West Indies, including Dominica, and to the United States. Of the impending trip, Rhys wrote to Evelyn Scott, "I suppose going back to Dominica is foolhardy but I want to so much—I can't help risking it—you can imagine the wild & fantastic plans and hopes" (JRL, p. 27). It was Rhys's first return to Dominica since she had left as a young girl and clearly, in her words to Scott, she recognized her tremendous investment in her memories of home. She was then over 40. There is a picture of her, taken in Dominica, which appears in her autobiography: a woman, still quite handsome, looks over the edge of a hammock in which she seems uncomfortably poised. There is also included in *Smile Please* a photo of the ruined gardens of Geneva—an estate that appears set in such deep clefts of overgrown mountains that it could fall off.

Rhys has spoken about this trip in several interviews and about her disappointment and resentment over the changes she found in Dominica. In the *Paris Review* interview she says flatly: "I went back to the West Indies and I hated it" (p. 236). But in a letter to Evelyn Scott written soon after their arrival on the island she seems almost euphoric, claiming misanthropically that "the wonderful thing is to wake up and know that nobody can get at you—nobody." At the conclusion of the letter she mentions her future travel plans but adds: "But I don't want to think about going away yet" (JRL, p. 29). About the entire trip, however, Staley concludes:

The people, their language and customs, still interested and even charmed her, but as much as anything else it was the island itself which stirred in Jean both memory and emotion. Even so, after spending so many years in Europe, the slow, languid life of Dominica now seemed to her remote and even boring. By the end of May she was anxious to leave. (p. 17)

When Rhys revisited Dominica this one and only time she had already published *The Left Bank, Quartet, After Leaving Mr. Mackenzie* and *Voyage in the Dark*. She was then at work on *Good Morning, Midnight*, which was published in 1939, several years after this return. She later used the visit as the basis of several stories in *Sleep It Off, Lady* and, most importantly, perhaps it gave her the wider range of vision and point of view evident in *Wide Sargasso Sea.*

After the publication of *Good Morning, Midnight* in 1939, Rhys's publications stopped for over 25 years. The war not only terminated Rhys's periodic visits to the Continent, it also interrupted her intermittent relationship with her daughter, who left from a holiday visit to her mother on the last boat from England to Holland to join her father. While Rhys never assumed the primary care of her daughter her letters to Evelyn Scott indicate her continuing concern about Maryvonne and her pleasure in her daughter. In a 1935 letter to Scott, she writes of a pre-War visit from Maryvonne:

She is so tall and gawky and sweet and sings so loudly all over the place that she's bringing me to life again—She is of a hopeful disposition I notice spent hours yesterday making a contraption with chalk and cotton wool to clean white shoes with!—hopeful and practical. So unlike me thank God. (JRL, p. 26)

During the war, according to Staley, Tilden Smith served in paramilitary work and Rhys "spent time in London and began to write again, but she all but gave up on the prospects for success. It was more a matter of an unquenchable need to write" (p. 17). Her husband complained that she was closing him off and Rhys, in an interview with Staley "agreed, because [she said], 'I don't see how you can write without shutting everything else out' " (p. 17).

While Rhys for much of her life seemed not to have termed herself a professional writer, and stopped writing professionally for many years, she reveals in interviews and conversations her strong dedication to writing. David Plante records some of Rhys's statements regarding this aspect of herself. Rhys told Plante: "You have to be selfish to be a writer. . . . Monstrously selfish" (p. 37). She also reveals in her conversations with him an intimate knowledge of the constancy necessary for writing. However, in other interviews she was often more cavalier about the writing process, suggesting that it came simply and *only* from particular events which made her "unhappy." However, in *Difficult Women* Plante records a conversation that indicates her understanding of what it meant for her to be a writer. Rhys said to him: " 'People think they can sit down and

write novels. Nonsense. It isn't done that way. It's not a part-time occupation, it's your life' " (p. 41). At another point, describing her frenzy
and near madness in the months after her third husband's death and the
events that finally led her to finish her last novel, *Wide Sargasso Sea,*
Rhys said: " 'Only writing is important. Only writing takes you out of
yourself" (p. 50).

When Tilden Smith died in 1945 Rhys was offered help by his cousin
Max Hamer, whom she married in 1947. Hamer, in a sad replay of her
first marriage, became involved with an apparently minor theft from his
firm and was eventually sent to prison for two years. In a conversation
with David Plante Rhys said:

'I have always been attracted, I suppose, to thieves and saints, not that they were
thieves exactly, and they weren't saints. I didn't know, and I don't know now,
why my first and third husbands were sent to prison. I don't know much about
my husbands, and I don't know much about my parents. Perhaps I wasn't curious.
My daughter once told me my first husband, Jean, was in the French Intelligence.
I didn't know. Max was married before, but whether he had any children or not
I don't know—perhaps a boy or girl. Men used to come to the house. I didn't
like them, especially one. I didn't know what Max did with them. He went to
prison.' (p. 54)

Rhys seems to have been, like her heroines, a remarkably self-absorbed
woman, unaware even, to use Ford's phrase, of the "topography" of her
own life. Certainly one can begin to understand her insistence on the
concept of fate. To be so uninformed about the conditions of one's own
private life may mean that one experiences events as if they happen outside
of one, beyond one's control and comprehension. Many of Rhys's heroines
seem to "choose" to remain ignorant of what to the reader are obvious
realities and then are shocked when those realities have consequences—
as if they live outside a logical order, outside of the most simple cause
and effect. While her heroines are often absorbed with their own pasts,
events themselves seem to occur without a relationship to the past—at
least in the unanalytic minds of her heroines. For Rhys to be able to
represent this added dimension in her fiction, one must suppose that the
naiveté of the above statement (her absolute ignorance of details of her
husbands' lives) is perhaps an unconscious exaggeration.

After Hamer was released from prison, Rhys and he settled in 1953 in a cottage in Cornwall, sight unseen. Rhys reports never having liked the cottage and spending most of her time in the kitchen. She told Plante that she had been trying to write *Wide Sargasso Sea* and after many interruptions in the work " 'in this cottage I quite gave up. . . . As usual, I took refuge in bottles of wine, and would get pretty drunk every night' " (DW, p. 48). In 1964 her husband, who had been ill for some time, died. Rhys said to Plante, " 'I was left completely alone. . . . Alone, when I had nearly finished a bottle of wine, I'd pin on all the medals Max had had, for he had been in the RAF in the First World War, go out of the door, and shout, 'Wings up! Wings up.' I think I must have been pretty nearly crazy at this time' " (DW, p. 48). Rhys describes further to Plante the trouble she had writing her last novel after her husband's death. She tried "to escape" to London for a while and suffered a heart attack. Later she returned to Devon, where they had moved in 1956, and tried to work again on the novel. She describes those attempts:

'Sitting at the long table in the kitchen, I did manage to fill two exercise books, but when I stopped and reread what I had done, I discovered that I had written one short chapter, and then about six more versions of it. It wasn't the chapter that appalled me so much as the fact that every one of the versions was the same. I had merely written the same thing over and over again, not changing a word. After that I gave up. It seemed to me that it would be impossible ever to write again. I had no money; it would be quite useless for me to borrow money from my brother to go up to London. I had only a few books, which I knew almost by heart. I spent my time walking up and down the passage, afraid of the spiders and the mice, and all the people in the village. I think it was one of the worst times of my life." (DW, p. 49)

Rhys's recounting of this episode is sadly reminiscent of episodes earlier in her life and in the lives of her heroines. It seems as if she was bound to repeat it "over and over again," to use the refrain that punctuates *Voyage in the Dark*. Rhys told Plante that it was only after a village clergyman called on her and offered her communion that she was able to resume work on the novel.

Most sources assume that the British actress Selma Vaz Dias "rediscovered" Rhys in 1957. Until recently, only Thomas Staley wrote of an earlier encounter, in 1949, with Vaz Dias. Staley was correct, as the letters at the MacFarlin Library verify. However, that it was not common knowledge may, in fact, be due to an article Vaz Dias herself wrote in 1957 for

Radio Times, a publication of the BBC.[27] Her article appeared prior to the BBC production of her adaptation of *Good Morning, Midnight.*

In her article, "In Quest of a Missing Author," Vaz Dias summarizes some aspects of her search for Jean Rhys, including inquiries to publishers, the examination of death records, and finally the placing of an advertisement in the *New Statesman and Nation,* an ad which Rhys herself answered. Vaz Dias's article records Rhys's words to her after their contact: " 'It seems that it is easy to disappear' " (p. 25). Further on, Vaz Dias briefly summarizes Jean Rhys's background and describes a little of Rhys's current situation. Vaz Dias writes:

In Cornwall she [Rhys] has no radio, but she is having one 'laid on' for the broadcast. 'It is all like a dream,' she tells me. 'You have lifted the hopeless feeling that stopped me writing for so long. You have made me want to write again.'

We have got together and exchanged ideas, and she is now busy writing a novel on a most exciting subject. She is full of a new enthusiasm, and I hope and pray that the reemergence of *Good Morning Midnight* [sic] as a radio monologue will give her sufficient encouragement to write a great deal more and come out of hiding. (p. 25)

For some reason, Vaz Dias disguises the fact that by the time of the appearance of this article, she had been a longtime correspondent and acquaintance of Rhys's and that, in fact, after locating Rhys in 1949, she had lost touch with the writer several times, apparently because Rhys moved without leaving adequate forwarding information. Yet Vaz Dias's article suggests that there was only one "rediscovery" of Rhys and that it occurred shortly before the article appeared, rather than almost a decade earlier. In fact, she clearly suggests that Rhys's words above have been uttered only recently. But in fact they were written by Rhys in letters to Vaz Dias in 1949, eight years before Vaz Dias's article (JRL, Nov. 7 and 9, pp. 60–61).

Vaz Dias's clouding of the facts may simply have been the result of a desire to present a fresh discovery to her audience and to potential publishers of Rhys's work. Furthermore, she might have wanted to conceal that the first production of her *Good Morning, Midnight* adaptation had actually occurred in 1949 at the Anglo-French Art Centre. Apparently neither Jean Rhys nor Selma Vaz Dias did much, later on, to dispel this misunderstanding. Indeed, in his introduction to *Wide Sargasso Sea* in

1966, Francis Wyndham, who was by then a longtime correspondent of Rhys, writes that "as the result of a dramatized version of *Good Morning, Midnight* broadcast on the Third Programme in 1958, she was finally traced to an address in Cornwall."[28] And in a 1984 letter to me, in which she discusses Jean Rhys's difficulty in sorting out dates, Diana Athill writes that not until Francis Wyndham and she had gone through the entire collection of letters did they realize that "there were two 'discoveries' " of Rhys by Vaz Dias.[29]

The initial contact with Vaz Dias, to which Rhys responded so enthusiastically, lasted less than a year. As Rhys's letters reveal, and as Francis Wyndham notes in his edition of the letters, Rhys had been found guilty of assault and placed on probation in the spring prior to the November ad in the *New Statesman and Nation*. During the proceedings, her sanity had been questioned and she was placed in Holloway Prison hospital for a determination of her mental status. In a letter to her longtime friend, Peggy Kirkaldy, written the month before the *New Statesman* ad appeared, Rhys writes of her malaise following the Holloway incident. She tells Kirkaldy that she has no desire to write and adds that it is the first time in her life that that has happened (JRL, pp. 55–56). In a letter to Kirkaldy written after the contact with Vaz Dias, Rhys again refers to the Holloway episode and to the apathy that followed. She then writes that when Vaz Dias contacted her she began to "wake up and make plans and come alive again" (JRL, p. 61).

However, by the time Rhys wrote the second letter, she was again in trouble. This time, in February of 1950, just four months after Rhys's first letter to Vaz Dias, Hamer was charged with check fraud. For a long time after that, Rhys was involved with the fate of her husband and with the problems of her own survival during his imprisonment. Her last letter to Vaz Dias during this period is dated 1950 and anticipates Hamer's upcoming trial (JRL, p. 72). During Hamer's two-year imprisonment, Rhys and Vaz Dias apparently had no contact with each other.

Max Hamer was released in the spring of 1952. At the beginning of 1953, Rhys contacted Vaz Dias again. It would seem that she and her husband may have decided to contact people who had previously expressed interest in her writing; at the same time, her husband wrote to the writer, Morchard Bishop, who had earlier had a correspondence with Rhys. Hamer indicated in his letter that Rhys was anxious to return to her work as a writer (JRL, p. 98). Rhys's renewed correspondence and contact with Vaz Dias lasted until about June of 1953, during which time the two women exchanged ideas regarding productions of Rhys's work and the possibilities of publication. Rhys's last letter from this period acknowledges receipt from Vaz Dias of stories that Rhys had sent her in the hope that the BBC might be interested but which had been rejected (JRL, pp. 108–109).[30]

During the time of this second "silence," Rhys's letters reveal that she, as always, continued to write to her daughter. Those letters, full of love and an impotent concern for both her daughter and grandchild, also reveal her constant preoccupation with trying to find a place to live and trying to eke out enough money to survive. Her letters to her daughter are painful with their lists of unbought presents—the things she'd like to send her daughter and grandchild if she had the money. It is difficult to know exactly why Rhys did not pursue the contact with Vaz Dias during these years, but it may have been due to a combination of factors: the disappointment of the returned stories from the BBC, her poor health and the obstacle that not having a suitable place to write places in the path of a writer. This last problem was one about which Rhys wrote often in her letters: sharing one rented room with her husband made writing very difficult.

Rhys's final resumption of the relationship with Selma Vaz Dias was prompted by another ad placed in the *New Statesman,* this time by Sasha Moorsom of the BBC. Rhys, recognizing that Vaz Dias must have had some involvement, answered the BBC ad and wrote to Vaz Dias at the same time. Her letter is again hopeful and she writes that it is "the first time I've felt half alive for months" (JRL, p. 133).

Until 1973, the two women continued to correspond. But while the initial friendship and collaboration was fruitful and positive for both women, there occurred a serious falling-out between them. Thomas Staley talks about some "misunderstandings" between the two women and alludes to Selma Vaz Dias's "later obsession for claiming she was the sole discoverer of Jean Rhys" (p. 18). In the introduction to his recently published bibliography on Rhys, Elgin Mellown discusses the relationship between Rhys and Vaz Dias and says that they "drifted apart." He also states that there is

a less attractive story that remains to be told, the story of an aging woman whose talent and helplessness invited the unscrupulous—and sometimes even the well-meaning and good-intentioned—to prey upon her. . . . For example, . . . she assigned her writings to different agents so arbitrarily that no one was quite sure who was responsible for which titles, and she irresponsibly signed away rights in her own work. Since all of the evidence is not available—and presenting that which is would be an embarrassment to persons still alive—the story of the lawsuits and the unhappinesses of Jean Rhys's last years cannot yet be fully detailed.[31]

Francis Wyndham, in a long note in the *Letters,* says that in 1963, Vaz Dias had Rhys sign an agreement which gave Vaz Dias "fifty percent of all proceeds from any film, stage, television and radio adaptation of any work by Jean, anywhere in the world, to last until the works came out of copyright, and also granting Selma artistic control of such adaptations" (JRL, p. 289). According to Wyndham, Rhys said that she had regarded the document as a "joke" and that she had been "rather drunk at the time" (JRL, p. 289). He says that Rhys later understood the implications of the document she had signed and felt "tricked" by Vaz Dias. According to Wyndham, Vaz Dias was later persuaded to give up the stipulation that she have complete artistic control and to settle for thirty-three and a third percent rather than fifty. Wyndham sadly notes that this "final agreement is still in force, and a large proportion of the posthumous earnings, which Jean was so anxious should go to Maryvonne, goes instead to Selma's heirs" (JRL, p. 289).

The 1957 broadcast on the BBC was nevertheless an important turning point for Rhys's reputation. That performance brought her public recognition and allowed her access to people in publishing, several of whom had admired her early books. Among those was Francis Wyndham and, later, Diana Athill. Wyndham became a correspondent and later, together with Diana Athill, encouraged Rhys and helped her to continue work on her last novel, *Wide Sargasso Sea.*

Rhys was quite frail and weak during the last fifteen years of her life, suffering heart attacks and injuries from falls. Although *Wide Sargasso Sea* was published in 1966, according to Athill, the novel was ready for publication by 1963, but Rhys would not allow it to be published until she was absolutely certain she had finished polishing the novel. Certainly the many letters in which she writes about *Wide Sargasso Sea* attest to the long time she spent working on it and the painstaking meticulousness she brought to her craft.

Following *Wide Sargasso Sea,* Rhys published two more collections of short stories—*Tigers Are Better Looking* (1968) and *Sleep It Off, Lady* (1974)—both of which contain older stories, some written apparently many years before their publication and some, especially in *Sleep It Off, Lady,* garnered from old autobiographical notes and early drafts, some of which are in the McFarlin Library collection. Rhys was apparently disappointed in the last collection of stories, of which she said to David Plante, " 'And these stories they want me to publish. Not good. I don't want to publish them. I've wasted two and a half years on them' " (DW, p. 19). But Rhys, though she had trouble writing, both physically and otherwise in her later years, needed to continue. It had become her raison d'être. Even in the 1940s diary included in *Smile Please,* when she had lost hope of ever having an audience for her work, she wrote:

I am tired. I learnt everything too late. Everything was always one jump ahead of me. . . . The trouble is I have plenty to say. Not only that but I am bound to say it. . . . I must. . . . I must write. If I stop writing my life will have been an abject failure. It is that already to other people. But it could be an abject failure to myself. I will not have earned death. (p. 163)

And more than three decades later, convinced for the moment that she was "nothing," David Plante reports her saying:

'Listen to me. I want to tell you something very important. All of writing is a huge lake. There are great rivers that feed the lake, like Tolstoy and Dostoevsky. And there are trickles, like Jean Rhys. All that matters is feeding the lake. I don't matter. The lake matters. You must keep feeding the lake. It is very important. Nothing else is important. (DW, p. 22)

During these last years Rhys was forced to use various amanuenses. Without David Plante, in particular, she probably would not have been able to assemble the vignettes that comprise her posthumously published autobiography.

In *Difficult Women* Plante mentions that as he worked with her to assemble her autobiography, Rhys was going through old notes and manuscripts for material. However, his essay gives no idea of the extent to which she used old material, especially from the Black Exercise Book and the unpublished conclusion of *Voyage in the Dark.* Discussing this aspect of Rhys's work, in an answer to my query about the extent of Rhys's "borrowings" from her earlier pieces, Diana Athill gives information about

Rhys's method of working and her relationship to writing in her last years. Athill says:

Jean's subject was—as she often said—herself; so of course she had 'used' everything of importance to her in earlier work either published or abandoned unfinished. . . . She was far from being impelled to write an autobiography in the way that she had been impelled to write her novels. Chiefly—or so it seemed to me—it was a matter of feeling that she had to be writing *something* or her days would be quite empty. . . . All the small amount of energy left to her was up to was the little bit of writing and the piecing together of stuff written earlier which we have. . . .

'Writing' [for Rhys] was rarely an uninterrupted process of putting words down on paper. A little bit here—a little bit there—and long intervals of feeling the existence of the work inside her but not actually *doing* anything about it. . . . I doubt whether she would have thought of herself as 'borrowing' for *Smile Please*. It would have been more a case of 'Now here's the place where *that* piece will fit in, at last.'[32]

After the publication of *Wide Sargasso Sea* and the subsequent reissuing of her early novels, Rhys figured in many interviews, often echoing each other verbatim and ultimately showing up in her autobiography. Concerning those interviews, Diana Athill says: "Those disconcertingly identical interviews represented what she was prepared to divulge, and blocked other enquiries."[33] Of those years, David Plante quotes, in *Difficult Women,* from a letter he received from Sonia Orwell about Rhys and written after Rhys's death of a heart attack on May 14, 1979. Orwell writes:

'She was, towards the end, so very old and so senile so much of the time. And I think that people who live so much alone tend to 'highlight' just a few incidents or thoughts in their lives and come out with these over and over again while other things, since they've not been used to talking about them, never, never get mentioned—they've been buried too deep to dig up again. Jean was the sort of essence of someone who'd forgotten how to talk naturally through having been isolated, which accounts for the yards of subconscious she dragged up when drunk, her endless thoughts about the "unfairness of it all", blacks, politics, etc., because this is the way a lonely person behaves when she finds herself at last in company.' (pp. 65–66)

In her long letter, Orwell also writes about Rhys's fear that Plante's helping Rhys write her autobiography would involve the supplanting of her writer's voice with his—" 'her terror that two writers never have the same 'voice' and that, without meaning to, you were in fact writing her book for her in a way she wouldn't have written it herself' " (pp. 65–66).

Jean Rhys's own voyage out took her from the tiny, insular and provincial world of her home, took her from its narrow sphere to an ever-expanding geography. But for Rhys, as the surrounding territory increased and the physical space widened, the internal closure tightened and her spirit straitened. On her island, though alienated and "outcast," Ella Williams lived with a sense of expanding possibility. Her voyage to England and the subsequent decade spent there resulted in disappointment, disillusionment and spiritual contraction, and with that, the need to cling to and yet transform the myth of home.

Rhys's escape to the Continent and especially to Paris, with its language that surely suggested home, offered the possibility of hope. It was there, in the company of Jean Lenglet and later Ford Madox Ford that the young provincial, Ella Williams, became the writer, Jean Rhys. Even after returning once again to England, she apparently needed to visit the Continent frequently in order to continue writing. In fact, one tends to overlook that Rhys lived on the Continent for no more than ten years and that, except for her first two books, all of her work was published while she lived in England.

Rhys herself remained, until her death, peculiarly homeless and placeless, but her work is informed by her unending sensitivity to place—to topography and climate, to language and people and to an island self haunted by the memory of a place that never had been as she had wanted.

For Jean Rhys, writing involved addressing the few important images that triggered and necessitated her craft. In so doing, she created a mythology for herself. It is in *Voyage in the Dark* and *Wide Sargasso Sea,* that Rhys touched most deeply those sources and impulses. Those loci defined her and her work and provided a way to regard the past and the present, both of which existed in a paradoxical dynamic of stasis and change.

In *Voyage in the Dark* and *Wide Sargasso Sea,* Rhys gives figure to the past, and thus shapes the present. These two novels reveal the writer as a child, as a young woman, and finally as a very old one bearing history. To look again at the past means at once to re-view the present, to understand the significance of both and, hence, to shape and control them. But the very act of controlling and shaping means to come to a new understanding and, perhaps, to a reconciliation with the forces that are exerted on the self—hence, a reconstructed reality. Myth, legend, and reality become one and constitute the "truth" of one's history. By summoning the past, Rhys made sense of the present. It could, though despised, become understandable through contrast and through an almost choric reiteration of the emotional "facts."

Fifty years after composing *Voyage in the Dark,* Jean Rhys returned in *Wide Sargasso Sea* to the same physical location—the West Indies. But that novel places the islands in a time that preceded her own youth. She re-placed the world she had known in a time about which she had heard only in story and legend. In so doing, she refixed that world, thus revealing it in a new way. Between the distant past (represented by *Wide Sargasso Sea*) and the immediate present of England, Rhys's childhood Dominica remained a pure, still point against which to measure all her experience.

Rhys's writing, however, reveals another level, an unconscious level, one might say, of what "home" was like. While both novels recall an island paradise, in both, that paradise is revealed as one that has early been tainted and corrupted. By examining these two novels in depth, we can understand the relationship of the West Indies to Jean Rhys and her work and the meaning of the West Indian experience for her as her life and her art converged. It is the image of Dominica that opens *Voyage in the Dark* and it is that image, as attested to in the Black Exercise Book, in her incomplete autobiography and in her short fiction, that spurred her until the end of her life.

In *Voyage in the Dark* and *Wide Sargasso Sea,* Rhys returns to her island sources—as a writer, as a colonial, and as a child who cannot forget her indifferent mother, nor dissociate that mother from the island. In both works she represents the island as an encapsulated and immutable place, a place which provides a counterpoint to England in terms that are geographical, historical, social, psychological and temporal.

Voyage in the Dark and *Wide Sargasso Sea* (the first close and personal, the latter distant and less personalized) bracket Jean Rhys's career as a novelist. The burden of her tale remained the same and the story essentially unchanged, though altered by the passing of time and the re-view that time passing and relocation allow. They mark the range and span of her fiction and illuminate all of her other works.

Part Two

Sojourn:

Voyage in the Dark

4

The Exile Looks Back

*As it was in the beginning, is now and ever
shall be, world without end.*
from the *Book of Common Prayer*

Voyage in the Dark is Jean Rhys's most clearly autobiographical novel,
the facts of its heroine's life almost completely paralleling those of the
young Jean Rhys. The novel recounts the physical and spiritual dislocation of Anna Morgan, who, at the age of 16 and following the death of
her father, is uprooted from her West Indian home and taken to England
by her stepmother. She becomes a touring chorus girl, living a dismal
and nomadic life. Much of her time is passed in grim rooming houses
monitored by unsympathetic landladies. She drifts into an affair with
Walter Jeffries, an older and well-to-do Englishman whom she has picked
up on the street. After he breaks with her, she becomes obsessed with
and then crushed by the experience. She passes into a life of genteel
prostitution and, at the end of the novel, undergoes an abortion. The
year is 1914.

Anna's story focuses on her life in England from her eighteenth to her
twentieth years but her narrative is punctuated by intensely nostalgic
memories of "home"—of her childhood and youth passed on the small
West Indian island of Dominica. Neither Rhys nor Anna ever name the
island, but Anna mentions its latitude and longitude, which are the same
as Dominica's.

Although Jean Rhys used her early diary as the basis for her fourth
novel, when she returned to her early manuscript she brought to that
original rendition the perspective afforded by the passing of time and the
experience of a discriminating writer. Furthermore, the novel reveals the
effects of Rhys's wide reading of literature and includes some very clear

ideas about writing. In fact, *Voyage in the Dark,* aside from being a fictionalized account of Rhys's early life, also contains and is shaped by some very clear ideas about what makes literature and what makes it good. It shows the writer taking the facts of her life and by careful shaping and pruning turning them into art.

Voyage in the Dark falls into four clearly defined parts. All four parts repeat an epicyclic structure and a downward spiral which mirrors the thought processes of someone who can neither escape from nor return to the past.

Part One is the longest section of *Voyage in the Dark,* ending almost exactly at the novel's center. It recapitulates Anna's present and past problems, mirroring the past in the present. It reflects her deterioration and degeneration and the exacerbation of her fragile state by events in England. Anna's crisis is precipitated by separation: first from a nurturing mother, second from her father and then from her lover (events which become synonymous for her), and third from her home. Although Anna desperately clings to the memory of home, her recollections show it to be a tainted Eden and thereby pose a paradox: the memory of home involves a loss of the very idea of home.

In Part Two, through a pattern of childlike regressions, Anna attempts to find an anodyne in a series of thoroughly inadequate and unsatisfying mother substitutes.

Having failed to obtain relief in the present (Part Two), Anna, unaware of the unconscious denial implicit in her memories of home in Part One, seeks to invent in Part Three a mythology of herself, a mythology that encompasses her unnamed and unspecified female sources, both in her compulsively rehearsed remembrance of the ride to her real mother's old estate and in her insistence on the power of obeah women. That matrilinear myth is counterpointed in Part Three with a dream representing the British patriarchy. The dream, following her clear entry into a life of prostitution, represents an unconscious exploration of the male/female conflict.

Part Four, only a few pages long and unseparated into chapters, is a painful coda in which rational thought is reduced to an uncontrolled mixing of the present and the past. Its ironic closure circles back to the beginning of the novel and restates the problem in a still more debased form. Perhaps the best way to understand the nature of Anna's memories of her lost island is to examine the structure and the specific parts of *Voyage in the Dark* as those divisions inform Anna's recollections and as her memories affect those divisions.

Part One

Part One recounts Anna's meeting with Walter Jeffries, the progress of their affair, and his eventual abandonment of Anna. That is the forward movement of what I call the linear narrative. Interwoven with this narration are breaks with the present in which Anna remembers home and even some of her initial impressions of England.

There are many passages in *Voyage in the Dark* which Rhys has separated by italics or sometimes by italics and ellipses and sometimes only by ellipses. Some of these passages involve Anna's memories and some involve a kind of stream of consciousness. Rhys uses at least four devices for invoking Anna's memories: the three mentioned above and a more conventional language of recollection within the linear narrative. It is not clear in all cases why she uses one rather than the other, nor have other critics discussed this.

Anna's thoughts and memories occur seemingly beyond her control. They are often not introduced with the conventional language of recollection (e.g., "I remember . . ."); and especially as Anna's despair and obsessiveness escalate, they occur in these unintroduced passages. They also become more frequent, longer, and refer to more distant and inchoate events, mirroring the increasing lack of order (the "non-fitting together" of things), and Anna's increasing inability to separate dream from waking life which, paradoxically, of course, involves a "fitting" together."

In the opening passage of *Voyage in the Dark,* Anna states her conflict clearly. It is a conflict signified by place and the language used to evoke the lost place, the childhood paradise, is sensual, colorful, melodic and certainly involved with the perpetuation of her myth and her myth-making impulse. She says:

It was as if a curtain had fallen, hiding everything I had ever known. It was almost like being born again. The colours were different, the smells different, the feeling things gave you right down inside yourself was different. Not just the difference between heat, cold; light, darkness, purple, grey. But a difference in the way I was frightened and the way I was happy. I didn't like England at first. I couldn't get used to the cold. Sometimes I would shut my eyes and pretend that the heat of the fire, or the bed-clothes drawn up around me, was sun-heat; or I would pretend I was standing outside the house at home, looking down Market Street to the Bay. When there was a breeze the sea was millions of spangles; and on still days it was purple as Tyre and Sidon. Market Street smelt of the wind, but the narrow street smelt of niggers and woodsmoke and salt fishcakes fried in lard. (When the black women sell fishcakes on the savannah they carry them in trays on their heads. They call out, 'Salt fishcakes, all sweet an' charmin', all sweet an' charmin'.') It was funny, but that was what I thought about more than anything else—the smell of the streets and the smells of frangipanni and lime juice and cinnamon and cloves, and sweets made of ginger and syrup, and incense after funerals or Corpus Christi processions, and the patients standing outside the surgery next door, and the smell of the sea-breeze and the different smell of the land-breeze.

Sometimes it was as if I were back there and as if England were a dream. At other times England was the real thing and out there was a dream, but I could never fit them together. (p. 3)

In the first two sentences of her opening Anna presents her situation as neutrally perhaps as she can: the loss ("hiding") of the past and the possibility of that signifying rebirth. However, neither are certain; both are "like" and "as if." Thus, in addition to presenting the conflict of place, she also uses language that reveals her underlying uncertainty about what is real. But in this opening to her narrative, Anna's language is reflective, even thoughtful and controlled, as she attempts to establish in logical terms the conflict and the representations of that conflict as she experiences them. While she says that at times she could not separate the dream from "the real thing" she says so in rational language that expresses the problem rationally and reasonably. And, while there is nostalgia and perhaps sadness, fear, and yearning, there is not as yet disorder.

Also woven into this opening are references to Catholic and Christian theology—an influence which later figures in Anna's references to sex and which also connects to the last section of *Voyage in the Dark* (e.g., the Corpus Christi procession that occurs seven weeks after Easter and which is, if we follow the subtly included calender in *Voyage in the Dark*, about the time of Anna's abortion). Anna's references to Tyre and Sidon reflect her need to make a grand and sustaining myth of her home.

In the first chapter Anna moves from this description of home to one of her life touring England prior to meeting Walter Jeffries. By the time she presents, near the end of that chapter, one of her first impressions of

England, the language, the tone, and the coherency are much deteriorated. The sentences are chopped and punctuated by dashes. Prior to her memory of her first sight of England, Anna recalls again the island and says: "A curtain fell and then I was here" (p. 9). But this curtain, unlike the more benign one of the opening, falls like a guillotine, cutting off the past that Anna in the previous paragraph has desperately been trying to objectify by refering to literature about the island and the facts of its latitude and longitude. This curtain triggers, not a lyrical memory of the island, but instead a rushing, hysterical montage of England:

> . . . This is England Hester said and I watched it through the train-window divided into squares like pocket-handkerchiefs; a small tidy look it had everywhere fenced off from everywhere else—what are those things—those are haystacks— oh are those haystacks—I had read about England ever since I could read—smaller meaner everything is never mind—this is London—hundreds thousands of white people white people rushing along and the dark houses all alike frowning down one after the other all alike all stuck together—the streets like smooth shut-in ravines and the dark houses frowning down—oh I'm not going to like this place I'm not going to like this place I'm not going to like this place—you'll get used to it Hester kept saying I expect you feel like a fish out of water but you'll soon get used to it—now don't look like Dying Dick and Solemn Davy as your poor father used to say you'll get used to it . . . (p. 9, Rhys's ellipses).

This passage, which gains its momentum and its sense of panic in part from the rushing images and in part from the repetition of those images and choric phrases, forecasts the kind of language Anna often uses when she speaks of England and London and reflects her obsession with the claustrophobic darkness of the entire country and its lack of expansiveness. Its black and whiteness, its greyness serve as stark contrast to the technicolor-like initial vision of Dominica. Even the phrase "all alike" which Anna constantly repeats about England is counterposed by the opening description of Dominica in which, for example, she uses the words "different" and "difference" five times in the opening four sentences. The phrase also indicates Anna's alien position: strangers to a land are less likely to distinguish diversity, while the native inhabitants are more aware of the variances within a small radius, just as Anna is of her tiny island.

While Anna later on adopts her stepmother's language and often says of England that she has "got used to it," one cannot believe her: the contrast in the languages she uses for the two places, and the very existence of her continuous lament, assure us that she has not, in fact, gotten used to it at all. Underlying Anna's absorption with her affair with Walter Jeffries and her continuous comparison of England and Dominica, both of which are developed in Part One, is her unconscious but continuing and mounting concern with her father, with being female, and with sex, aging, and death. Anna is at first covert in her allusions to her father. In the opening, Anna mentions "the surgery next door." Rhys's father was a doctor who maintained a surgery next to the house but Anna never mentions that *her* father actually is a doctor. But in Chapter 5 Anna's father becomes a central concern. Her response to his death and her eventual identification of him with Walter precipitate her crisis.

In chapter 5 several of the themes developed in Part One begin to merge. First, there is in this chapter the first, or the first extended, mention of Anna's father. Anna, just prior to sleeping with Walter, begins talking to him about "home," and about her father. All of this talk of home has stemmed from Walter's admonition to Anna that she should not drink too much or too early. He uses the same words that her father used and this leads to her certain identification of one with the other.

Second, in this chapter Anna recalls the "walls of the Old Estate house" (p. 32) with its foundations overgrown with exotic flowers and ferns. She also remembers an old slave list kept at the estate and recalls the name of a slave on that list: "Maillotte Boyd, aged 18" (p. 32), the same age as Anna. Later, after making love with Walter, that name suddenly occurs to her. In this chapter, Anna has begun to identify Walter with her dead father and herself, in relation to Walter, with the unknown slave girl.

The past involvement of Anna's family with slavery and her memories of her dead father surface as her own growing servitude becomes apparent in the affair with Walter, a man almost 20 years older. Anna's feelings about sex and her family's past involvement with slavery apparently involve feelings of guilt (as is probably the case with Antoinette in *Wide Sargasso Sea*). Like Antoinette, Anna is in between two places: her family history identifies her with the oppressors, the slaveowners, and her race reinforces that identification; yet her private thoughts, her own actions, place her with those who are victimized, those whose bodies are bought and sold for money. Anna has been enslaved, not only in body, but in mind and spirit; furthermore, she seems to embrace that enslavement, perhaps even wills it on herself. After making love with Walter, she again recalls the slave's name, this time adding, *"But I like it like this. I don't*

want it any other way but this" (p. 34; Rhys's italics). In the Black
Exercise Book Rhys describes parts of the sexual serial story that
Mr. Howard used to relate to her and concludes similarly to Anna, "Always in the end punished—That is love—And only that. To give yourself
up entirely, inevitably, hopelessly. Not for the fear of hell, not for the
hope of heaven" (fols. 28–29). Further on, she writes of Mr. Howard's
tale: "Cruelty, submission, utter submission, that was the Story"
(fols. 28–29). Later she adds:

But the terrible thing was the way something in the depths of me said, 'Yes, that
is true. Pain, humiliation, submission, that is for me.'

It fitted in with all I knew of life, with all I'd ever felt. It fitted like a hook fits
an eye. (fol. 33)

Both Rhys and her young heroine identify their older "lovers" as masters
of their bodies and souls and recognize in themselves the terrible desire
for that enslavement.

But Anna's enslavement to her lover has another aspect: his appearance
in her life has signified the first experience of being cared for in England.
In her second encounter with him, he appears at her room when she is
ill and begins to nurse her, sending food and a doctor. In addition, he
promises to curb her unpleasant landlady. After Walter leaves, Anna says,
"He went out. The room looked different, as if it had grown bigger"
(p. 20). For the moment, Walter's attentions expand the walls of her
enclosure. Although Anna is aware of Walter's prurience (she feels he
assesses her as if she were a bottle of wine), he joins the only two figures
who have ever offered her warmth and kindness: her dead father and the
vanished Francine. For this reason, and her identification of him with her
father, she is totally bereft when he leaves.

In addition to the memories that inform chapter 5, another recollection,
one connected to the Catholic and Christian theology underlying *Voyage
in the Dark,* haunts Anna. She thinks about "the Four Last Things," part
of the teachings, it would appear, from the catechism she probably learned
in her convent school. The passage occurs suddenly as Anna goes upstairs
with Walter:

'Children, every day one should put aside a quarter of an hour for meditation on

the Four Last Things. Every night before going to sleep—that's the best time—
you should shut your eyes and try to think of one of the Four Last Things.'
(*Question:* What are the Four Last Things? *Answer:* The Four Last Things are
Death, Judgment, Hell and Heaven.) That was Mother St. Anthony—funny old
thing she was, too. She would say, 'Children, every night before you go to sleep
you should lie straight down with your arms by your sides and your eyes shut
and say: "One day I shall be dead. One day I shall lie like this with my eyes
closed and I shall be dead." ' 'Are you afraid of dying?' Beatrice would say. 'No,
I don't believe I am. Are you? 'Yes, I am, but I never think about it.'
   Lying down with your arms by your sides and your eyes shut. (p. 34)

Rhys writes about Mother St. Anthony in the Black Exercise Book too.
She says that the nun was "a convert and when she really got going about
hell, was most impressive" (fol. 17).
   Following this passage, after Walter and Anna have made love, Anna
thinks: "*Lying so still afterwards. That's what they call the Little Death*"
(p. 34, Rhys's italics). In this episode Anna identifies sex with death and
sleeping with death. The three are intertwined and related to Anna's
Catholic education in which sex for money and sex without marriage are
sinful. Toward the end of the chapter Anna says, "I am bad, not good
any longer, bad. That has no meaning, absolutely none. Just words"
(p. 35). In this probable reference to her own recent loss of virginity, as
well as her final loss of sexual innocence and her entrance into the adult
world of corruption and further loss, Anna's Catholic education, her memories of the catechism and the punishment for carnal sin, are stronger
than she tells us; that is why she considers the question of whether she
is "bad."
   There are recurring sub rosa religious references in *Voyage in the Dark.*
Rather than being comprised of an intellectual dialogue such as occurs in
James Joyce's *A Portrait of the Artist as a Young Man,* the religious matter
in *Voyage in the Dark* is often of a more popular kind and appears to be
less considered by its heroine, just as the literary references differ between
the two novels.[1] In Joyce's work, for example, a clear argument is pursued
regarding the role of the Catholic church and Stephen's relationship to it
and to religion. In *Voyage in the Dark,* the religious references deal more
with the inconsistent and oddly mixed-up religious education that Anna
probably received. For example, as a student at a French-Catholic convent, she was exposed to some teachings of the Catholic church; as a
British colonial, she might have attended Protestant church services; as

a young child, she was exposed to the obeah and witchcraft of the black islanders and the mixture of Catholic/Christian theology and native custom in such practices as Carnival, a festival related to Easter and occurring in Dominica three days before Lent. Of her own schooling at the convent, Rhys says in the Black Exercise Book "I chiefly learnt there all the ins and outs of the Catholic religion. We were excluded from the Catholicism being heretics but, Mother St. Anthony got her own back during sewing" (fols. 16–17).

Much of the religious subtext is suggested in chapter 4. In fact, the events of chapter 4 all take place on a Sunday and much of the chapter is concerned with the nature of Sunday. In addition, this particular Sunday is Anna's nineteenth birthday and, because she gives us the date, we also know it is the first Sunday of the year. She says: "That year my birthday was on Sunday. The seventh of January. I was nineteen" (pp. 24–25). It is also, as both Anna and Rhys would know, the Sunday after Epiphany, suggesting the anticlimactic quality of Anna's birthday, a rainy Sunday on which, as she waits for a visit from her friend Maudie, Anna tries to sleep but can't. She says, "A church bell started with that tinny, nagging sound they have. The feeling of Sunday is the same everywhere, heavy, melancholy, standing still. Like when they say, 'As it was in the beginning, is now, and ever shall be, world without end' " (p. 25).

Certainly Anna's feeling about conventional, church-going religion is unhopeful and uncharged, cynical and deadened. She connects conventional religion to class, money, and bourgeois constriction and restriction. In fact, it is in this chapter that she reminisces about Sundays at home and contrasts the dramatic difference between the airlessness of the enclosed church service and the grandeur of the natural and open space in the churchyard outside. And yet, nevertheless, something of her conventional religious training has influenced Anna, and stays with her. Despite herself, she remains a Christian, perhaps even a most conventional one.

Toward the end of the "Sunday chapter (chapter 4)," as Anna is walking with her friend Maudie near Hyde Park, they pass a Sunday speaker. Anna says, "Some distance away from the crowd round the speakers, there was a man standing on a box, bawling something about God. Nobody was listening to him. You could only hear 'God . . . God. . . . The wrath of God. . . . Wah, wah, wah, wah. . . ." (p. 29, Rhys's ellipses).

When Maudie begins to laugh at the man, Anna says, "He got wild and shrieked after us, 'Laugh! Your sins will find you out. Already the fear of death and hell is in your hearts, already the fear of God is like fire in your hearts' " (p. 29). Maudie, a foil for Anna, has a reaction which is typical for her. She becomes angry and says to Anna, "Insulting us just because we haven't got a man with us. I know these people, they're careful who they're rude to. They're damned careful who they try to convert. Have you ever noticed? He wouldn't have said a word if we'd have had a man with us" (p. 29). Anna doesn't respond to Maudie, but she wants "to go back and talk to him and find out what he was really thinking of, because his eyes had a blind look, like a dog's when it sniffs something" (p. 30).

In some ways this episode is reminiscent of another scene between Maudie and Anna, in which Anna is reading Emile Zola's *Nana* and Maudie says: " 'I bet you a man writing a book about a tart tells a lot of lies one way and another' " (pp. 4–5). Her remark is almost proto-feminist, much like the Wife of Bath who refers to the fable in which a lion is shown a picture of a slain lion and asks who painted it, lion or man. But Anna, who ignores Maudie's socio-sexual viewpoint, senses instead that the speaker knows something, or, like a hound, is on to her scent— that he is aware perhaps of her transgressions. Anna, unworldly and innocent, cannot abandon her guilt or see things for what they are, or at least how Maudie, in her greater worldliness, sees them.

In chapter 4, the remembered words of the doxology, words that Christian children learn by rote ("As it was in the beginning, is now and ever shall be"), contain in a compressed form the entire structure of Rhys's novel, the words now ironically reinterpreted as signalling hopelessness and despair. They echo Anna's opening lines and anticipate both the doctor's cynical closing remarks (" 'She'll be all right, . . . ready to start all over again in no time.' " [p. 115]) and Anna's last words: "I lay . . . and thought about starting all over again, all over again" (p. 115). Finally, if we recall the day on which these ruminations occur, we are doubly reminded of the hopelessness of Anna's situation. It is the first Sunday of the new year and her birthday—a double beginning. But, as we are here reminded in an early part of Anna's narrative, with the twisted meaning of the doxology, all beginnings end the same.

Chapter 6 is perhaps one of the most important in *Voyage in the Dark* in terms of establishing the essential conflicts that Anna must later deal with in England. The chapter itself is composed of two parts: the first is a "frame" in which we see Anna meeting with her stepmother in London in what is obviously their last encounter. The second part of chapter 6, occurring within the frame of this meeting, consists of a long recollection Anna has of her first menstrual period.

She remembers that the black servant, Francine, had explained it so that "it seemed quite all right and I thought it was all in the day's work like eating or drinking" (p. 42). But when her stepmother comes to talk to her about it Anna is devastated. She says of the effect of Hester's talk, "But I began to feel awfully miserable, as if everything were shutting up around me and I couldn't breathe. I wanted to die" (p. 42).

Later Anna seeks solace with Francine in the kitchen. She says:

But I knew that of course she disliked me too because I was white; and that I would never be able to explain to her that I hated being white. Being white and getting like Hester, and all things you get—old and sad and everything. I kept thinking, 'No. . . . No. . . . No. . . .' and I knew that day that I'd started to grow old and nothing could stop it. (p. 44, Rhys's ellipses)

Following this sudden consciousness of her own aging Anna leaves Francine and, walking in a certain section of the estate, begins to talk about her father who "grew cocoa and nutmegs . . . on the slopes of the hill" (p. 45). She interrupts the movement of her narrative of that day to talk tangentially again about her father. She says:

When the young nutmeg trees flowered for the first time he used to take me with him to see if the tree was male or female, because the buds were so small that you had to have sharp eyes to see the difference. 'You're young and you have sharp eyes,' he would say. 'Come along.'

'I'm getting old,' he would say. 'My eyes aren't as good as they used to be.' I always felt so miserable when he said that. (p. 45)

This seemingly irrelevant discussion in Anna's narrative occurs as she has been talking about the day of her first menstruation. Prior to this, sexuality was limited to the making of distinctions in the sexual organs of young nutmeg trees, something that Anna could share with a male, her father. But Anna in undergoing menstruation—her own sexual differentiation—feels herself separated from the natural world and from a world of polymorphous sexuality, even from a natural mixing between blacks and whites. The separation of the nutmeg trees becomes linked with her father's aging, and probably with his death, and also with her awareness that the one woman who has shown her nurture and kindness, Francine, must dislike her because she is white.

Following this Anna has a very clear death wish which culminates in a long illness. She says:

I got well away from the house. I sat down against a rock in the shadow. The sky was terribly blue and very close to the earth.

I felt I was more alone than anybody had ever been in the world before and I kept thinking, 'No. . . . No. . . . No. . . .' Just like that. Then a cloud came in front of my eyes and seemed to blot out half of what I ought to have been able to see. It was always like that when I was going to have a headache.

I thought, 'Well, all right. This time I'll die.' So I took my hat off and went and stood in the sun.

The sun at home can be terrible, like God.

I stood there until I felt the pain of the headache begin and then the sky came up close to me. It clanged, it was so hard. The pain was like knives. And then I was cold, and when I had been very sick I went home.

I got fever and I was ill for a long time. I would get better and then it would start again. It went on for several months. I got awfully thin and ugly and yellow as a guinea, my father said.

I asked Hester if I had talked a lot when I was bad and she said, 'Yes, you talked about cats and a great deal about Francine.' It was after that she started disliking Francine so much and saying she ought to be sent away. (p. 45)

This extreme response to the onset of menstruation is, according to Simone de Beauvoir, not an unusual occurrence. Beauvoir writes in *The Second Sex*, "If the young girl at about this stage frequently develops a neurotic condition, it is because she feels defenseless before a dull fatality that condemns her to unimaginable trials; her femininity means in her eyes sickness and suffering and death, and she is obsessed with this fate."[2] Certainly Anna's response incorporates Beauvoir's analysis. Beauvoir also says, in referring to the work of psychologist Helene Deutsch, "Instances of attempted suicide are not unknown, and indeed it is natural enough for the young girl to be frightened as her life blood seems to be flowing away, perhaps from some injury to the internal organs" (pp. 348–349). But for Anna, the fear may go even deeper than Beauvoir describes here. She has agreed to die by her own will on the first day of her menarche; but she has also marked it as the beginning of her own uncontrollable decay, both physical and spiritual. For Anna, the natural process of menstruation does not simply suggest death but rather has become symbolic of the entire process of dying. Furthermore, as Anna grows out of adolescence, she does not seem to grow out of her adolescent response to it.

Anna not only regards the menarche as an initiation into womanhood and sexuality, but also as an initiation into aging, sadness, loss and death and, worst of all, isolation. She can no longer count on the love of the naturally maternal Francine and the world that Francine represents: the warm natural world of the island. Instead she is separated by her color into the world of her stepmother, the world of the white, of England, and the world of repression and unnaturalness that Hester represents. Beauvoir also considers this reluctant entrance into the world of women. She writes:

Previously the little girl, with a bit of self-deception, could consider herself as still a sexless being, or she could think of herself not at all; she might even dream of awakening changed into a man; but now, mothers and aunts whisper flatteringly: 'She's a big girl now'; the matrons' group has won: she belongs to it. And so she is placed without recourse on the women's side. (p. 350)

Anna can no longer stay in the nonmatronly world she previously occupied, but she never accepts or enters into the worlds of the women she fears, neither the world represented by Hester, nor the world of Maudie and Laurie.

The menarche marks the beginning of Anna's fall from grace, the beginning of her fear of, and her yearning for, death. From this point on, until the close of *Voyage in the Dark,* when Anna is twenty, all of her new beginnings are no more than a series of false starts; her life becomes a progression of "little deaths," perhaps best characterized by her brief and isolate sexual encounters, each of which leaves her further and further removed from paradise. If Anna could shut out the past, then she could possibly really start over again. But the past imposes itself on her so that she continues to live between it and the present, between black and white, between dream and reality, between childhood and adulthood, between innocence and worldliness. There is no place to go unless she can find some way to affirm, to realize, the present and the future. While the onset of menstruation has marked the onset of separation, the dividing of things into parts, she has not found a way to synthesize these parts back into a working whole.

If we return to the frame of chapter 6, within which occurs the story of her menarche, we learn something else about Anna's actual physical separation from the island. In the course of their conversation, we discover that Anna has apparently been forced to leave home after, and because of the death of her father, and that she has been deprived of her inheritance by Hester. Ultimately, forced into the world of her step-mother, Anna has been betrayed by her.

The final three chapters of Part One, the last of which ends just at about the center of the novel, mark the inevitable and downward movement of Anna's life and her inability to confront and cope with a world that Rhys associates with male and British domination, the latter perhaps especially an outcome of her colonial sensibility. In fact, Germaine, a woman who is "half-French" and who accompanies Walter's cousin Vincent to Savernake, perhaps more than any other character may represent the point of view of *Voyage in the Dark* and of Rhys herself. Germaine says that Vincent is the perfect specimen of an Englishman, men whose faces reveal " 'scorn and loathing of the female' " (p. 50). She adds that there are no pretty women in England, that they all have a " 'beaten, cringing look' " (p. 51) or they are " 'cruel and dried-up' " (p. 51). Her strongest indictment is directed toward the men who have made the women like that " 'because most Englishmen don't care a damn about women. They can't make women happy because they don't really like them' " (p. 51). One is reminded of the Englishman Heidler in *Quartet* who "wasn't a good lover of course. He didn't really like women . . ." (p. 190) and of Rochester's hatred for his beautiful and sensual wife in *Wide Sargasso Sea.*

Walter interprets Germaine's remarks as signifying her bitterness at not getting as much money from Vincent as she wanted. Not only do both Vincent and Walter view the relationships between the sexes as monetary, but all the women also view it that way. On the other hand, Anna, who eventually falls into prostitution, deludes herself with fantasies of romantic love even though all of her relationships with men are based on money.

In *Voyage in the Dark,* the men have the money and the power to withhold it. The women who survive are those cunning and experienced enough to know how to extract that money from men.

In the last few chapters of Part One, Anna is completely out of kilter. Her dependency on Walter has become uncontrollable. When Vincent sends Anna a cloying and hypocritical letter terminating the affair with Walter, the memories of her father and his death begins to escalate, as does her own identification with him. Her father, like Anna, rejected the smug nationalism, coldheartedness, and vulgar chauvinisms of the Vincents and Hesters, but like her he remained their prey, resisting only passively. Anna's identification becomes so strong that at the end of Part One she feels that she, like her father, will die and she recalls a funeral—possibly her father's—at which people said, "so young to die . . ." (p. 61). Though the subject of this funeral is never identified, it would appear to be Anna's father. However, in a manuscript copy of an unpublished version of Part Four in the University of Tulsa collection, the funeral is apparently Anna's mother's. The Tulsa manuscript is a far longer version of the section than the published one. It may be that in the final version of *Voyage in the Dark* Rhys decided that it was artistically more useful to leave the mother completely unmentioned and to leave the funeral attributable to the father. This would appear to be the case since the next reference, following the funeral, connected with her sense that she is drowning, is clearly a reference to her father. Anna's identification with her father becomes complete with the double abandonment, first by her father and now by Walter. Anna wishes to die, though she states that wish as a fear.

At the end of Part One, Anna is barely holding on. She leaves her rooms once again, but the streets are scenes of paranoia for her as her fear fills the entire world. The first section ends in dramatic contrast to its opening. Whereas Anna begins with a lyrical evocation of place and a presentation of her dilemma, she ends by saying, " 'Anywhere will do, so long as it's somewhere that nobody knows' " (p. 63). She is cut off from everyone and every place she has known. She has completed the first part of her voyage: a journey toward no place, toward detachment, darkness, and death. While the opening lines of the first chapter have half-promised a new beginning, it is the beginning of an end, a journey to a cold country of sexual and sensual deprivation. For Anna, sexuality and adulthood have come to signify death and separation. Every rebirth or potential new start

that Anna has in Part One has also been accompanied by a "curtain falling." The present cannot connect, as it must, to the past. At the conclusion of Part One, everything of importance to Anna has died or ended
and Anna, who was so obsessed in the beginning with defining and understanding place, ends by seeking placelessness and anonymity.

For Anna, her memory of the island from her present point of view in
England is of an unreal world—mythic and "something else." She says
of her island: "If England is beautiful, it's not beautiful. It's some other
world' " (p. 32). It is also, compared to England, timeless. For example,
Anna marks episodes in England by dates, by days of the week, by months
and by statements like "three weeks later." But the world of the island
has no such timing. It is out of time and out of this world. The "real
world," the world of England is, for Anna, unbearable. Having been cut
off from that other world, from the safety of the island, Anna has become
like that island—insular, turned inward, cut off. The further Anna moves
in time, space, and relationships from the world of the island, the further
she moves into a world foreign to its primordial beauty, and the more
deeply she is locked into its memory.

Part Two

Part One is a failed attempt to understand and to transcend the past, in
part, through the male/female sexual relationship. Part Two reveals an
attempt by Anna to recover that past and her childhood through regres-
sion and the simulation of motherly nurturing from other women. She
seeks an anodyne in the recapitulation of the child-mother relationship,
but that too is doomed to failure.

The opening of Part Two, which begins with an unappetizing description of the food on her plate and of her equally unappetizing landlady,
followed by a description of her rooms, is, compared to the impassioned
opening of Part One, anticlimactic indeed. In Part Two Anna's very conflicted feelings about women and men and about being a woman are
revealed. There are two very strong elements throughout the section. The
first is her relationship to the women, all of whom in some way offer
unsatisfactory care and nourishment and toward whom Anna remains
antipathetic. Though she wants something from them, like a suckling
infant she offers nothing in return. She is at best indifferent to them.
Second, counterpointed to this world of (incomplete) mothering and

women is the world of men—which we see in Part Two in the persons of Carl Redman and his secretary Joe. While they are Americans and therefore more sympathetic (in Anna's mind) than Walter and Vincent of Part One, the duo they comprise is not dissimilar.

Unlike the women, the men rarely seem to be loners. They back each other up and pursue women as assessable objects. Carl, like Walter who "took care" of Anna's troublesome landlady, presumably by giving her money, "takes care" of Ethel in the same way. And Ethel, like the previous landlady, becomes more deferential to Anna. Unlike Maudie, who sees men as a way of protecting her from other men, Anna's men protect her from women.

In Part Two, the longest conversation among the foursome is about the sexes, just as Vincent, Walter, Anna, and Germaine have such a conversation at Savernake in Part One. But Anna's response to men is far less critical than her response to women, perhaps because of her deep desire for women to mother her. In the restaurant, with Laurie and the two men, Anna looks at a woman at another table and thinks to herself that the woman is "terrifying." She says:

> But I was thinking that it was terrifying—the way they look at you. So that you know that they would see you burnt alive without even turning their heads away; so that you know in yourself that they would watch you burning without even blinking once. Their glassy eyes that don't admit anything so definite as hate. Only just that underground hope that you'll be burnt alive, tortured, where they can have a peep. And slowly, slowly, you feel the hate back starting. . . . (p. 74, Rhys's ellipses)

What is strange is that in her narrative, except for her stepmother Hester, Anna has never encountered a woman who is truly cruel to her or who uses her in the way men do. And even her stepmother is not sufficient to the above description of women. Anna's most scathing criticisms are always directed at white English ladies. She becomes dependent on men and is ultimately "smashed" by them, as are Rhys's other heroines, but it is English women who loosen her real anger. The men, to whom she willingly falls victim, receive none of this vituperation. These gentle-women, who live on the edge of poverty and who are strict enforcers of the bourgeois code, occur often in Rhys's fiction (e.g., Julia's sister in *After Leaving Mr. MacKenzie,* Lois's friend in *Quartet* and other minor

characters in both the novels and the short fiction). It is for them that
Rhys's heroines' greatest scorn is reserved.

When Joe is alone with Anna, he tells her that she shouldn't hang
around with Laurie because she's a "tart" (p. 79). Later on, in an encounter with Vincent, he too criticizes Laurie as he looks at a photograph
of her. These male judgments are also reminiscent of Walter's assertion
to Anna that her virginity is " 'the only thing that matters' " (p. 22). Anna
never makes overt commentary about these male remarks and shows none
of the scorn and loathing that she shows for women, though it is the males
who set the standards for *all* of the women.

The women who are excluded from Anna's attacks are the women who
remain outsiders, women who disdain or are disdained by the bourgeoisie,
like Maudie, Laurie, and the black Francine. Sometimes these women
are tough survivors; sometimes they are like "flowers." In the first cate-
gory is Laurie, who says about the woman in the restaurant whom Anna
has found terrifying: " 'Terrifying? . . . She doesn't terrify me. I'm not
so easily terrified. I've got good strong peasant blood in me' " (p. 75).
Later, in the following chapter, it is Laurie who summarizes Anna. Without judgment, she says to her, " 'I think you're a bit of a fool, that's all.
And I think you'll never get on, because you don't know how to take
people' " (p. 80). Later, she kisses Anna and says," 'You know I'm fond
of you' " (p. 129). But despite her and Maudie's fondness for Anna, they
cannot help her. Like the woman in the story "Tigers are Better Looking,"
Anna cannot "adapt." Although women like Laurie and the black women
of the islands (Francine and Christophine in *Wide Sargasso Sea*) are
outsiders and unacceptable to the white bourgeois ladies, they have a sense
of their own power, based on a practical relation to the world around
them. It is not that they do not see what Anna sees. Rather, they have
defied it, are not intimidated or terrified by it, and have learned to care
for themselves. In that sense they have become adults while Anna remains
a child.

Many of the descriptions, especially of the women, in Part Two involve
animal or grotesque metaphors. Laurie has a voice "as hoarse as a crow's"
(p. 70) and puts makeup on so that her face "looked like a clown's face"
(p. 77). Even Laurie refers to another woman in the restaurant as having
a "face like a hen's—and like a hen's behind too" (p. 74). The landlady
in the first set of rooms, ironically named Mrs. Flower, "had bulging eyes,
dark blobs in a long, pink face, like a prawn" (p. 64). Ethel Mathews,

who is "short and fat" with a "long face and a long body and short legs," has "deep rings under her eyes and her hair looked dusty" (p. 66). And Anna concludes "An ant, just like all the other ants; not the sort of ant that has too long a head or a deformed body or anything like that. She was like all women whom you look at and don't notice except that she had such short legs and that her hair was so dusty" (p. 66). All these images indicate Anna's further distance from the people around her. Earlier, after she has described Ethel, who is visiting her for the first time in the rooms at Mrs. Flower's, Anna is about to dismiss her and then stops herself, saying: "Because after all she was a human being" (p. 66). Later, in Part Three, Anna loses all sympathy for others so that human beings comprise nothing more than an ant-like community of which she is not a part.

Even Anna's reveries of her island change. In a recollection of the Caribs, whom Anna recalls first as fierce warriors who resisted " 'white domination' " (p. 65) and who nevertheless are " 'oceans away from despair' " (p. 65), Anna identifies death as the cure for hopelessness.

In Part Two Anna is giving up the hope that her memories of the island have given her. Whereas before the memories contained sustenance, in Part Two the material in the memories themselves is different and can no longer provide momentary respite from the present. On a visit to the cinema with Ethel, one senses that giving up in the words that occur to her as she sits in the darkened theater. She says, as the lights go out: "The piano began to play, sickly-sweet" (p. 67). Anna has had memories before of home or of time passing triggered by piano music. This time the music triggers the words: "Never again, never, not ever, never. Through caverns measureless to man down to a sunless sea. . . ." (p. 67; Rhys's ellipses). The piano, just as in Part One, has reminded Anna of the passing of time and of death and darkness and primarily, of loss. But the words "ever" and "never" also draw Anna to the poem "Kubla Khan" by Samuel Taylor Coleridge, which bears clearly obvious similarities to *Voyage in the Dark*. That poem, like Anna's story, moves between light and dark as it recalls an exotic landscape. On the surface then, Anna's recollection of the lines from "Kubla Khan" emphasizes her despair and her voyage into the dark, precipitated at this moment by the immediate darkness of the cinema. On a larger scale it recalls her voyage from the island to England—which has now become a symbol for her own internal emotional voyage.

"Kubla Khan" contains two important symbols for Anna, the sea and the sun; it describes a landscape which is, like the topography of Anna's own island, deeply sexual and female. But Coleridge's poem finally summons up the damsel with a dulcimer. The poet's despair leads him to a vision in which he can triumph by making poetry. Anna, on the other hand, can do no more than compose letters to Walter which she writes and then destroys.

The opening and closing of chapter 1 set a pattern recreated throughout Part Two: the unsatisfied quest for sustenance and mothering represented by food and drink served to Anna by various women. At the end of each chapter, Anna approaches such a repast with a desire for sleep. At the end of this first chapter, after leaving Ethel's room, Anna returns to her own. She says:

I got down to my room and there was some bread and cheese on a tray and a glass of milk. I felt very tired. I looked at the bed and thought, 'There's one thing—I do sleep. I sleep as if I were dead.'

It's funny when you feel as if you don't want anything more in your life except to sleep, or else to lie without moving. That's when you can hear time sliding past you, like water running. (p. 70)

The next chapter is, in some way, a replay of chapter 1, though it contains the important addition of men and male power. As in chapter 1, Anna's only respite comes in the form of female attendance and the chapter culminates with Anna being served food before lying down to sleep. She says:

The window of the bathroom was open and the soft, damp air from outside blew in on my face. There was a white bath-wrap on the chair. I put it on afterwards and went and lay down and the old woman brought me in some tea. I felt emptied-out and peaceful—like when you've had a toothache and it stops for a bit, and you know quite well it's going to start again but just for a bit it's stopped. (p. 73)

What is important here is that Anna's pain is temporarily relieved by women mothering her, "putting her to bed" like a child. In this case, the housemaid is literally called "Ma."

Chapter 4, the penultimate chapter of Part Two, also ends on the same note as chapters 1 and 2. Anna says, "It was the first fine day for weeks.

The old woman spread a white cloth on the table in the sitting-room and the sun shone in on it. Then she went into the kitchen and started to fry bacon. There was the smell of the bacon and the sound of the water running into the bath. And nothing else. My head felt empty" (p. 81).

The last chapter of the section again repeats the pattern of the food offering but suddenly slides into a revealing epiphanic vision. Anna, having decided to move into Ethel's rooms, returns with her things and goes to bed. Ethel offers to bring her something to eat. Anna says, "I was lying down thinking about money and that I had only three pounds left when she came in with bread and cheese and a bottle of Guinness. She sat by my bedside while I ate and began to tell me how respectable she was" (p. 84). Anna, like a child, makes no comment on this courtesy of Ethel's, treats it as an expected event. But after Ethel leaves her room, the chapter and Part Two end in a final fantasy toward which the entire movement of Part Two has been leading. Anna says:

She went out. And I lay there and thought.

. . . She'll smile and put the tray down and I'll say Francine I've had such an awful dream—it was only a dream she'll say—and on the tray the blue cup and saucer and the silver teapot so I'd know for certain that it had started again my lovely life—like a five-finger exercise played very slowly on the piano like a garden with a high wall around it—and every now and again thinking I only dreamt it it never happened. . . . (p. 84; Rhys's ellipses)

This ending chapter of Part Two suggests again the yearning and nostalgia, the need to separate dream and reality and the anticipation of beginning again that we saw in the opening of Part One. We are reminded of Anna's false hope of starting again, of beginning all over. ("I'd know for certain that it had started again my lovely life.") And yet the image of the piano in this final paragraph, like the sound of running water, symbolizing the passing of time, reminds us that the dream she has is an impossible one. In Part Two Anna has again come full circle. The first chapter opened with Anna in a new place, and the last chapter has ended with the same situation: Anna in new rooms.

As Anna's condition deteriorates she becomes more and more childlike. She may hope that if she can sink back into her past, into her childhood and her sources, she can renew herself. Perhaps sinking deeper and deeper into darkness, into night and sleep, brings the false promise of waking to a new beginning where there will again be light, color, and life.

In sum then, Part Two has presented the dichotomy of Anna's world: her inability to function profitably in the male-controlled world and her contradictory desire for nourishment and mothering by women she despises. The section is compounded of a series of repeating images that contain food, the sound of running water, the possibility of sleep, and women serving Anna. All are unable to provide her with the satisfaction that she experiences in the final fantasized vision of Francine in which she is a child once more and the present reality nothing but a bad dream. The movement in these chapters is toward Anna's being able to sleep (to die or to dream), to turn from the present to the past, to become a child once more in a time that predates sexual consciousness.

By the end of Part Two, Anna is seeking sleep and the absence of pain, not happiness. The moments of quiet, verging on rest, that Anna attains are simply stations on her downward voyage. With each pause, each respite, there is less hope. Anna's education and initiation have become an introduction not to evil or disenchantment but to despair and hopelessness. Like the hero of "The Iron Shroud," a Gothic tale of terror Anna recalls about a man who is crushed to death by the walls of his prison,[3] the world closes in on her and there is neither escape nor meaning.

Anna's remembrance of "The Iron Shroud" is prompted by her recollection of a room in which she once stayed. Her concern with rooms, with their similarity and their individuality, is shared by almost all of Rhys's heroines and is a major theme in her work. In fact, except for Part One of *Voyage in the Dark,* which begins with a religious and mythical invocation of home, all of the remaining sections, and many of the chapters within, begin with a description of the rooms in which Anna happens to be living; they heighten the glory of the opening passage of Part One by their bleak contrast. In the short essay written while her third husband, Max Hamer, was in prison, which appears at the end of *Smile Please,* Rhys wrote "The place I live in is terribly important to me, it always has been, but now it is all I have. The table, the chair, the tree outside my bed upstairs, it is all I have" (p. 165). We might say that that description serves Anna too: her rooms and her memories of home are all she has, and neither provide what Anna seeks from them.

Like Anna, all of Rhys's heroines suffer in these claustrophobic, these dead and deadening rooms, cubicles that heighten their desire for escape while literally cutting off its possibility. Anna, who constantly changes rooms, seeks in each one both refuge and anonymity. At the end of Part One, she again leaves her lodgings precipitously and, once in the street, feels paranoic. She says, "I got out into the street. A man passed. I thought he looked at me funnily and I wanted to run, but I stopped myself. I walked straight ahead. I thought, 'Anywhere will do, so long as it's somewhere that nobody knows' " (p. 63). Outside is dangerous; inside is deadly.

Anna seeks solace and nurturing. Often that unconscious quest is ironically signified by these ungiving and sterile rooms. They represent, among other things, her inward turning, her psychological imprisonment, her enclosure and, through that enclosure, her separation from others. At the same time, the temporary nature of Anna's English rooms signify her rootlessness and her exile, her separation from the "normal" community. In *The Vagabond,* Colette's heroine René, another wandering showgirl, says that these rooms and hotels are the places that one stays in when there is no real home, no permanent place. René says when you are a "lady on your own . . . you take what you find, lodge where you may and put up with newly-plastered walls."[4] And for both René and Anna, a permanent place may signify capitulation to the bourgeois world. The dispossessed maintain their integrity, if nothing else. But while Colette's vagabond both laments and glories in her detachment, and hence her freedom, Rhys's heroines often become a victim of it. Instead of remaining free they become prisoners of the very rooms that initially may have signified freedom from bourgeois constraints.

For Anna these rooms are not only representations of her own insularity, her self-enclosure and transitoriness; they are also symbolic of the England she detests. Their spatial dimension and their particular physical characteristics are part of that symbolic function. But in *Voyage in the Dark,* descriptions of these rooms are also an aspect of Anna's own rhetoric. That is, Anna has a compulsive need to describe and re-describe them. That need reflects her desire to stop feeling, to stop seeing anything beyond the walls that confine her.

In an essay on Doris Lessing, like Rhys a British colonial writer who eventually made her home in England, Frederick Karl has made some interesting observations about what he terms "the literature of enclosure."[5] Though Karl makes his remarks in the context of the 1960s, some

of them shed light on Rhys's work too. Karl points to the obvious connection between the development of the room as a theme in modern
literature and "the Freudian reliance on the regressive tendencies of the
adult to return to the womb . . ." (p. 20). He continues his argument by
pointing to the room as "the place in which one can dream, in which one
can isolate himself as a consequence of neurosis or withdrawal symptoms,
all as part of that desire to seek refuge from external onslaughts which
are too much for the individual to withstand" (p. 20). Certainly in *Voyage
in the Dark,* especially in Part Two, Anna withdraws to her rooms as if
they could offer a womb-like safety and sustenance. But for Anna, this
womb-like aspect of the room contains also, as it does for Vivenzio of
"The Iron Shroud," the opposite: the deathlike symbol of being crushed
by forces outside. Unlike the possibility that Karl suggests, that the room
may provide "refuge from external onslaughts," for Anna and many of
Rhys's heroines the room finally provides not a refuge but a shroud.

In *Good Morning, Midnight,* the novel that followed *Voyage in the Dark,*
Rhys explores this preoccupation with rooms even further in the character
of Sasha Jansen, who is occupied and preoccupied with finding the "right
room." Trying to get "a light room," in a Paris hotel, Sasha is first promised room 219 and then told it is still occupied. She says:

Suddenly I feel that I must have number 219, with bath—number 219, with rose-
coloured curtains, carpet and bath. I shall exist on a different plane at once if I
can get this room, if only for a couple of nights. It will be an omen. Who says
you can't escape from your fate? I'll escape from mine, into room number 219.
Just try me, just give me a chance. (p. 365)

Sasha, however, is refused the room. When the girl shows her another
"which looks on to a high, blank wall" (p. 38), Sasha leaves the hotel in
a panic. And then, perhaps seeing into herself, as Anna never does, she
says:

A beautiful room with bath? A room with bath? A nice room? A room? . . . But
never tell the truth about this business of rooms, because it would bust the roof
off everything and undermine the whole social system. All rooms are the same.
All rooms have four walls, a door, a window or two, a bed, a chair and perhaps
a bidet. A room is a place where you hide from the wolves outside and that's all
any room is. Why should I worry about changing my room? (p. 366, Rhys's
ellipses)

Later, Sasha returns to her old room, having been unable to obtain a new one. She says, as she imbues the room with an almost human quality:

The room welcomes me back.

'There you are,' it says. 'You didn't go off, then?'

'No, no. I thought better of it. Here I belong and here I'll stay.' (p. 367)

In *Voyage in the Dark,* the repetitive and ungiving picture of the rooms in which Anna stays counterpoint her memories of her island landscape and its fleeting, paradisial quality. Anna's rooms lack the visual and sensual variety of the island. They are, to use phrases that Anna repeats chorically, "all the same," "all alike." This refrain of doom punctuates Anna's depiction of England increasingly in the way her memories of home punctuate the entire novel. Karl, again speaking in reference to the work of Lessing, remarks on the repetitive nature inherent in the literature of enclosure. He says, "This sense of nightmarish repetitiousness, of destiny repeating itself inexorably, is of course very much part of the literature of enclosure. With spatiality, one can avoid repetition through novelty of choice or act, but enclosure negates personal expansion" (p. 26). Furthermore, Karl discusses how the use of the room tends to inform the entire work: "Its physical desolation is indeed a counterpart of the character's psychological state. . . . The enclosure fixes the limits of sexuality, threatens and reassures within bounds, freeing as it limits. As a consequence, the novel becomes personal, subjective, solipsistic, even when externals like political events are of significance" (p. 21). Certainly his last observation on the "personal" nature of these novels is true for all of Rhys's works. For example, the only date ever mentioned in *Voyage in the Dark* is 1914—the start of World War I. And yet this date is given to us in an offhand way (it figures at the top of a letter from Anna's one-time "roommate," Ethel Mathews) and its inclusion at all is saucy in its insinuation that all external events are of no importance to Anna. There is in Rhys's work until *Wide Sargasso Sea* rarely (perhaps never) a mention of external political events. In a few short stories, some pretentious men discuss local politics.

If depression is often anger turned inward against the self, Anna rarely reveals her subterranean rage. Once she describes wanting to hit a man on the street with her bracelet, the one Walter had given her, but generally she does not betray what anger she might feel. Instead, she remains a hurt and depressed creature, constantly turning further inward within the confines of these London rooms. Again, Karl points to the room as an entity that contributes to that pattern. He says:

The room bottles up rage, leaves no escape for anger except when it is directed back into the self. The lair is itself a physical symbol of impotence [recall Sasha Jansen's description of a room as "a place where you hide from the wolves outside"]—lack of choice, will, determination; identity is indistinguishable from one's furnishings. . . . Clearly, the panoramic novel is snuffed out, for adventure is lost; there is no struggle. (p. 21)

Karl also believes that the room acts as a possible symbol for the "profane city" whose "space is not infinite, but geometric . . ." (p. 22). Certainly *Voyage in the Dark* (and to some extent *Quartet, After Leaving Mr. MacKenzie* and *Good Morning, Midnight*) contain indictments of the urban landscape. Karl also asserts that at one time when the room or house was "sacred" (because in it occurred the "act of creation itself"), "one's conception of space was "infinite" and "one could as it were breathe in something coexistent with the cosmos" (p. 22). His comment suggests something about the nature of the relationship for Anna between her island and England. Her memories of the island have a mythic and religious quality to them. In fact, part of Anna's concern in *Voyage in the Dark* is the shaping and reshaping, the forming and intensifying of her own myth: her myth of her home, her father, her sources, and ultimately herself. It is ironic that at the end of the novel, as Anna finally and momentarily fits all the pieces together, as she has said she cannot do in the opening to her narrative, the myth itself, in effect, self-destructs, leaving her bereft of the one thing that has apparently sustained her all along. That myth and myth-making process, rather than sustaining her, has in fact led her to the edge by providing a means for her *not* to make a supportable and self-supporting adjustment to the present. In a letter to Evelyn Scott, written shortly before the publication of *Voyage in the Dark,* Rhys says about her intention in the novel:

The big idea . . . [has] something to do with time being an illusion I think. I mean that the past exists—side by side with the present not behind it—that what was—is—.

I tried to do it by making the past (the West Indies) very vivid—the present (downward career of girl) dreamlike—starting of course piano and ending fortis- simo.

Perhaps I was simply trying to describe a girl going potty. (June 10, 1934; JRL, p. 24)[6]

Anna's memories of the island are often embodied in language that is mythic and religious, both in tone and references. In the passage below, Anna recalls some conflicting images of Sunday at home. She describes the preparations for church, the restriction of clothing and the reprimands of her elders, the ennui created in her by the formal religious service, and then she describes the out-of-doors in language that is rich in female sexual imagery and variously reverent, lyrical, and almost naturalistically reli- gious. The vision Rhys creates here, though written a decade or more earlier, reminds one of the lyrical invocations of her father's countryman, Dylan Thomas, in his poem, "Fern Hill." Anna says:

And the sky close to the earth. Hard, blue and close to the earth. The mango tree was so big that all the garden was in its shadow and the ground under it always looked dark and damp. The stable-yard was by the side of the garden, white-paved and hot, smelling of horses and manure. And then next to the stables was a bathroom. And the bathroom too was always dark and damp. It had no windows, but the door used to be hooked a little bit open. The light was always dim, greenish. There were cobwebs on the roof.

The stone bath was half as big as a good-sized room. You went up into it by two stone steps, cool and lovely to your feet. Then you sat on the side of the bath and let your legs dangle into the dark green water. . . .

During the Litany I would bite the back of the pitchpine pew in front, and sigh, and read bits of the marriage-service, and fan myself with an old wire fan with a picture on it in faded blues and reds of a fat Chinese woman toppling over backwards. Her little fat feet, with slippers turned up at the toes, seemed to be moving in the air; her little fat hands clutched at nothingness. . . .

Always, just when I had fallen into a sort of stupor, the Litany would end.

Walking through the still palms in the churchyard. The light is gold and when you shut your eyes you see fire-colour. (pp. 25–26)

Toward the end of this revery, for the moment, things fit together for

Anna in a moment of grace and splendor. As Anna escapes from the church, her revery ends with a vision of light and heat—the entire opposite of the cold and dark of England. The movement in this entire passage is like a real birth, as Anna moves from the damp, dark, and wet bathhouse which is like a sensual womb, through the moments in the church, and then out into a glorious natural paradise of light and warmth.

The vision Anna has of the churchyard is immediately undercut by the next scene, a recurring device in Rhys, in which her friend Maudie enters her rooms in London. Maudie's talk about economic survival and in what ways women in their position can get the most from men destroys Anna's glorious vision.

Part Three

In Part Two, all the "false" mothers have failed to provide Anna with the ideal maternal care she seeks. Part Three contains two responses by Anna to that failure: the first is a long fantasy in which she dives mythopoeically into her past as she rehearses the remembered ride to her mother's old estate; the second is a dream that seals Anna's future as it reflects her position in the patriarchy.

The fantasy of the ride to Constance constitutes a deeper and more mythic exploration of Anna's desire for a core or "essential" mother and the conflict that desire would present within the existing patriarchal world in which Anna finds herself. The fantasy of that journey immediately follows Anna's remembered image of still another antagonistic landlady and another unsustaining meal. Of the meal Anna recalls, "And the breakfast-tray dumped down on the bed, two plates with a bit of curled-up bacon on each. And if the landlady smiled or said 'Good morning' Maudie would say, 'She's very smarmy. What's the matter with her? I bet she puts that down on the bill. For saying Good Morning, half-a-crown' " (p. 92). It is immediately following this unmotherly image that Anna launches into a particularly compulsive recollection of home. This recollection is one of the most centrally important to *Voyage in the Dark*. In fact, fragments of it turn up later in Part Four. The entire recollection follows:

And then I tried to remember the road that leads to Constance Estate. It's funny how well you can remember when you lie in the dark with your arm over your forehead. Two eyes open inside your head. The sandbox tree outside the door at the home and the horse waiting with his bridle over the hook that was fixed in the tree. And the sweat rolling down Joseph's face when he helped me to mount and the tear in my habit-skirt. And mounting, and then the bridge and the sound of the horse's hoofs on the wooden planks, and then the savannah. And then there is New Town, and just beyond New Town the big mango tree. It was just past there that I fell off the mule when I was a kid and it seemed such a long time before I hit the ground. The road goes along by the sea. The coconut palms lean crookedly down to the water. (Francine says that if you wash your face in fresh coconut-water every day you are always young and unwrinkled, however long you live.) You ride in a sort of dream, the saddle creaks sometimes, and you smell the sea and the good smell of the horse. And then—wait a minute. Then do you turn to the right or the left? To the left, of course. You turn to the left and the sea is at your back, and the road goes zigzag upwards. The feeling of the hills comes to you—cool and hot at the same time. Everything is green, everywhere things are growing. There is never one moment of stillness—always something buzzing. And then dark cliffs and ravines and the smell of rotten leaves and damp. That's how the road to Constance is—green, and the smell of green, and then the smell of water and dark earth and rotting leaves and damp. There's a bird called a Mountain Whistler, that calls out on one note, very high-up and sweet and piercing. You ford little rivers. The noise the horse's hoofs make when he picks them up and puts them down in the water. When you see the sea again it's far below you. It took three hours to get to Constance Estate. It was as long as a life sometimes. I was nearly twelve before I rode it by myself. There were bits in the road that I was afraid of. The turning where you came very suddenly out of the sun into the shadow; and the shadow was always the same shape. And the place where the woman with yaws spoke to me. I suppose she was begging but I couldn't understand because her nose and mouth were eaten away; it seemed as though she were laughing at me. I was frightened; I kept on looking backwards to see if she was following me, but when the horse came to the next ford and I saw clear water I thought I had forgotten about her. And now—there she is. (pp. 92–93)

Before I discuss this passage further, it should be placed in context. Following the fantasy, Anna is visited by Carl Redman, who is an American version perhaps of Walter Jeffries; like Walter, he is a worldly-wise and self-assured representative of the patriarchy. Though kind to Anna he is, like Walter, primarily interested in buying her sexual favors. She knows that he too will eventually abandon her, though she fantasizes he will marry her. In her meeting with him, following the Constance fantasy, Anna sleeps with him for money, confirming her entry into prostitution. The chapter, then, divides itself essentially between the world of Anna's obsessively remembered ride to her mother's family's old estate and the world of Carl Redman—that is, between her female sources and the existing patriarchy.

The remembered ride to Constance indicates Anna's overwhelming need to return to her past—specifically, to the primordial quality of the lost island. The language she uses is of someone obsessed. She must repeat the ride and the journey exactly as it used to take place. She must re-see and re-feel each turning exactly as it was.

It is important that this ritualistically recalled ride is to her mother's place, although her mother has barely been mentioned except to reconfirm Anna's indigenous relationship to the island. Anna, in Part One, stresses to Walter that she is " 'a real West Indian.' " She says, " 'I'm the fifth generation on my mother's side' " (p. 33). It is her mother who connects Anna, like Antoinette Cosway's in *Wide Sargasso Sea,* to the island, who gives her whatever claim she has as one who belongs to it. It is her descent from her mother that connects her to the land and to Nature. And yet Anna's mother remains peculiarly unnamed, unmentioned, unspecified as a particular human being. All we know is her family name, Costerus—a Dutch name and word related to the custodian of the church. (I have been unable to understand Rhys's choice of this unusual name.)

It is also Anna's mother who connects her to the blacks of the island, both negatively and positively. Although Anna's mother is descended from slave owners, she nevertheless provides a link with the island blacks. Furthermore, the only continuing attachment Anna still has to the island is through her mother's brother, the Uncle Bo whom Hester castigates earlier for drinking too much and for having and then acknowledging half-black, illegitimate children. Hester says, "The Costeruses seem to have populated half the island in their time' " (p. 39). It is Anna's stepmother who dislikes Anna's mother's family, who links Anna and her mother with " 'niggers,' " who hates the land, especially the countryside, and who despises the flowers of the island (like Rochester in *Wide Sargasso Sea*).

Anna's memory of the ride to Constance Estate is also linked to her prepubescence and her puberty. Part of the memory concerns the time before she was twelve. It is only following her mention of being twelve that she introduces the element of dread to the ride and only after this that she describes the terrifying picture of the woman with yaws, perhaps a representation of the taint and corruption introduced into Anna's life at puberty.

The language Anna uses to describe the ride is both sensual and sexual.

The descriptions of the earth are particularly female, similar in kind to the topographical imagery in Coleridge's "Kubla Khan," which Anna has remembered earlier. In particular, after she falters and must think about whether to turn left or right, the language is concerned with fertility, with growth, with darkness and dampness. The place, as Anna describes it, seems peculiarly evocative of female sexuality; perhaps we could say that the imagery is vaginal or womblike. ("Everything is green, everywhere things are growing. . . . And then dark cliffs and ravines and the smell of rotten leaves and damp. . . . green, and the smell of green and then the smell of water and dark earth and rotting leaves and damp.")

Adjoining the sensual and sexual nature of this interior journey is Anna's very deep connection to nature, to things natural, to the earth, even to the animal on which she is riding. It is a primordial and at times sexually androgynous world; it counterfigures the unnatural response she has had to the onset of her menstruation after her stepmother destroys the "natural" response Francine has engendered. Even Anna's portrayal of the island, after the talk with Hester, contrasts vividly with this later description of the ride to her mother's estate. The landscape Anna sees after the talk with her stepmother is barren, harsh, almost desertlike. Unlike the representation of the island in the fantasy, the island then was murderous and oppressive. But in the island connected to Anna's mother, the world is soft and alive. It is a lush and growing, green world into which Anna desires to immerse herself and perhaps find renewal. But this possibility of renewal or revival where Anna might gain sustenance and fertility ends with an image of the woman who appears, as a presentiment perhaps, to the adolescent Anna. The mutilated and diseased face of the woman on the road, disfigured by a tropical disease particularly associated with the West Indies, reminds one of Anna's earlier reading of Emile Zola's *Nana,* whose heroine's end involved the disfigurement of her face by smallpox, suggesting in Rhys, that this disfigurement may represent a woman's punishment for extra-marital sex or prostitution.

That this fantasy is followed by Anna's emergence into the world of Carl Redman and prostitution signals the end of any attempt to return to the island or to the female sources that might re-empower her. And if we remember that all of Part Two has been moving toward the final vision of female sustenance in the person of Francine, a "natural" mother of sorts, it might also signify the end of her search for her natural mother.

Annis Pratt has noted similar patterns in many novels by women. She notes that often in such novels there are "recurrent moments of epiphanic vision uniting a woman hero's consciousness with the world of nature, in a relationship that has characteristics unique from that of male heroes as they experience both nature and woman. Young adolescent women, in particular, engage in fantasies of having a powerful place in the Green World and in nightmares of losing it. . . ."[7] Certainly Anna's journey is a seeking backward into a "green world." In fact, we might regard her entire narrative as the nightmare following her loss. Pratt equates this "green world" with matrilinear connections. In an earlier article, "Women and Nature in Modern Fiction," Pratt, in an attempt to define possible differences between the male and female *bildungsroman,* notes, "The first vision [heralding the advent of selfhood] most often occurs in a natural setting and is accompanied by a feeling of ecstasy, the idyllic aspect of the 'green world' with its budding trees and flowers apparently expressing the first sensual blossoming of the psyche."[8] Pratt contrasts Simone de Beauvoir's analyses with Joseph Campbell's; the latter, Pratt says, posits the hero's quest as a "'road of trials' or initiatory adventures that consummate in the simultaneous discovery of woman and earth . . ." (p. 477). In contrast to that is Beauvoir's comments on women writers. As Pratt points out, Beauvoir writes in *The Second Sex:*

Nature is one of the realms they have most lovingly explored. For the young girl, for the woman who has not fully abdicated, nature represents what woman herself represents for man: herself and her negation, a kingdom and a place of exile; the whole in the guise of the other. It is when she speaks of moors and gardens that the woman novelist will reveal her experience and her dreams to us most intimately. (Beauvoir, p. 790)

Anna's journey back into a world where "everything was green, everything was growing" is an attempt to get back to that part of herself which is essentially female and fertile. As long as she still has that desire she has not "abdicated." This, I believe, is one of the essential aspects of the island—that and its opposing connection to her own discovery of sexuality and death.

In her article on the *bildungsroman,* Pratt says that the "communion with the authentic self" that a heroine first achieves in "early naturistic epiphanies" enables her to maintain herself "in the face of destructive roles proffered to her by society" (p. 488). Anna's fantasy of Constance Estate serves as an alternative vision to the life suggested by the "models" offered by Hester, Ethel, Laurie, Maudie, and the other female characters in *Voyage in the Dark.* In the same article Pratt notes, "Models for false selves are constantly being brought forth, most scathingly in the author's delineations of alternate female characters playing inauthentic roles and tempting the heroines to do likewise" (p. 488). While Anna is presented with models for "false selves," unlike the heroines Pratt refers to, her diving into her sources, her past, and the natural world of the island is unable to sustain her because it has already been tainted before her exit from it.

Anna holds up to herself, like the mirrors in which she obsessively examines herself, the memory of the island. That memory contains, in part, another "self" for Anna and she holds on to it as a defense against her present world and the people who occupy it. Her memories in Part One were a way of combatting Walter (e.g., at Savernake she is both with him and away from him as she reveals to the reader her inner thoughts about the island; in many of the exchanges with him, it is the island of which she speaks; later it is the world to which she retreats when he abandons her). When Anna "retreats" to her memories of the island, she is always searching for the time that preceded her sexual development— the time before the sexes became separated, the time before she realized that she would have to grow old and more importantly, the time before she would be expected to enter the world of the Hesters or, barring that, the world of Laurie and Maudie. Thus far, in an act of passive resistance, she has avoided both. Anna's island, on the other hand, is associated with her "real" mother's land; since that mother remains unspecified and undefined, she offers for Anna the possibility of infinite expansion.

Anna has originally defined her problem as being one of place and her ability to fit the two places together. What we know by now is that the two places are of course symbols for Anna's inner state, representations of the opposing desires in herself: to be apart and different from the rest of society, to oppose the bourgeois and genteel mold offered by Hester— in short, to experience adventure—and yet to remain a child, cared for and looked after in a world in which there is no sexual differentiation. After examining the development of parts One, Two, and Three we can also say that the places signify her own search for her authentic female self or identity, and the counterposing authority of a patriarchal, materialistic, and uncaring society in which women who do not play the role delineated by Hester become items of trade.

Maudie has clearly defined this world, in which women are "cheaper than things." When she visits Anna on her birthday, she tells Anna a funny story:

'My dear, I had to laugh,' she said. 'Do you know what a man said to me the other day? It's funny, he said, have you ever thought that a girl's clothes cost more than the girl inside them?

'. . . You can get a very nice girl for five pounds, a very nice girl indeed; you can even get a very nice girl for nothing if you know how to go about it. But you can't get a very nice costume for her for five pounds. To say nothing of underclothes, shoes, etcetera and so on. And then I had to laugh, because after all it's true, isn't it? People are much cheaper than things. And look here! Some dogs are more expensive than people, aren't they?' (p. 28)

Later, Maudie tells Anna that she's met a man she'd like very much to have marry her. She tells Anna that she's afraid she'll lose her chance at securing him because she's " 'so damned shabby' " (p. 98). She says, " 'He said . . . , 'If there's anything I notice about a girl it's her legs and shoes.' Well, my legs are all right, but look at my shoes. . . . Isn't it rotten when a thing like that falls through just because you haven't got a little cash? Oh God, I wish it could happen. I want it so to happen' " (p. 98). Anna, who has just received fifteen quid as what we might call severance pay from Carl Redman, gives Maudie the money and concludes with a statement that reminds one of Stella Bowen's description of Jean Rhys. Anna says: "It's always like that with money. You never know where it goes to. You change a fiver and then it's gone" (p. 98).

Just as Bowen states that Rhys appeared to be proud of her ethos, so one senses that while Anna can neither function in the role prescribed by Hester or the roles delineated by Maudie or Laurie or Ethel, though all of them give her very clear instructions on how and what to do, there is an element of pride in her own solitary and outcast position. Even among the outcasts, Anna remains outcast, reminding one too of Rhys's description of the other "outcast" girl in the convent school who wanted to befriend her. Despite Anna's economic dependence and her inability to deal with the harshness of the adult society in which she finds herself, one senses that she—and Jean Rhys—acknowledge it as a positive limitation. Better to be a miserable victim in this society, better not to "know exactly what's going to happen . . . each day" (p. 46) than to be either a victimizer or one of those who, like Hester, rigidly maintains the proper order of things.

Chapter 4, the central chapter of Part Three, contains in symbolic form the conflict and difference between the two worlds and the two places with which Anna contends. The two episodes that comprise chapter 4— one a revery of a woman from Anna's childhood, the other a dream— contain within them the two opposing poles of power that permeate Anna's world. The two episodes contrast matriarchal origins, already suggested by the previous revery of the ride to Constance Estate, and patriarchal governance, represented by men who purchase women.

The first episode, a revery of Colonel Jackson's illegitimate and half-black daughter, is triggered by a song that a customer of Anna's asks her to play on the gramophone. The song, which she refuses to play because it gives her "the pip" (p. 99), is "Connais-tu le Pays," which is probably a French rendition of Goethe's well known poem "Mignon," which begins in English with the line: "Knowst thou the land of flowering lemon-trees?" Goethe's poem contains a remembrance of a sunny land where the citrus grows, a reminiscence that must remind Anna of her own island. The poem also contains the lines, "What have they done, poor child, to hurt thee so?"9 which echo Carl Redman's earlier words to Anna: "'Now, what have they been doing to you?'" (p. 94).

Anna recalls the opening line again, this time in French, after her customer leaves. The memory of the song leads Anna to recall, in a long, unpunctuated passage introduced by ellipses, Colonel Jackson's illegitimate daughter and the sad songs she sang. In particular Anna recalls the name of a song, "By the Blue Alsatian Mountains I Watch and Wait Alway" which is, though Anna doesn't mention it, a song about a maiden abandoned by her lover. But the title of the song leads Anna to begin to name the mountains on her island. The names she lists are actual mountains in Dominica, including the last she comes to, Morne Diablotin. What is important about this particular recollection is her observation that Morne Diablotin was "obeah" (West Indian black magic). Anna says, "It's a high mountain five thousand feet with its top always veiled and Anne Chewett used to say that it's haunted and obeah—she had been in gaol for obeah (obeah-women who dig up dead people and cut their fingers off and go to gaol for it—it's hands that are obeah) . . ." (p. 100). Obeah,

which is particularly connected in Rhys with the power of black West
Indian women, becomes the focus of her recollection. But shortly after,
she reports a dream which serves as a direct rebuttal to the previous
thoughts of obeah and hence female power. The dream, in contrast to the
preceding thoughts of obeah women, deals with the power of the patriarchy. About that dream, which comprises the conclusion of chapter 4,
Anna says:

I dreamt that I was on a ship. From the deck you could see small islands—dolls
of islands—and the ship was sailing in a doll's sea, transparent as glass.

Somebody said in my ear, 'That's your island that you talk such a lot about.'

And the ship was sailing very close to an island, which was home except that
the trees were all wrong. These were English trees, their leaves trailing in the
water. I tried to catch hold of a branch and step ashore, but the deck of the ship
expanded. Somebody had fallen overboard.

And there was a sailor carrying a child's coffin. He lifted the lid, bowed and
said, 'The boy bishop,' and a little dwarf with a bald head sat up in the coffin.
He was wearing a priest's robes. He had a large blue ring on his third finger.

'I ought to kiss the ring,' I thought in my dream, 'and then he'll start saying
"In nomine Patris, Filii. . . ." '

When he stood up, the boy bishop was like a doll. His large, light eyes in a
narrow, cruel face rolled like a doll's as you lean it from one side to the other. He
bowed from right to left as the sailor held him up.

But I was thinking, 'What's overboard?' and I had that awful dropping of the
heart.

I was still trying to walk up the deck and get ashore. I took huge, climbing,
flying strides among confused figures. I was powerless and very tired, but I had
to go on. And the dream rose into a climax of meaninglessness, fatigue and
powerlessness, and the deck was heaving up and down, and when I woke up
everything was still heaving up and down.

It was funny how, after that, I kept on dreaming about the sea. (pp. 101–102)

This dream contains many elements already developed in *Voyage in the*

Dark. It reflects Anna's continuing conflict about the past and the present, about England and the island. And, I think, especially if taken in conjunction with the preceding revery of obeah women, *female* priests perhaps, it reveals the underlying power struggle between men and women, if we can say that in *Voyage in the Dark* there really is any struggle at all. Perhaps rather, the dream represents, among other things, the power that men can have over women. Furthermore, the dream also reflects Anna's recent discovery of her pregnancy (the inclusion of the dolls and the *boy* bishop) and perhaps her presentiment about her coming abortion (the child's coffin).

The boy bishop, who is perhaps a mixture of Anna's own childish and child concerns and a reflection of her concern with the male world, stands in particular opposition to the obeah women. This figure, who literally represents the Father and the Son, is the spirit of the male world. He wears a priest's robes and has large "light eyes in a narrow cruel face." Many of Rhys's male victimizers have light eyes—Heidler in *Quartet* has eyes "like blue glass' (p.106). My own feeling is that the source for this recurring image in Rhys goes back to Mr. Howard. In the Black Exercise Book, recollecting the picture of herself as a child with Mr. Howard, she writes: "God I can see these two—a very tall very upright old gentleman with a white moustache one blue eye one glass one" (fol. 28).

Furthermore, Anna's thought that she should kiss the boy bishop's ring seems deliberately to echo her first sexual encounter with Walter when, after she sees him in the mirror placing some money into her handbag, she thinks she ought to stop him; instead she describes an act of fealty. She says, "But when I went up to him, instead of saying, 'don't do that.' I said. [sic] 'All right, if you like—anything you like, any way you like.' And I kissed his hand" (p. 23). With that echo in mind, this dream of Anna's seems clearly to seal her obeisance to the male world and male power and the connection of that to sexual involvement with men. The Catholic hierarchy also seems to reflect the fears with which Anna has fallen asleep—fears of the judgments to be pronounced on her for her pregnancy and possibly for her as yet unplanned abortion. Finally, it is Anna herself who states that the dream is about power. She concludes by saying that she was "powerless and very tired" and that the dream climaxed into "powerlessness."

I think that a further division is present in this dream, a division that presents the difference between the quality of the male and female worlds, the difference between the land and the sea and specifically between trees and the sea. In her memories of home, Anna has often ritualistically and obsessively recalled its plant life, in all its variety, especially the flowers and the flamboyant flowering trees which, in Rhys, are often associated with women. They have served as a symbol for her island, for her childhood, and for her female sources. She has also spoken about English trees as either "tidy" or, in a more grim mood, dead and deadly. On a ride she takes with Laurie and two men Anna notices the trees, "The long shadows of the trees, like skeletons, and others like spiders and others like octopuses" (p. 87). Later, chapter 6 opens, just before the abortion but after it is planned, with another reference to English trees. Anna says, "The big tree in the square opposite d'Adhémar's flat was perfectly still, and the forked twigs looked like fingers pointing. Everything was perfectly still, as if it were dead" (p. 104). The trees of England represent a strange and alien world, a world which stands in particular opposition to the fecundity of the island.

After detailing her dream, Anna says that she continued to dream about the sea all the time. These dreams continue the concerns which are evident in this one: her separation, by the sea, from her island; that she cannot get ashore; and that she is close to drowning. Anna has made references to her drowning as early as Part One and has told Ethel that she doesn't leave her simply because she " 'can't swim well enough' " (p. 89). Last, it is not far-fetched to assume that Anna, in dreaming about the sea, is also dreaming about her father. Anna's surname Morgan means "the one from beside the sea" in Welsh. Anna, and Rhys, learned some Welsh from their fathers. Anna has mentioned earlier that *hiraeth* is the Welsh word for grief. Rhys gave her address in Roseau, her family home, to the RADA in Welsh ("Bod Gwilym")[10] and Rhys seemed particularly fond of associating the name Morgan with her own father, who ran away to sea. In *Smile Please,* she says that she "will call" her father's smaller estate "Morgan's Rest" and never gives the actual name by which it was known, nor why she chooses to refer to it in that way (p. 81).

Anna concludes her dream by describing her own inability to get to shore, to get her feet on the ground, so to speak. "What's overboard?" she asks in the dream. Certainly we can say that it is, at least, everything that has ever meant anything for Anna. Her past, hope, possibility, love, and meaning—all are overboard.

After Anna's abortion there is only one subsequent recollection of home in Part Three. This time, however, and for the first time, it is a totally negative memory. As Anna leaves Mrs. Robinson's she is in a paranoic state and fears she is dying. She says:

I got outside. I was afraid to cross the street and then I was afraid because the slanting houses might fall on me or the pavement rise up and hit me. But most of all I was afraid of the people passing because I was dying; and, just because I was dying, any one of them, any minute, might stop and approach me and knock me down, or put their tongues out as far as they would go. Like that time at home with Meta, when it was Masquerade and she came to see me and put out her tongue at me through the slit in her mask. (p. 110)

In some way, perhaps in the most negative way possible, things are starting to come together for Anna; the past and the present are merging, but not as she once hoped. Even the memories of the past are becoming dark, threatening, frightening, and noncomforting. In starting the abortion, in beginning to cut the child out of herself, if we think of the growing child inside as another aspect of Anna, the island has started to become a malevolent aspect of her life, as England already is.

It is interesting that Rhys has used the name of her own childhood nurse here, a person whom she points out in her autobiography as being unwontedly cruel to her and who, in fact, showed her "a world of fear and distrust" (p. 32). As a counterpart to that, Rhys also tells in her autobiography of a maidservant in the house, Francine, who was very kind to her and often told her stories. Years later she learned when "reading about obeah" that "Bois sèche," one of the ritual words Francine began stories with, was an obeah god (p. 31). Further on, Rhys writes, "I grew very fond of Francine and admired her; when she disappeared without a word to me I was hurt. People did disappear, they went to one of the other islands, but not without saying goodby. I still think of Francine and now I can imagine other reasons for her complete disappearance from the house and from my life" (p. 31).

Clearly, Rhys has taken the names of two of the most important black women of her childhood and used them (actually reversed them) in *Voyage in the Dark*. Francine takes the place of the bad nanny Meta and Meta becomes an acquaintance who is cruel. The nurse, Meta, terrified the young Ella Williams so much that she would yell, "Black Devil Black Devil," until she had no breath left (SP, p. 31). The ghoulish and unkind face of the black woman Meta becomes the final image that stays with Anna in Part Four. If Rhys has taken the good and the bad caretakers in her life and transposed them in *Voyage in the Dark,* she has, like Anna perhaps, tried to make a wish come true. But it is the face of Meta who finally pops up cruelly in the end of Part Three, though she has never been mentioned before; we never hear of Francine again in *Voyage in the Dark.* The benevolence of the island seems to have been totally destroyed by Anna's abortion. The dream has lost its power, or rather it has lost its healing or restorative properties and instead has assumed the face of the terrible masks, which engender in Anna the same kind of paralysis and fear that she experiences in England. In that mask, the past and the present have finally come together in a terrifying and hostile image. In the world of Anna's island, power, whether it be the good and restorative power of Francine or the evil and malevolent power of Meta, or the religious power of the obeah woman, is essentially black and female. Power in England is white and male, though often enforced by the gentlewomen of Hester's ilk. What is important in Anna's desire to be black is a desire for place and, more importantly, a desire for personal power.

The ending of Part Three also returns, like parts One and Two, full circle back to the opening of *Voyage in the Dark.* Anna concludes with a description of yet another new set of rooms and the statement that everything, the rooms, the houses, the streets, are "always so exactly alike" (p. 111). Her final words in Part Three ("And the cold; and the houses all exactly alike, and the streets going north, south, east, west, all exactly alike" (p. 111) are almost exactly the same words Anna used at the beginning of her narrative in Part One to describe her first shocking experiences of England.

Part Four

The final section of *Voyage in the Dark,* Part Four, is different in structure from the preceding divisions. It consists of one unnumbered chapter which is about half italicized flashbacks, punctuated only by dashes, and about half continuation of Anna's narrative. The chapter incorporates the actual time of the completion of Anna's abortion and flashes back to reveries and memories, some of which have already occurred in previous sections of *Voyage in the Dark.* In this sense, while Anna is undergoing the end of her abortion, things come together in a way that they have not previously. In fact, there are also no ellipses separating the past and the present in this section. In this final chapter, the divisions between memory and present have all but disappeared. However, unlike the earlier sections, during the entire section there is not one pleasant or gratifying memory.

The chapter opens with Anna in a "nearly dark" room with "a long yellow ray coming in under the door" (p. 112). Anna is lying watching the light; for the first part of the chapter, she is conscious and clearly reporting the dialogue between Laurie and the landlady as they await the doctor. Then, after she takes a drink, she falls into a semiconscious state so that the words and actions of the present trigger memories and associations on another level of consciousness. In the beginning part of her flashback Anna is still conscious and the clock ticking reminds her of a time when she was having sex with a man who is apparently older than she. He says to her that he is " 'too old for this sort of thing' " (p. 112) and Anna adds: "His face was white." (p. 113) Rhys uses this as a somewhat awkward transition to the italicized and scarcely punctuated passage which begins with a vision of a white mask seen by the child Anna as she watches the Carnival masquerade in which the images of home and of both the blacks and whites there have degenerated into a series of frightening cartoon figures. Of the blacks in the Carnival Parade, Anna says:

they passed under the window singing—it was all colours of the rainbow when you looked down at them and the sky so blue . . . the masks the men wore were a crude pink with the eyes squinting near together squinting but the masks the women wore were made of close-meshed wire covering the whole face and tied at the back of the head—the handkerchief that went over the back of the head hid the strings and over the slits for the eyes mild blue eyes were painted then there was a small straight nose and a little red heart-shaped mouth and under the mouth another slit so that they could put their tongues out at you—(p. 113, my ellipses)

As she watches the macabre and dark scene, Anna also listens to the voices of the adults behind her discussing the blacks in condescending and hateful terms. She says, *"I was looking out of the window and I knew why the masks were laughing and I heard the concertina-music going"* (p. 113). This image of the blacks is different from the previous ones in parts One, Two and Three, except for the final image in Part Three where Anna, in a state of paranoia, recalls Meta. All the blacks have taken on, in this final section, a frightening aspect and have become a depersonalized mob. In *Smile Please,* Rhys has described the carnival in Dominica and says the masks terrified her. She also, and in *Wide Sargasso Sea* this becomes a major theme, describes nights when there were small riots in Dominica. On one night in particular the young Rhys was awakened and dressed, apparently in order to flee should that prove necessary. Rhys says that after that "a certain wariness did creep in when I thought about the black people who surrounded me" (p. 48). Generally, even in some of the short fiction and in *Wide Sargasso Sea,* blacks, in groups especially, seem to be a dangerous and frightening element in Rhys's work, understandably linked to the possibility of rebellion and riot—an event which at least once destroyed the Lockhart estate. The blacks in the scene that Anna describes are laughing and Anna says she knows the reason why. We can assume that they are perhaps laughing at the whites sitting in their houses, watching but not participating in the Carnival. (In an unpublished longer version of part Four now in The McFarlin Library, Anna says: "they were laughing at the idea that anybody black would want to be white.")[11]

The italicized and almost unpunctuated stream of consciousness in Part Four is twice interrupted by Anna calling out that she is giddy. These moves to the surface and then Anna's subsequent submersion remind one of the last attempts of a person drowning. In the third submersion into unconsciousness, Anna returns to a recapitulation of the ride to Constance Estate which is more fragmented than previously and now contains new material. The final words of that stream of consciousness contain a new and negative vision. Anna says:

do you turn to the right or the left—the left of course—and then that turning where the shadow is always the same shape—shadows are ghosts you look at them and you don't see them—you look at everything and you don't see it only sometimes you see it like now I see—a cold moon looking down on a place where nobody is a place full of stones where nobody is

I thought I'm going to fall nothing can save me now but still I clung desperately with my knees feeling very sick. (p. 114)

In what might be described as a negative epiphany Anna, in this last semiconscious revery, "sees" into things. She sees what there is not, sees the nonexistence, the denial within things, sees the absolute barrenness and hopelessness—"a cold moon looking down on a place where nobody is." These last three words with their unusual juxtaposition of negative and then positive sound like an impressionistic definition of a shadow—and the "place full of stones" sounds very much like the ruins of Anna's mother's old estate, where nothing is left but shadows and memories. The stones stand like inconsequential and ungiving monuments to the past, like the stones that commemorate those long dead.

Following this final stream of consciousness Anna says, "I fell, . . . I fell for a hell of a long time then" (p. 114) and Laurie translates Anna's words into a warning that she tell that to the doctor—that she had a fall. This line about falling occurs in the original version of the ride to Constance in a less "universal" context. Just at the beginning of the section, as she tries to reconstruct the path in her mind, she says, "It was just past there [near a big mango tree] that I fell off the mule when I was a kid and it seemed such a long time before I hit the ground" (p. 92). This time Rhys takes the line and puts it toward the end. Instead of being, as it is in the original version of the ride, a foreshadowing of Anna's "fall," it becomes a statement summing up all of her experience because, if nothing else, *Voyage in the Dark* has been the story of Anna's fall from grace, out of the Paradisial world of the preadolescent island of her childhood. It has been the story of her fall from the innocence of childhood and its accompanying deep connection to nature, into the mortal knowledge of sex and its accompanying spiritual and sexual degradation.

As Anna returns to consciousness, she hears the doctor's voice again, " 'You girls are too naive to live, aren't you?' " (p. 114). Then she hears him laughing with Laurie "and their voices going up and down" (p. 114).

The last words of the book are Anna's and they take us full circle both in language and content to the opening of *Voyage in the Dark*. She says:

When their voices stopped the ray of light came in again under the door like the last thrust of remembering before everything is blotted out. I lay and watched it and thought about starting all over again. And about being new and fresh. And about mornings, and misty days, when anything might happen. And about starting all over again, all over again. . . . (p. 115, Rhys's ellipses)

Like the opening two lines of *Voyage in the Dark,* in which Anna talks about ending and beginning, about memory and the past and about the possibility of being born again, here too in her last line she talks about losing memory and knowledge of the past and the possibility of beginning again, of being "new and fresh." But given the epicyclic movement of the novel, given the series of false beginnings and new starts that Anna has experienced throughout *Voyage in the Dark,* we cannot but think that even this possibility is without hope. There is nothing to suggest otherwise. This entire last section reinforces the sense of the epicyclic repetitions Anna has experienced, even to the interior monologue which recounts in dizzying repetitions and rhythmical language many fragments that have already occurred in the previous three sections.

In fact, in the last section, at least one recollection indicates, because of the purposeful inaccuracy it contains, that Anna is already making into mythic memory the stuff of the linear narrative of *Voyage in the Dark.* In Part Four, in the flashback section, Anna recalls words Walter has said to her in Part One. In the passage in Part One in which these words first occur, Anna has said that it is 3:30 and that she ought to be leaving and Walter replies: ' 'you mustn't be sad, you mustn't worry. My darling mustn't worry' " (p. 22). However, in the flashback in Part Four, Anna changes the facts so that it is Walter who tells her that is is nearly 4:00 and that she ought to leave. It would seem that Anna has already taken this experience and made it more negative, changed a recollection of her own leave-taking into another aspect of Walter's rejection of her. Given the obvious care with which *Voyage in the Dark* is constructed, this change in the text can hardly be an oversight. It suggests a distance perhaps between Rhys and Anna; that Rhys, although she admittedly used much of the material of her own life and her own journals for *Voyage in the Dark,* was aware that a character like Anna might make the worst of things and might be distrustful, if not paranoic, as in this case where Anna has remembered an incident as worse than it was.

When Anna undergoes her abortion, she is twenty and it is the month of April. We can assume this by counting from March 26, the date of Ethel's letter to Laurie, prior to the abortion. Like *A Portrait of the Artist as a Young Man,* Anna's coming of age story ends in April—a time obviously connected with beginnings and rebirth. But for Anna, unlike for Stephen Daedelus, it is a time of death—literally because of the abortion and metaphorically because of the effect it has on her: she feels as though she is dying. Certainly this episode and the events that have led up to it signify the certain passing of Anna's youth. Even the seasonal aspect of Anna's narrative acts in counterpoint to what happens to her. Her story, about "being born all over again," begins in the fall as does the "new beginning" heralded by her affair with Walter; she concludes with the abortion of a real birth in the spring. Even Vincent, when he talks to Anna about her career, says: " 'We're trying to make a start in the autumn' " (p. 53). Everything is reversed. Anna's life, its beginnings and endings, its starts and little deaths, are usually in counterpoint to the natural world. Before the start of her abortion, Anna expresses this dislocation. She too feels far from the natural world when, as Vincent is leaving, she says to him: " 'It must be lovely in the country' " (p. 108).

In some sense, though, the time of the island and the time in England do, however, finally and ironically fit together. It is the Carnival that Anna recalls in this final section, the Carnival which in Dominica occurs as part of the pre-Easter holiday. But the Carnival, a joyful event, becomes equated with fear and death.

Anna's story has been, in part, about loss through time. Perhaps we should look at the "time" when she ends her story because the one date given, 1914, is, as V. S. Naipaul has said, "startling."[12] Though Naipaul doesn't detail his reasoning, we come across the date with a sense of shock because in the entire narrative, there has been no mention of war, no political or social effects described or detailed, an indication perhaps of Anna's overwhelming self-involvement. But the date itself also signifies an end and a beginning: the end of an era and the end of the kind of world that produced Anna. The date indicates a dividing line between one epoch and another. As Walter Allen says in *The Modern Novel:*

After the first World War, the age that had ended in July 1914 seemed as remote as the far side of the moon. The War split the landscape of time like an enormous natural catastrophe, obliterating long-established boundaries, blowing sky-high landmarks that for years had been taken for granted. It lay like an unbridgeable chasm between the present and the past, so that present and past seemed almost laughably different in kind. . . . It affected everything and everybody. Nothing was as it was before.[13]

In this sense, Anna's personal and individual story also comes to a changing point that is reflected, but only by the date Rhys includes, by the coming war. In Rhys's own life, the war did signify, in her meeting Jean Lenglet, an opportunity to leave England. But Walter Allen's description of the effects of the war could serve just as well as a description of the cataclysmic effects of Anna's personal experiences on her.

What Anna's future promises is left only slightly ambiguous at the conclusion of *Voyage in the Dark*. One may doubt that Anna does have the chance or the promise, as she half-heartedly imagines, "to feel new and fresh." One may doubt too that it is possible for her to start over in such a way that the fresh start would not contain within it an inevitable "fall"—as all her previous starts have. Certainly one would have to perceive some change in Anna in order to believe that such a change in her life would be possible. But the only changes that one perceives are slight and hardly positive signs. At the beginning, Anna has been unable to "fit things together"—the past and present, England and Dominica. In the final sections, things do come together: the time remembered on the island (Carnival) is literally connected to the present time in England (April). Furthermore, the final section, rather than being divided into parts, is one entire whole with no chapter divisions. The internal monologue contained in that section is not separated by ellipses, though it does occur in italics. Finally, Anna merges together many of the incidents and memories of her past in this final section, but that fitting together is so extraordinarily negative that one cannot see it as a hopeful synthesis. Anna says that she sees something which she does not usually see. However, that image of what she sees, nothingness, is hardly an image to restore one's faith that Anna will do any more than survive. Anna says, as she comes to, that she "had a fall," perhaps indicating that the fall is over. But there is no substantial change in Anna that would lead us to think that she will be better equipped to deal with a world that she, and the point of view of the book, presents so negatively and so fatalistically.

As is now rather well known, Rhys had originally intended another ending for the novel but her publishers felt that it was too negative. That ending, which is in the Jean Rhys collection at the University of Tulsa, is a much lengthier version of Part Four and contains far more "explanations" and new information not included in the previous three sections of the novel. Most importantly it suggests that the corpse that the young Anna mentions in Part One as being "too young to die" is the body of her mother. In fact, in the original Part Four the mother is developed far more than in the published verion of *Voyage in the Dark*. Furthermore, the character Meta, who appears briefly in Part Three of the published version, is also more fully developed and identified. In general the manuscript also contains more social and political commentary, particularly about the relationship between blacks and whites.

In 1963, when Rhys and Selma Vaz Dias were corresponding about a proposed dramatization of *Voyage in the Dark,* Rhys sent Vaz Dias the unpublished ending. In a letter to Vaz Dias she writes that perhaps Vaz Dias "will see no difference between the two versions" but that "all the same I still think it better" (August 30, 1963; JRL, p. 236). Perhaps the most significant change is the actual closing paragraph. The unpublished version of that paragraph follows:

And the concertina-music stopped and it was so still, so still and lovely like just before you go to sleep   and it stopped   and there was the ray of light along the floor like the last thrust of remembering before everything is blotted out and blackness comes. . . . .[14]

In that same letter Rhys makes suggestions for a stage production of *Voyage in the Dark* and suggests there be a "dead girl" or "certainly a dying girl" on stage.

In a letter to Evelyn Scott written before the publication of *Voyage in the Dark,* Rhys writes about her feelings concerning the changed ending:

I don't know what to do. I suppose I shall have to give in and cut the book and I'm afraid it will make it meaningless. The worst is that it is precisely that last part which I am most certain of that will have to be mutilated.

My dear it is so mad—really it is not a disgusting book—or even a very grey book. And I *know* the ending is the only possible ending.

I know if I tinker around with it I'll spoil it without helping myself a bit from the being popular point of view. (June 10, 1934; JRL, p. 25)

Rhys's preferred ending literally ends on a dark note rather than a light one, though the published ending is hardly metaphorically "light." It seems to me that this unpublished ending, even though Rhys may have intended that the young Anna be dead or dying, does not eliminate the ambiguity which is also present in the published version. I do not think that whichever version one uses to read the novel is a serious problem in terms of understanding because the fact of the abortion and the vision that accompanies it before Anna returns to consciousness are the most crucial aspects of the conclusion. I would also say that the published version contributes more brilliantly to the structure Rhys has developed in the rest of the book—a structure that depends on epicyclic false starts and beginnings. The published ending restates that structure in an almost perfect spiral that recalls the novel's opening. I think that because of this recapitulation of structure, the published version is in fact superior to Rhys's manuscript version—a rendition which also lacks the terseness and maintenance of tone of the published version.

In an unpublished paper on *Voyage in the Dark,* Joan Givner agrees with Rhys's contention that the unpublished version is superior.[15] She writes that the "unsatisfactory nature" of *Voyage in the Dark* is the publisher's fault. Givner says that "Rhys had written a tragic ending, similar to the ending of *Wide Sargasso Sea,* in which her heroine moves irrevocably into death" (p. 5). She interprets Rhys's preferred conclusion as containing a "description of death as the result of a botched abortion" (p. 5). Givner's reading of the unpublished ending has Anna definitely dead. But, despite what Rhys says about the ending, a precise reading of it certainly leaves more ambiguity than Givner accords it. While Givner is correct in stating that Rhys's preferred ending approaches her treatment of Antoinette's death in *Wide Sargasso Sea,* it is also true that Rhys handles the ending in *Wide Sargasso Sea* quite differently too. Givner also does not deal with the problem of a first person narrator who would not only be dead but would be witness and narrator of the moment of her death—a problem Rhys solves in *Wide Sargasso Sea* with a dream-vision and a reliance on intertextual references.

In the introduction to her recently published transcription of the original ending to *Voyage in the Dark* Nancy Hemond Brown, like Givner, states that the published version is the inferior one. She says that it "altered and diminished the achievement of the novel as a whole" (p. 41). Brown also asks why, with the typescript in her possession, Rhys did not, upon republication of her novels by André Deutsch, restore the original ending. In partial answer to her question, Brown notes that Diana Athill "speculates that by this time [1964] Jean Rhys no longer preferred the original ending." Athill told Brown that it was "her impression that the story of how she [Jean Rhys] was forced into changing the ending became one of 'her automatic "anti-*them*" stories, rather than a comment on the book' " (LM, p. 43). Brown, however, feels that other factors, such as Rhys's involvement with her work on *Wide Sargasso Sea,* as well as personal problems, may have induced her to leave the originally published version unchanged. Certainly Rhys's letter to Vaz Dias about the possible production of *Voyage in the Dark* is in agreement with Brown's thinking about Rhys's continued preference for the unpublished conclusion.

Though no critic has noted it, perhaps one of the most interesting aspects of this unpublished version of Part Four, aside from the light it throws on *Voyage in the Dark,* is that Rhys apparently used it as an important source for her autobiography. The opening line of the manuscript provides the autobiography's title; the opening page, with minor alterations, is the same as the opening page of *Smile Please,* suggesting again the ways in which Rhys's fiction and autobiography overlap.

The Writer Looks On

Rhys often reveals the emotional tone of Anna Morgan's life through the use of literary reference. The Gothic tale of terror "The Iron Shroud," though only passingly mentioned by Anna, is a fitting paradigm for her narrative. In the tale, written more than fifty years earlier than *Voyage in the Dark,* William Mudford describes the torture of Vivenzio, a prisoner who is cruelly crushed to death by the slowly collapsing walls and roof of his dark prison cell. Anna, "imprisoned" in one of her boarding house rooms, forever exiled from her native island, recalls Mudford's story. She says: "I lay down and started thinking about the time when I was ill in Newcastle, and the room I had there, and that story about the walls of a room getting smaller and smaller until they crush you to death. *The Iron Shroud,* it was called. It wasn't Poe's story; it was more frightening than that" (p. 18). Anna never mentions the story again, though she is passingly aware perhaps of the parallels between Vivenzio and herself. Both Vivenzio and she are victims of an apparently arbitrary punishment; both dream of their homelands and of the bright sensuality of a warm and benevolent Nature. But both are doomed to a dark relentless despair and are powerless to affect the seeming inevitability of their fates. However, Vivenzio's doom is sealed wholly from without, while Anna's comes at least in part from within.

Voyage in the Dark records Anna's escalating sense of loss, her despair, and her downward spiral in terms of hope, possibility, and attachment to the quotidian world. She is, like the zombies and souciants of the black religion of her island, one of the living dead. She lives between dream and reality, in a "lethargy of the soul"—the term Mudford uses to describe Vivenzio's state of mind when he finally abandons all hope. Vivenzio's torturer, anticipating this mental state, has a loud and unsettling bell ring periodically to ensure that the torture will not be diminished by Vivenzio's deadened spirit. Mudford writes:

His wasted spirits and oppressed mind no longer struggled within him. He was past hope, and fear shook him no more.

> But such a lethargy of the soul . . . had entered into the diabolical calculations of Tolfi. . . . The tolling of an enormous bell struck. . . . The sound was so close and stunning that it seemed to shatter his very brain. . . . (p. 68)

Anna's affair with Walter Jeffries serves a parallel function to Tolfi's bell; it awakens a sense of yearning and passion in her so that she cannot, at least not at first, immure herself against the pain by blotting out feeling. But, paradoxically, her affair with him ultimately increases her paralyzing despair and her inertia.

Vivenzio's tormentor has fashioned his bed with a contrivance of hidden springs so that on the last day of his torture it is transformed into a bier,

> in order to heighten . . . all the feelings of despair and anguish. . . . For the same reason, the last window was so made as to admit only a shadowy kind of gloom rather than light. . . . [At the end], as he lay gathered up in lessened bulk, the bell beat loud and frequent—crash succeeded crash— and on, and on, and on came the mysterious engine of death, till Vivenzio's smothered groans were heard no more! He was horribly crushed by the ponderous roof and collapsing sides— and the flattened bier was his *Iron Shroud*. (pp. 68–69)

Vivenzio's fate is undoubtedly and quite literally sealed: Anna's at the conclusion of *Voyage in the Dark* is more ambiguous. But the psychological reality and the concrete and physical presentation of asphyxiating enclosure that Vivenzio experiences is, nevertheless, a suitable metaphor for Anna's torment.

As with many Gothic tales, Mudford does not treat us to a prolonged description of the reasons why Vivenzio must suffer. The point of the story seems to be to create a psychological realism that renders the intensity of the emotions of fear, powerlessness, and existential suffering counterpointed with a vision of human community, physical warmth, and the natural world of the sun and growing things—a clear parallel to Anna's obsessive returns in thought to her sunny homeland. Mudford writes, "The evening sun was descending, and Vivenzio beheld its golden beams streaming through one of the windows. What a thrill of joy shot through his soul at the sight! It was a precious link that united him, for the moment, with the world beyond. There was ecstasy in the thought" (p. 66).

While Anna is not so literally crushed to death, she is enshrouded in her dark rooms and, at least once, while in Walter's bed, as in a bier, she simulates death. Anna's world is full of enclosing and suffocating walls. Even England itself and its people remind her of walls. Of the unsympathetic British voices she says that "their damned voices [are] like high, smooth, unclimbable walls all round you, closing in on you" (p. 90). For Anna, these walls, signified by voices, and sometimes the look of someone's eyes, besides crushing her also signal her isolation and her own inarticulateness and powerlessness. For example, Walter's cousin Vincent, a cold and haughty man who patronizes Anna and who wants to protect Walter from her, though there is little need of such defense, has a "look in his eyes . . . like a high, smooth, unclimbable wall. No communication possible" (p. 106). But sometimes for Anna, walls like rooms, *seem* to symbolize refuge and peace.

Vivenzio's reactions to his confinement and severance from family and friends are similar to Anna's. His are natural reactions to an unnatural and insupportable situation; he begins to talk to himself and manifests the behavior that we normally attribute to those who are mad: "He remained on the ground, sometimes sitting, sometimes lying; at intervals, sleeping heavily; and when not sleeping, silently brooding over what was to come, or talking aloud, in disordered speech, of his wrongs, of his friends, of his home, and of those he loved, with a confused mingling of all" (p. 67). Like Vivenzio, Anna lives hazily in the present recalling without control the past; like him, she continually desires sleep. Vivenzio says: "Oh! for a deep sleep to fall upon me! That so, in death's likeness, I might embrace death itself . . ." (p. 64). Anna, in a similar spirit tells us:

I felt very tired. I looked at the bed and thought, 'There's one thing—I do sleep. I sleep as if I were dead!

It's funny when you feel as if you don't want anything more in your life except to sleep, or else to lie without moving. That's when you can hear time sliding past you, like water running. (p. 70)

Both Mudford's hero and Rhys's heroine in *Voyage in the Dark* are tortured in the darkness of the present and by the fleeting visions of a light, natural world of the past. The tortures that Anna suffers, both from the present and the past, remarkably echo Mudford's tale. Even Anna's opening memory of home finds its parallel in Mudford's story. When Vivenzio catches a glimpse of the outside world from his cell, Mudford's recapitulation of that vision bears a strong resemblance to Anna's opening vision of her island in Part One. Mudford writes:

At the extremity of a long vista, cut through the solid rocks, the ocean, the sky, the setting sun, olive-groves, shady walks, and, in the farthest distance, delicious glimpses of magnificent Sicily, burst upon his sight. How exquisite was the cool breeze as it swept across his cheek, loaded with fragrance! And there was a fresh-ness in the landscape, and in the rippling of the calm green sea, that fell upon his withering heart like dew upon the parched earth.[1]

When Vivenzio faints because of that vision, his subsequent revival and state of mind mirror and abbreviate Anna's experience in England and her confusions between dream and rality. Of Vivenzio, Mudford writes:

When he recovered, the glorious vision had vanished. He was in darkness. He doubted whether it was not a dream that had passed before his sleeping fancy. . . .

Yes! he had looked once again upon the gorgeous splendor of nature! (p. 67)

It is no accident that Rhys has Anna compare her life to the fate of a literary figure. On close examination, *Voyage in the Dark* contains several clear and conscious subtextual dialogues and arguments with many other works of literature, many of them in popular genres. While several of these texts offer heroes or heorines whose lives parallel and contrast with Anna's (Vivenzio in "The Iron Shroud," Nana of that novel), others suggest opposite lives, values, and attitudes and opposite ideas about what makes good literature. Interestingly, in Rhys's first West Indian novel this intertextual discussion occurs on a nearly subtextual level while in her last, the interliterary reference provides the actual framework.

Anna continually denies that she reads anymore. She betrays almost a phobia for books, saying "But I never read now, so they can't get at me like that, anyway" (p. 46). But despite her disclaimers, we find her in the opening pages reading *Nana,* another parallel to her own life; in fact, they are obvious namesakes. Anna says:

It was a paper-covered book with a coloured picture of a stout, dark woman brandishing a wine-glass. She was sitting on the knee of a bald-headed man in evening dress. The print was very small, and the endless procession of words gave me a curious feeling—sad, excited and frightened. It wasn't what I was reading, it was the look of the dark, blurred words going on endlessly that gave me that feeling. (p. 4)

It is rather difficult to believe that what frightens Anna is only the look of the words; the parallels between Anna's and Nana's lives are too close. Both are 18 when the novels commence; both move from careers as showgirls to a life of prostitution; both live in cities foreign to them. However, Anna does not have the sexual and personal power of Nana nor does she have her namesake's high spirits and energy. Anna turns more and more inward as she severs all ties with the world. On the other hand, Nana becomes more and more public until, at her death, she is a myth. While there are parallels, Nana's career serves too as contrast to Anna's. Most interesting is Anna's friend Maudie's response when she sees Anna reading the book. She says that she knows it's " 'a dirty book' " and then adds, " 'I know; it's about a tart. I think it's disgusting. I bet you a man writing a book about a tart tells a lot of lies one way and another. Besides, all books are like that—just somebody stuffing you up' " (pp. 4–5). While the sex of the author does not seem to concern Anna, it certainly appears to be an issue in *Voyage in the Dark* which, after all, is a "book about a tart" written by a woman who, we might say, had also been a "tart."

While Rhys often betrayed a strong distrust and hostility to women, both in her fiction and interviews, she makes some rather different observations about women and female and male writers in the Black Exercise Book. For example, in one section she says: 'I wish that somewhere sometime some place a man would write about women fairly. I suppose it's an impossible [thing] to ask. Some Frenchmen almost do it though" (fol. 30). In another, at times incomprehensible, section she describes a dialogue between herself and "L." The discussion is about women writers and male critics, particularly one who hates women writers. Rhys betrays much bitterness, perhaps about her own treatment as a writer, when she says, "In fact the thing is to shut them [women writers] up if they threaten to be good except of course if they have money or a clique of friends or something. Then one's got to be careful" (fol. 50). At the conclusion of this discussion appears the words: "A successful day. Not one yelp at women from the papers. Not one growl either" (fol. 51).

Walter's cousin Vincent also comments on a book that serves a similar function to *Nana* in terms of the sex of its author, the contrast of its heroine's life to Anna's and the very type of fiction it represents. When Vincent recommends *The Rosary,* Anna responds as usual by saying later " 'I haven't read any of these books you're talking about. I hardly ever read' " (p. 54). Vincent adds that he thinks that " ' "the man who wrote this book should be knighted (p. 52)." ' " Walter chides him with the fact that it was not written by a man at all.

Written by Florence Barclay, published in 1904, and popular after its appearance, *The Rosary* sentimentally extols the virtues of "Christian womanhood" in the person of its heroine, Jane Champion.[2] Jane and her lover communicate to each other through Christian hymns, "The Rosary" being one such song, and their talk of God is poorly masked sexual play. We do not doubt that the author intended no irony toward her outspoken heroine, who is, even to her surname, a winner. The overbearing sanctimoniousness and hypocritical tone of the novel is similar to Vincent's and reveals the crude level of his literary tastes. *The Rosary,* with its ornate Victorian diction, its smug and vulgar extolling of middle-class virtues and optimism, stands in contrast to the spare prose of Rhys's novel and to its heroine, who lives outside acceptable bourgeois norms. *The Rosary* is about the winners in British middle-class society; Rhys's novel is about the losers. *The Rosary,* both in its style and content, represents the world from which Vincent and Walter come and of which Anna is the victim. We can assume that from Rhys's point of view, a novel (such as *The Rosary*) written by a woman can also "stuff you up" and be used to extol and enforce the moral and immoral rules of the bourgeoisie—just as women like Anna's stepmother Hester do.

One has the impression that Anna has obtained a lot of her ideas, especially her ideas of romantic love, from books and that perhaps now she intuits that those ideas are part of the cause of her misery. In *Smile Please* Rhys recounts her own experiences with books both as a young girl and as a chorus girl. The former experiences she describes thus:

So as soon as I could I lost myself in the immense world of books, and tried to blot out the real world which was so puzzling to me. Even then I had a vague, persistent feeling that I'd always be lost in it, defeated.

However books too were all about the same thing, I discovered, but in a different way. I could accept it in books and from books (fatally) I gradually got most of my ideas and beliefs.

. . . I liked books about prostitutes, there were a good many then, and vividly recollect a novel called *The Sands of Pleasure* written by a man named Filson Young. It must have been well written otherwise I would never have remembered it so perfectly to this day. It was about an Englishman's love affair with an expensive demi-mondaine in Paris. (pp. 62–63)

Concerning her relationship to books while a chorus girl, Rhys writes:

In England my love and longing for books completely left me. I never felt the least desire to read anything, not even a newspaper, and I think this indifference lasted a long time. Years. I don't remember reading anything on tour except *Forest Lovers.* . . . The company tart, whom I liked very much, would sometimes lend me a book. I wouldn't really read it and sometimes forgot it. . . . However abominable and dull my life was, it never occurred to me to buy a book or even a newspaper, which now seems very strange to me. (p. 111)

Even without Rhys's testimony about her own life—which of course is also a parallel to Anna's—we can assume from what Anna tells us that she has been "fatally" deluded by some of her readings as a young girl and that at some times, her life entails an acting out of those books, while at others it renders her like the subjects of the popular songs that constantly occur to her.

Voyage in the Dark is, to use Wayne Booth's term, a story told by a "narrator-agent."[3] She is the center of consciousness through which we see the world both philosophically and phenomenally. Rarely does Rhys falter in her maintenance of this consciousness. We see only through Anna and thus a problem in understanding *Voyage in the Dark* involves knowing where, and if, there are distances, places of nonidentification, between the author (the second narrator) and Anna. In other words, how are we to respond to Anna's perceptions, judgments, and behavior? Is her view of the world and of particular characters consistent with the author's "norms" (again, Booth's word)? Are there differing paradigms of the norm for Anna and the second narrator or are they the same? Of course this is often, as Booth notes, a problem in reading a novel that reflects reality through the consciousness of a protagonist within the work.

If we can point to no place of possible divergence, no irony, then we must assume their voices are congruent. In *Voyage in the Dark,* there appears to be little, if any, divergence between Anna's perception and evaluations and Rhys's. When Anna perceives the world as cruel, brutal, economically determined, there is nothing within the book either overtly and covertly to refute that. In fact, the "outside evidence" introduced in the letters of Vincent and Ethel corroborate for us their insincerity and self-interest. These letters condemn their writers far more than anything Anna says about them. But it is possible that *Voyage in the Dark* suggests that it is a different consciousness that one must have in order to deal with this world effectively. The few points of nonconvergence between Anna's voice and the voice of the author point to this difference.

The main point of distance between Anna and her creator seems to be the level of her naiveté, a naiveté that the author of *Voyage in the Dark* does not have. Anna denies familiarity with certain literary works with which we must assume Rhys is familiar. For example, although Anna says that she is not familiar with *The Rosary,* we must assume that the author of *Voyage in the Dark* is, and that she is aware of its significance concerning Vincent's character and literary acumen and aware of its structural irony concerning the "story" we hear in *Voyage in the Dark*. And earlier when Anna says she is reading *Nana* and that she was frightened, but not by what the book was about, we can either believe her or not believe her. But we cannot be unaware of the analogues between the two stories, analogues that Anna has no apparent interest in but which we are encouraged to consider because Anna tells us, so early in her narrative, that the book frightened her. When Maudie remarks that *Nana* is a book about a tart, written by a man, there is an implicit comment on *Voyage in the Dark* and its author and all books either by or about women.

Anna's literary naiveté and her inability to produce or make anything— possibly the major difference between her life and the life of Jean Rhys— perhaps contains an implicit statement about writing. There is a more literary consciousness operating behind Anna's, the consciousness that includes the literary references that abound in *Voyage in the Dark*. Sometimes this commentary comes in the person of Maudie, sometimes Vincent, sometimes Anna. To that extent the book contains commentary about literature, beyond Anna's denials of interest in reading, beyond her uncritical acceptance and absorption of the easy sentiment of the lyrics of popular songs which are also woven throughout *Voyage in the Dark*. This commentary may include, by inference, the notion that perhaps the making of literature out of such debilitating losses as Anna experiences is a way to salvation or, at the least, a mode of survival. If the voice of *Voyage in the Dark* is, in fact, in sympathy with Anna's perception of the cruelty and meaninglessness of the world and does, in fact, view her passivity and turning inward as a "normal" response, then one way to transcend is to withdraw into the creative isolation of the artist. In the world of *Voyage in the Dark* there does not seem to be any alternative described or available. No one is happy and nobody is nice. That Rhys identifies in most ways with her heroines, that they reflect her world-view, seems to be implicit within the books, especially as one can discern so little irony. The autobiographical tone is striking and the biographical "truth" well documented. And of course, external to *Voyage in the Dark,* we can recall Rhys's own stated reasons for writing—to rid herself of unhappiness.

Anna never really leaves her island; she finally becomes like it—insular and apart. And like the island, a dependent colony, she is subsumed and intimidated by the mother country—in Rhys, always male-identified. But Anna's personal stance and posture has wider implications: the individual self bears the burden of society, of culture, and of political realities, and becomes their index. In *Voyage in the Dark* those realities locate themselves in the person of Anna Morgan.

Through a character like Anna, Rhys was able to probe the terror of the condition of passivity, a condition which was an aspect of her own life. Perhaps the act of writing and revealing such crippling passivity rids the writer of it. At the very least, it becomes objectified and distanced, allowing the writer, for the moment, to take control of it. Certainly the refined and carefully crafted structure of *Voyage in the Dark* suggests such control and reveals the connections between the psychological, the social, the political, and finally, the creative aspects of existence. A woman like Anna cannot control her life; her fate is sealed because she cannot adapt. But Rhys's novel about this most autobiographical heroine suggests that at the very least, and perhaps at most, in carefully delineating the world and lives of characters of fiction, there lies for the writer and artist the possibility of rational control. That is, the activity of shaping and forming becomes a corrective to passivity. The realization of that possibility marks the border between Anna Morgan and her creator.

Part Three

The Long View:
Wide Sargasso Sea

The Caribbean Jane Eyre:
The West Indies and England

'The devil prince of this world.'
from *Wide Sargasso Sea*

In her last novel, *Wide Sargasso Sea,* Jean Rhys returns again to the themes and subjects she first dealt with in detail in *Voyage in the Dark.* But whereas *Voyage in the Dark* is a monochromatic rendering of the suffering of a displaced and disjointed heroine, the lament of a single voice, *Wide Sargasso Sea* is lush and multifaceted, a technicolor nightmare. And though it is based on Charlotte Brontë's fiction it, like *Voyage in the Dark,* makes use of the facts, though this time perhaps more psychologically true, of Rhys's own life.

In *Wide Sargasso Sea,* perhaps for the first and only time in Rhys's fiction, other voices are strongly articulated. In fact, the novel's structure is based on those voices. Unlike *Voyage in the Dark, Wide Sargasso Sea* is an attempt to give separate and equal voice to elements which comprise the conflicts in the life of its heroine, including the conflict about what is real. As does *Voyage in the Dark, Wide Sargasso Sea* recounts and portrays the causes of its heroine's downfall and the sources of her madness. But whereas *Voyage in the Dark* is the recounting of a personal alienation and separation from society, *Wide Sargasso Sea* examines the historical, cultural, and social context of isolation.

The conflicting forces in Antoinette Cosway's life encompass many of the same conflicts as Anna Morgan's: the struggle between men and women, between blacks and whites, between those who feel and those who are cold, between the warm, Eden-like atmosphere and topography of the semitropics and the cold hell of England. In *Wide Sargasso Sea,* each of these "places" is given an independent voice; indeed, the most outstanding characteristic of this novel is Rhys's intricate weaving of those voices. The heroine's allies and enemies express counterpointed and counterposing points of view.

Wide Sargasso Sea is separated into three parts. The first section, comprising less than a quarter of the novel, is narrated by Antoinette Cosway, the given and family name Rhys accords Bertha Rochester. She describes, often in a mournful and nostalgic voice, her youth on the island of Jamaica, a youth shared with her mother and some servants just following the Emancipation Act of 1833. The family lives in post-Emancipation poverty and isolation. The first section ends when Antoinette is about 17, when she is to be removed from her convent school by her stepfather for the purpose of an arranged marriage. Her mother, no longer sane after the burning of the family estate and the death of her son, remains shut up in the country, looked after by sinister and exploitative blacks.

Section Two, which comprises the main part of the novel, opens with the voice of Antoinette's husband, the Mr. Rochester of *Jane Eyre*, though he is not identified as such until Part Three. He recounts the days spent in Jamaica with his new wife, the schism that occurs between them, and their eventual removal to England. A small section of Part Two shifts to Antoinette's narration.

Section Three, less than a tenth of the novel, provides a surreal and dreamlike coda comprised of Antoinette's caretaker's voice, Grace Poole of *Jane Eyre*, and the now-mad Antoinette's account of her enclosure at Thornfield Hall. In that section, Antoinette recounts a dream she has that precedes and forecasts her burning of Thornfield.

In the *Paris Review* interview in 1979, Jean Rhys, in discussing *Wide Sargasso Sea*, indicated her long-held resentment over Brontë's treatment of Rochester's mad West Indian wife:

When I read *Jane Eyre* as a child, I thought, why should she think Creole women are lunatics and all that? What a shame to make Rochester's first wife, Bertha, the awful madwoman, and I immediately thought I'd write the story as it might really have been. She seemed such a poor ghost. I thought I'd try to write her a life. Charlotte Brontë must have had strong feelings about the West Indies because she brings the West Indies into a lot of her books. . . .[1]

In many respects, Rhys's "sequel" to *Jane Eyre* constitutes not only an explanation and defense of Bertha Rochester but provides an opposition to many of the givens of Brontë's novel. Brontë's heroine, the homely, impoverished, and motherless but independent girl battles the odds of culture, society, and economics and wins, whereas Antoinette Cosway, beautiful, passive, childlike, and dependent, succumbs to those forces represented for Antoinette in the person of Edward Rochester—the man who ultimately symbolizes, for Jane, her happy marriage to the world. And while *Jane Eyre* takes place in England and ultimately extols Britain and the British virtues of self-control and a belief in the "might of right," *Wide Sargasso Sea* occurs, for the most part in the West Indies, in a terrain which is the equivalent of Dominica and in a moral climate that suggests that the meek may never inherit the earth.

The Sargasso Sea, situated in the North Atlantic between the West Indies and the Azores, both divides and unites the opposite worlds of the old and the new hemispheres; in Rhys's novel it stands between the world of the whites and blacks, the colonizers and colonized, the English and the West Indian Creoles and ultimately, the worlds of evil and good, of hate and love, of power and meekness, of men and women, devils and innocents, the possessors and the possessed. *Wide Sargasso Sea* encompasses a Manichean world of dark and light symbolized ultimately by two places——Edward Rochester's England and Antoinette Cosway's island. How those forces mesh and confront each other and how they function is the matter of Rhys's last novel.

While these dichotomies are less obliquely presented in *Wide Sargasso Sea* than in any of Rhys's other works, they are also more complex. That is, the use of several narrators and the inclusion of Christophine's very strong voice, though she is never a first-person narrator, adds dimension, depth, and complexity to an essentially polarized world. And while evil triumphs—indeed is "prince of this world"—the harbingers of evil, the devils incarnate, so to speak, are neither, as Christophine describes Rochester, the best nor the worst, but rather, like Rochester, simply self-righteous and blind, insecure and unprepossessing men who can bring misfortune as much upon themselves as upon their victims. Like Rochester and Daniel Cosway, those who commit "evil" are often victims of family, history, and patriarchal systems—as is Antoinette Cosway, the most deeply wounded of all. Complexities of place and personality intertwine, to be resolved in a paradox of similarities and contradictions.

All the characters, male and female, black and white, oppressor or oppressed, are shaped and controlled by macrocosmic and microcosmic forces beyond their control and yet, as in Greek tragedy, their individual characters also determine their fates.

Place, specifically England and the West Indies, aside from symbolizing states of mind and attitudes in *Wide Sargasso Sea,* is also quite literally part of what shapes those attitudes. Rhys, besides vindicating Rochester's wife Bertha, also attempts to "explain" the place from which she comes. That place, as we learn early in *Wide Sargasso Sea* is, like Anna Morgan's island, a lost Eden, a world into which, even prior to the coming of Mason and Rochester, the Devil has already entered. Antoinette says, recalling the garden at Coulibri:

Our garden was large and beautiful as that garden in the Bible—the tree of life grew there. But it had gone wild. The paths were overgrown and a smell of dead flowers mixed with the fresh living smell. Underneath the tree ferns, tall as forest tree ferns, the light was green. Orchids flourished out of reach or for some reason not to be touched. One was snaky looking, another like an octopus with long thin brown tentacles bare of leaves hanging from a twisted root. (p. 466)

This wildness reflects a loss of that energy needed to produce order in nature, in politics, and in the social hierarchy. The destruction of her dead father's estate, according to Antoinette, is attributable to the lassitude that dominates her Jamaica after the Emancipation Act of 1833. She says, "All Coulibri Estate had gone wild like the garden, gone to bush. No more slavery—why should *anybody* work? This never saddened me. I did not remember the place when it was prosperous" (p. 466).[2] Antoinette, born before the Emancipation Act, though she does not remember that time, is already, like Anna Morgan, caught between two worlds: the world of slavery and the post-Emancipation West Indies. Her fate has already been, in part, determined because of this. She, like Anna, begins life in a sensual but corrupt paradise, a world that *begins* with a sense of loss. Caught between these two worlds, Antoinette too has trouble distinguishing the dream from reality, the past from the present. But while Anna's dislocation occurs both in time and in space, until the last section of *Wide Sargasso Sea* Antoinette's occurs only in time.

Like Anna, what registers to Antoinette as most "real" and concrete is the sensual lushness of her island and of Jamaica (which represent probably, in terms of its description and the "clues" Rhys includes, one and the same place, though certainly not Jamaica). It is the memory, the recollection and perception of all this, and only this, that offers her any security or center. It is her reference point, which Rochester later destroys. For example, as Antoinette and her stepfather, Mr. Mason, pass the huts of the black peasants, which are frightening to Antoinette, she says, "There was a smell of ferns and river water and I felt safe again, as if I was one of the righteous" (p. 475). Of course, as with all of Rhys's heroines, this feeling is quickly dissipated—this time by Antoinette's recollection of a black servant's drunken accusation that they are not part of the righteous and that they (meaning Antoinette and her family and perhaps all whites) are "all damned" (p. 476). And later, in a conversation with her husband, Antoinette says of her island: " 'I love it more than anywhere in the world. As if it were a person. More than a person' " (p. 510). Antoinette's pantheistic connection to her island and its natural beauty counterposes what, at times, amounts to a strong misanthropy. For example, she says: "And if the razor grass cut my legs and arms I would think 'It's better than people.' Black ants . . . rain . . . a snake. All better than people" (p. 472). This antipathy toward "people" is a common theme in Rhys's work and a feeling expressed by every one of her heroines at one time or another.

While Antoinette's attachment to her island is apparently stronger than any other she has—it constitutes, in fact, her most basic definition of reality—it and her relation to it and its history also leads, in part, to her destruction. Like Anna, who is falsely sustained by her apparently revivifying recollections of home, Antoinette too relies on the memories of her home to help her struggle against those forces that threaten to destroy her, to limit her natural sensuality, and to deprive her of autonomy and freedom.

Like Anna's island, Antoinette's is a lush green place richly described in images of fertility and femaleness. Antoinette too gains her right to the most sacred places in her iconography through her mother. The honeymoon house where she takes Rochester is a small estate that belonged to her mother. It is, even in terms of its inmates and like the convent of her childhood, a woman's house. There, Antoinette is in control, intimate with the topography, the people, and customs. In fact, from the time she and Rochester arrive there, she becomes his guide and protector. Rochester, who is both seduced and repelled by the retreat, reluctantly follows her leadership.

Rochester's initial response to the scenery he sees on the horseback ride to Granbois reveals his antipathy to this new land. And yet, as if Rhys's one return trip to Dominica has allowed her too to see her island in a different way, Rochester's view of it is both sympathetic and antipathetic. In other words, Rhys allows Rochester's vision to have some credibility. Of the ride Rochester says:

The road climbed upward. On one side the wall of green, on the other a steep drop to the ravine below. We pulled up and looked at the hills, the mountains and the blue-green sea. There was a soft warm wind blowing but I understood why the porter had called it a wild place. Not only wild but menacing. Those hills would close in on you.

'What an extreme green,' was all I could say. . . . (p. 498)

In the person of Rochester, Rhys allows, for the first time, a voice which with conviction rejects the beloved landscape of her West Indian heroines and defends the constructs of England. (" 'And how can millions of people, their houses and their streets be unreal?' " (p. 505) he asks Antoinette.) Rochester's reasons for disliking the tropical terrain are exactly the opposite of Anna's for disliking England. She despises the monochromatic sparsity, both urban and rural, while Rochester says of the island, "Everything is too much, I felt as I rode wearily after her. Too much blue, too much purple, too much green. The flowers too red, the mountains too high, the hills too near" (p. 498). The island, for Rochester, threatens suffocation and enclosure, the same danger to which Rhys's heroines are exposed in England. As England is male-identified in Rhys and the West Indian tropics female-identified, one might contend that this very fear of suffocation may well be connected to the fear of annihilation by the other, by the powers of the opposite sex which are for Rhys's women—and in *Wide Sargasso Sea,* for Rochester too—both seductive and repellent.

In fact, Rochester undergoes a kind of conversion for a time and becomes enchanted by the island's bright sensuality. The island represents Antoinette's powers. Rochester, who has wed the heiress for her dowry, is suddenly, because of his lack of familiarity and his own insecurity, thrust into the role of neophyte and dependent. He is awkward and self-conscious, unable to fathom how best to protect himself in this new and strange environment. His initial report of the ride toward Granbois reflects his dependency, his loneliness and insecurity. He says:

Meanwhile the horses jogged along a very bad road. It was getting cooler. A bird whistled, a long sad note. 'What bird is that?' She was too far ahead and did not hear me. The bird whistled again. A mountain bird. Shrill and sweet. A very lonely sound.

She stopped and called, 'Put your coat on now.' I did so and realized that I was no longer pleasantly cool but cold in my sweat-soaked shirt. . . .

She dismounted quickly, picked a large shamrock-shaped leaf to make a cup, and drank. Then she picked another leaf, folded it and brought it to me. 'Taste. This is mountain water.' (pp. 498–99)

And finally, as they arrive at the house he says, "Antoinette ran across the lawn and as I followed her I collided with a boy coming in the opposite direction" (p. 499). Antoinette initiates Rochester into the customs of the island and its people, instructs him about its flora and fauna, protects him from its dangers. For the time, their sex-defined roles are reversed. Sequestered in a female world and forced into a female's role, Rochester is both seduced and frightened. Ultimately, his paranoia and insecurity escalate so that, like Rhys's heroines in England, he fears that those who serve and administer to the native whites mock him and despise him, watching him with unfriendly and suspicious eyes. But Rochester's final response, an English and male response, is quite different from Rhys's women's. He wages war on his declared foes and finally escapes the alien land with a vengeance and deliberation of which no Rhys heroine is capable.

That the island and England symbolize the underlying and eventually mutually destructive differences between Antoinette and Rochester becomes clear early in their discussions. When Antoinette comments during the ride to Granbois that the earth is red, Rochester answers that it is red in parts of England too. " 'Oh England, England' " Antoinette responds "mockingly" and Rochester remembers that "the sound went on and on like a warning I did not choose to hear" (p. 499).

In their discussions of the differences between their homelands, Antoinette and Rochester fail to understand the other's idea of what is real. Their closed vision and their mutual inability to transcend the geographical and conceptual barriers between them, represented by the image and the literal presence of the Sargasso Sea, seals their doom. This failure is apparent in the following dialogue that Rochester reports between himself and Antoinette:

'Is it true,' she said, 'that England is like a dream? Because one of my friends who married an Englishman wrote and told me so. She said this place London is like a cold dark dream sometimes. I want to wake up.'

'Well,' I answered annoyed, 'that is precisely how your beautiful island seems to me, quite unreal and like a dream.'

'But how can rivers and mountains and the sea be unreal?'

'And how can millions of people, their houses and their streets be unreal?'

'More easily,' she said, 'much more easily. Yes a big city must be like a dream.'

'No, this is unreal and like a dream,' I thought. (p. 505)

This discussion not only reflects the couple's mutual lack of understanding but its conclusion also suggests Rochester's implicit and habitual dishonesty. Many of their conversations terminate with his *unspoken* words. Rochester obliquely reveals that he is biding his time and waiting for an opportunity to gain mastery.

Just as their ideas of each other and of themselves correlate with their ideas of their respective homes, and with their respective sexes, so, as Antoinette and Rochester develop in the novel, as they change and are changed, their respective ideas of the island and the West Indies (and, in Antoinette's case, her ideas of England) also change.

Rochester clearly identifies the island with his new wife. For him, both are "alien," a word he often uses in describing both. As he gains spiritual control over his wife—he has already gained legal control through marriage—he wants to possess and control the spirit of the place too. Of the bathing pool he frequents he says: "It was a beautiful place—wild untouched, above all untouched, with an alien, disturbing, secret loveliness. And it kept its secret. I'd find myself thinking, 'What I see is nothing—I want what it *hides*—that is not nothing" (p. 509).

Rochester's response to the island—both in his initial feeling that the colors and the lushness are foreign and alien and in his sense that it masks another reality—is mirrored in Antoinette's later perception of England, though her perceptions are, ironically, represented as "mad." She also expresses no concomitant desire for possession. She says, as she describes her nocturnal wandering about Thornfield:

Then I open the door and walk into their world. It is, as I always knew, made of cardboard. I have seen it before somewhere, this cardboard world where every-thing is coloured brown or dark red or yellow that has no light in it. As I walk along the passages I wish I could see what is behind the cardboard. They tell me I am in England but I don't believe them. We lost our way to England. When? Where? I don't remember, but we lost it. (p. 568)

While both Antoinette and Rochester have problems dealing with the other's reality, it is Rochester perhaps who is most blind because he has convinced himself that he is objective, logical, and dispassionate. In de-scribing Antoinette's ideas about England, he says:

She often questioned me about England and listened attentively to my answers, but I was certain that nothing I said made much difference. Her mind was already made up. Some romantic novel, a stray remark never forgotten . . . and her ideas were fixed. . . . I could not change them and probably nothing would. Reality might disconcert her, bewilder her, hurt her, but it would not be reality. It would be only a mistake, a misfortune, a wrong path taken, her fixed ideas would never change.

Nothing that I told her influenced her at all. (pp. 513–14)

Rochester believes that he has a neutral and accurate understanding of reality.

Although Antoinette has imbued her island with a person-hood, so has Rochester—but he attributes to it malevolence and hostility. And his identification of the island with his wife only serves to complicate his already complicated feelings. He believes that his wife cannot hear the "truth" from him but we see in another discussion that he cannot accept the "truth" about the place from her. Rochester says to Antoinette, in words that echo his opening language of war: " 'I feel very much a stranger here. . . . I feel that this place is my enemy and on your side' " (p. 537). But Antoinette replies with words that reflect Rhys's and Anna Morgan's sad perceptions of the "indifference" of home. She says, " 'It [the island] is not for you and not for me. It has nothing to do with either of us. That is why you are afraid of it, because it is something else. I found that out long ago when I was a child. I loved it because I had nothing else to love, but it is as indifferent as this God you call on so often' " (p.537). Antoinette's vision is of an uncaring, unmothering and unloving universe.

Ironically, both Antoinette and Rochester recognize that the other has fixed ideas and prejudices, which make it impossible to see reality clearly. Unfortunately, neither recognizes that truth about himself. Only Christophine, the uneducated black obeah woman, reflects objectivity and openness about what the reality symbolized by place might represent. Antoinette reports her conversation with Christophine about England in which Christophine reveals her empiricism and her skepticism:

'England,' said Christophine, who was watching me. 'You think there is such a place?'

'How can you ask that? You know there is.'

'I never see the damn place, how I know?'

'You do not believe that there is a country called England?'

She blinked and answered quickly, 'I don't say I don't *believe,* I say I don't *know,* I know what I see with my eyes and I never see it. Besides I ask myself is this place like they tell us? Some say one thing, some different, I hear it cold to freeze your bones and they thief your money, clever like the devil. You have money in your pocket, you look again and bam! No money. Why you want to go to this cold thief place? If there is this place at all, I never see it, that is one thing sure.' (p. 125)

Christophine's assertion that one must think for oneself has no effect on Antoinette, who wonders, " 'how can she know the best thing for me to do, this ignorant, obstinate old negro woman, who is not certain if there is such a place as England?' " (p. 112).

In an interior monologue, Antoinette reveals that Rochester is at least correct in his assessment that Antoinette's idea of England has been garnered from books and that not much will change that pastiche. Antoinette thinks to herself:

I will be a different person when I live in England and different things will happen to me. . . . England, rosy pink in the geography book map, but on the page opposite the words are closely crowded, heavy looking. Exports, coal, iron, wool. Then Imports and Character of Inhabitants. Names, Essex, Chelmsford on the Chelmer. The Yorkshire and Lincolnshire wolds. Wolds? Does that mean hills? How high? Half the height of ours, or not even that? Cool green leaves in the short cool summer. Summer. There are fields of corn like sugar-cane fields, but gold colour and not so tall. After summer the trees are bare, then winter and snow. White feathers falling? Torn pieces of paper falling? They say frost makes flower patterns on the window panes. I must know more than I know already. For I know that house where I will be cold and not belonging, the bed I shall lie in has red curtains and I have slept here many times before, long ago. How long ago? In that bed I will dream the end of my dream. But my dream had nothing to do with England and I must not think like this, I must remember about chandeliers and dancing, about swans and roses and snow. And snow. (pp. 524– 25, Rhys's ellipses)

In this remarkable collage, Rhys does several things that also occur in *Voyage in the Dark*. She contrasts the young girl's anticipation of England based on books and tales (probably the collective nostalgia of the colonial culture that surrounds her) plus a brave attempt at "objectivity" (the remembered geography lesson). But obviously the names of places and the descriptions written in the book have no reality for Antoinette who, as Rochester responds when she says she loves her island better than anywhere in the world, does not " 'know the world' " (p. 510). But for the sensual Antoinette, images do have a reality—images of snow and swans and images of bare trees and coldness. But all of this she can only imagine in relation to her knowledge of her own island—a knowledge that would hardly prepare her, as it hardly prepared the young Ella Williams, for England.

While Antoinette and Rochester confuse dream and reality, in this collage—and in Antoinette's final dream—dream becomes reality. In fact, Antoinette's final translation of her dream of burning Thornfield into the act of doing it, is prompted by her obsession with the red dress, a symbol of another reality, another time, and another place. Antoinette's confounding of time and place, dream and reality in this final episode is paradoxically both a mad action and the act that avenges her and, at least symbolically, sets her free—the latter perhaps represented in her own Phoenix-like fantasy of recapitulation and regeneration ("The wind caught my hair and it streamed out like wings. It might bear me up, I thought, if I jumped to those hard stones" [pp. 574].)

By the time Antoinette's and Rochester's relationship has degenerated into overt and active hate, their feelings about the island have also changed, reflecting their changed feelings about each other. Antoinette says to Rochester prior to the final breakdown of her own mind and prior to being forced to leave for England by him, " 'I used to think that if everything else went out of my life I would still have this, and now you have spoilt it. It's just somewhere else where I have been unhappy, and all the other things are nothing to what has happened here. I hate it now like I hate you and before I die I will show you how much I hate you' " (p. 548). Until this point her island has symbolized for Antoinette the last hope, the secret vestige of renewal and restoration always available to her. In taking Rochester to the island to begin with, Antoinette has exposed what is most precious. Certainly both Antoinette and Rochester identify her with this island. It is her self, her secret self. In destroying this place for Antoinette, Rochester precipitates her madness because he has destroyed her sense of hope, of belonging, of ownership, autonomy, and ultimately her own sense of personal power. Antoinette, like so many of Rhys's women, turns her hate for Rochester into hate for her beloved island and hence for herself.

That Rochester turns his hate for Antoinette into hate for the island is apparent in one of his last statements about it. He says:

And I hated the place.

I hated the mountains and the hills, the rivers and the rain. I hated the sunsets of whatever colour, I hated its beauty and its magic and the secret I would never know. I hated its indifference and the cruelty which was part of its loveliness. Above all I hated her. For she belonged to the magic and the loveliness. She had left me thirsty and all my life would be thirst and longing for what I had lost before I found it. (p. 565)

Rochester has come full circle. He entered the island with hostility—a hostility that he projected onto the place. Later, seduced by the sensuality of both his wife and her home, he starts if not to love them, at least to delight in his awakened senses. It is this and the possibility of closeness to Antoinette that frightens him. Both would mean divesting himself of the hate he carries with him, a hate that, like Daniel Cosway, he has malevolently learned to feed on. This hate, first borne for his father and brother and later transferred to Antoinette and the West Indies, is his true patrimony.

In finding false reasons for extricating himself from closeness with Antoinette, from what would have been a "humanizing" experience, Rochester must destroy both Antoinette and her representation. By the end of Part Two, as Rochester becomes irredeemable, his hatred is more extreme, more fixed, and more irrevocable. While he has begun his mission in the West Indies with an inherent sense of loss (first of money and second of his father's love) he ends his quest with wealth but further than ever from love. The dowry he receives from Antoinette includes a permanent sense of loss.

Just prior to the final breakdown of any possibility of understanding betweeen Antoinette and Rochester, before she gives him the obeah medicine and will try one more time to get him to "understand," Rochester's and Antoinette's voices become, at times, almost coincident as they describe the island retreat. For example, Part Two, which is predominantly Rochester's narration, has a brief section in Antoinette's voice in which she describes her visit to Christophine. As she leaves, Antoinette says:

> I can remember every second of that morning, if I shut my eyes I can see the deep blue colour of the sky and the mango leaves, the pink and red hibiscus, the yellow handkerchief she wore round her head, tied in the Martinique fashion with the sharp points in front, but now I see everything still, fixed for ever like the colours in a stained-glass window. Only the clouds move. (p. 529)

Antoinette's language is rich in concrete detail, both visual and sensual, and contains a nostalgic longing for and remembrance of the vision of the island and its parts. Right after the above section, Part Two switches again to Rochester. His language, for the first time, is remarkably similar to Antoinette's, both in terms of the kind of detail—the sensual, visual aspects of the flowers, the colours of the girl—and in terms of its wistfulness. He says:

> I sat on the veranda with my back to the sea and it was as if I had done it all my life. I could not imagine different weather or a different sky. I knew the shape of the mountains as well as I knew the shape of the two brown jugs filled with white sweet-scented flowers on the wooden table. I knew that the girl would be wearing a white dress. Brown and white she would be, her curls, her white girl's hair she called it, half covered with a red handkerchief, her feet bare. There would be the

sky and the mountains, the flowers and the girl and the feeling that all this was a nightmare, and the faint consoling hope that I might wake up. (p. 530)

Rochester's language here, so similar in tone and content to Antoinette's, reveals his conflicted state. In the first part of his statement, he reflects upon the sweet seductions of the island, seductions he did not recognize on first sight. But like Rhys's women in England, in the second part he expresses the hope that he will awaken from what he perceives as a nightmare. What is surprising in this statement (as compared to Anna Morgan, for instance, and Antoinette in Part Two of *Wide Sargasso Sea*), is that the "reality" he describes here does not appear to be nightmarish— sensual certainly, but neither hostile as he has described it before, nor suffocating, nor even "too much." One can only assume that Rochester does not want to like this place, does not want to like Antoinette, fears perhaps both closeness with her and, perhaps as Antoinette has guessed, the indifference of the land.

Rochester's and Antoinette's preoccupations center on their differences— their origins and culture as represented by place, and the wide barrier between them represented by the Sargasso Sea. But the Sargasso Sea is a place too. North of the Indies, where the trade winds—so important in the history of the West Indian islands—originate, the Sargasso Sea is an apparently dead ocean where flotsam accumulates, a mélange of derelict ships and the sargassum seaweed. It is said that one can walk on the Sargasso Sea; in the past, writers wrote ghost stories about it. Rhys's novel is, in some sense, a ghost story too. To Rochester's thinking Antoinette is, at the end, only a ghost, but he too is a pale reminder of what he was and what, had he and Antoinette been able to overcome their "differences," he might have been. In *Voyage in the Dark,* Anna is concerned that she has become like a soucriant. Rochester too reads about zombis after he visits the ruined priest's house. His book says:

'A zombi is a dead person who seems to be alive or a living person who is dead. A zombi can also be the spirit of a place, usually malignant but sometimes to be propitiated with sacrifices or offerings of flowers and fruit.' . . . ' "They cry out in the wind that is their voice. They rage in the sea that is their anger" ' (p. 122)

Rochester and Antoinette both, because of the island and because of who they are, become zombis too. In fact, all the major characters, except Christophine, come to inhabit the land of the living dead—Rochester and Antoinette, her mother, and Daniel Cosway.

Both Antoinette and Rochester contain within themselves aspects of the Sargasso Sea. Empty, stagnant, and bereft of "normal" life, they are isolated and separated, like alien and watery islands, neither land nor sea, caught between two "realities." Rhys's novel contains within it the loss of possibility for both Rochester and Antoinette. With their union, the dissolution and resolution of the opposites symbolized by their respective homes might have been possible. As they move further apart, they come to represent a dead and empty place, a lifeless chasm, ungiving and incapable of sustaining or producing life. Their personal failures and the reflected larger failure of history indicate the dynamic between person and place—that a person, shaped by home and homeland, in turn shapes those and other terrains with memories, perceptions, and prejudices that reflect or include those original progenitors. Or, as Milton's arch-hero proclaims (with an optimism that is the converse of Rhys's conclusions) about that interior-exterior dynamic:

> The mind is its own place, and in itself
> Can make a Heaven of Hell, a Hell of
> Heaven.[3]

7

Men: Sons and Fathers

Rhys's characterization of Rochester in *Wide Sargasso Sea* marks a distinct break with all her preceding male characters. The men in her earlier novels are often no more than shallow and indifferent representatives of the patriarchy—like the double couples of Vincent and Walter or Carl and Joe in *Voyage in the Dark*. But in *Wide Sargasso Sea*, Rhys unfolds not only the cultural history of Rochester but elements of his personal story as well. For in *Wide Sargasso Sea*, the problem between Antoinette and Rochester is neither only personal, nor only sociohistorical, but is rather a complicated mixture. Rochester and Antoinette represent their cultures and countries; they would not be who they are without those backgrounds. But they also bring with them a personal history that is congruent with the schema of Rhys's novel. Conversely, their personal and individual histories also reflect their cultures and those cultures' histories. One must account for the personal, the cultural, and the historical elements in *Wide Sargasso Sea* in order to understand its characters.

The counterposed voices of the various characters, as much as place, signify their differences. Rochester's voice, which we first hear only at the opening of Part Two, suddenly and immediately brings in a new note of cynicism, sarcasm, hate, bitterness, and interest in pecuniary matters. It is a stark contrast to the closing of the preceding section narrated by Antoinette, which concludes with the final conversation she has with Sister Marie Augustine—a philosophical discussion in an intensely female cloister about evil. The language is both evocative and sympathetic, whereas Rochester's narration begins in a jaded voice and uses the vocabulary of war. He begins: "So it was all over, the advance and retreat, the doubts and hesitations" (p. 495).

He then immediately betrays his unsubstantiated feelings about the blacks and the place. He says of the servant Amelie, "She was laughing at me I could see. A lovely little creature but sly, spiteful, malignant perhaps, like much else in this place" (p. 495). While Rochester's response to both the blacks and the place is the opposite of his predecessor Mason's benign and naive attitude, it is still as prejudiced and blind. Furthermore, it reveals Rochester's need to project his own feelings and attitudes onto others. (That is not to say that Amelie is not at times archly malicious, but certainly she often takes her cues from Rochester, indeed receives tacit license from him.) In not recognizing the blacks' potential for malevolence, Mason did not give credit to them as fully realized human beings. Conversely, Rochester does not give credence to their potential for dignity, generosity, intelligence, and wisdom. In that sense, both he and Mason represent the British colonial interloper, as opposed to the native white Creole who, like the black Creole, has become indigenous to the West Indies. The Creoles—like Antoinette, her mother, Christophine, Tia, and the other black servants—have an understanding, though at times it is an antipathetic one. They recognize each other's humanity and they know the place.

While Rochester eventually becomes, along with Daniel Cosway, the most malevolent character in *Wide Sargasso Sea,* Rhys portrays him at first with some sympathy: as a newcomer to a foreign place who is both frightened and insecure, and already deeply wounded. In fact, he shares some of the attributes of her heroines. But Rochester finally deals with his hurt and his fear, his dislocation and doubt, in a very different way from Rhys's women because he is, in Rhys's iconography, representative of the most dangerous of humans: he is English and male.

Rochester's motives and behavior are at first ambivalent and ambiguous. For example, when he tells us that at the last moment Antoinette wanted to withdraw from the marriage arrangement, he says: "This would indeed make a fool of me" to be "in the role of rejected suitor jilted by this Creole girl" (p. 503). While he shows no malevolence toward her— indeed it is difficult to know whether his feelings are anything but indifferent—we learn that he is " 'Stiff. Hard as a board and stupid as a foot . . . except where his own interests are concerned' " (p. 115). But for the moment he reveals only his essential indifference—an indifference that will be mutated into self-righteous cruelty by the end of Part Two.

To convince Antoinette to go through with the marriage he makes what becomes a false promise, though it is difficult to know whether he initially intends to break his word. He says to Antoinette: " 'I'll trust you if you'll trust me. Is that a bargain?' " (p. 504). What his statement does reveal though, is his use of the language of the merchant and the marketplace in making a marriage proposal and a covenant of trust, though it apparently reveals nothing to Antoinette, who later, in her behavior, takes him at his word. While she enters the marriage reluctantly (as all Rhys heroines enter their love relationships), she quickly succumbs to the spell of intimacy and sensuality and begins to trust him, revealing to him things about herself she has told no one else. The truth and openness with which she imbues her relationship to him, makes her, among other things, his slave and his victim.

Rochester is frightened by closeness and intimacy; his indifference turns to hostility. In fact, though he is the one to have suggested a compact of mutual trust, he is the first to find an excuse to betray it. Thus, when he receives Daniel Cosway's first letter, a transparently vindictive and untrustworthy account, he says: "I folded the letter carefully and put it into my pocket. I felt no surprise. It was as if I'd expected it, been waiting for it" (p. 517). Though he makes no move to respond to Cosway, Rochester immediately translates his response to it into overt hostility toward Antoinette. He says, "Then I passed an orchid with long sprays of golden-brown flowers. One of them touched my cheek [as Antoinette has also done in an act of sympathy toward him when she agrees to marry him] and I remembered picking some for her one day. 'They are like you,' I told her. Now I stopped, broke a spray off and trampled it into the mud" (p. 517).

Earlier, in a similar symbology, Rochester has already revealed his *unconscious* hostility toward Antoinette, who is clearly identified with the flowers. When they first enter the honeymoon house at Granbois, Rochester "crowns" himself with one of the wreaths of frangipani there. But when it falls to the floor he says: "As I went towards the window I stepped on it. The room was full of the scent of crushed flowers" (p. 500). The implications of Rochester's trampling on the flowers after receiving Cosway's first letter are several—among them being his continuing dishonesty, even to himself. One senses that he is hardly aware of the hostility he bears toward Antoinette.

Throughout Rochester's narration, many of his feelings and thoughts remain inexplicit. It is often difficult for us to understand his motivation. At other times the implications of his actions, though never clear to him, are transparent to the reader.

Rochester reveals often that both in Jamaica and at Granbois he is biding his time, waiting to act. Exactly why he feels hesitant to move is not clear. Perhaps he still carries with him a vestige of gentility which makes it necessary for him to rationalize selfish and cruel behavior. But he early and constantly reveals that he is waiting for the time when he can assume control. For example, at Granbois he reveals that he feels a need for secrecy, circumspection, and restraint in expressing his thoughts and feelings. When Antoinette tells Rochester how much she is indebted to Baptiste, he says:

I'd agree, keeping my opinion of Baptiste, Christophine and all the others to myself. . . .

She trusted them and I did not. But I could hardly say so. Not yet. (p. 511)

And again, like a domestic spy he says:

As for the money which she handed out so carelessly, not counting it, not knowing how much she gave, or the unfamiliar faces that appeared then disappeared, though never without a large meal eaten and a shot of rum I discovered. . . . If she asked no questions how could I? . . .

After breakfast at noon there'd be silence till the evening meal which was served much later than in England. Christophine's whims and fancies, I was sure. Then we were left alone. Sometimes a sidelong look or a sly knowing glance disturbed me, but it was never for long. 'Not now,' I would think. 'Not yet.' (p. 511)

Later, when they are leaving for England, Rochester in a soliloquy says, but too late: "Like the swaggering pirates, let's make the most and best and worst of what we have. Give not one-third but everything. All—all—all. Keep nothing back. . . ." (p. 563). But it is precisely Rochester—a pirate of a different order—who has kept things back when he should not have, who has distrusted his wife while she has naively kept their covenant of trust.

Rochester distrusts all human beings, black or white. In a classic case of projection, he thinks the blacks suspect him, while he reveals that it is he who distrusts them. From Rochester's point of view, everyone is either mad or mean. He fears that no one will reveal the truth to him. But it is Rochester himself who is ultimately the least desirous of either revealing or of learning the truth. Clearly Rochester has been deeply and early wounded, like Antoinette, but how he deals with his wounds is what makes the essential difference between them.

After Rochester receives Cosway's first letter, distraught, he goes for a walk in the forest. Interestingly, his thoughts turn to his father and brother, the cause and perpetrators of his first "wound." He says:

As I walked I remembered my father's face and his thin lips, my brother's round conceited eyes. They knew [probably the "truth" of Cosway's accusations]. And Richard, the fool, he knew too. And the girl [Antoinette] with her blank smiling face. They all knew.

. . . How can one discover truth I thought and that thought led me nowhere. No one would tell me the truth. Not my father nor Richard Mason, certainly not the girl I had married. (p. 520)

Rochester, in remembering his father's antipathy, translates it into Antoinette's crime. As he jumps at the possibility of the truth of Cosway's words, he seeks a scapegoat for his hate of his father and brother; Antoinette is a ready and willing victim. Rochester, like Cosway, turns his hate for his father into hate for Antoinette.

Cosway and Rochester share similar characters—even to their ultimate greed, which each gives rein to through a self-righteous desire for vengeance. Both Cosway and Rochester, each in his relation to Antoinette and her household, replicates his idea of his father's—indeed the entire world's—relation to him.

While Antoinette has revealed herself as an innocent, a naive who childishly reveals details of her fears and dreams to Rochester, Cosway's letter reflects a diametrically opposed stance. That Rochester is affected at all by Cosway's letter, so transparent in its manipulations, its bitterness and hatred, and so comic in its language, its self-importance and inconsistencies, indicates his own predisposition to spurn Antoinette. While Cosway's main intent is to damage Antoinette's reputation, the letter is hilarious in some of the attempts by Cosway at gentility and flattery. For example, Cosway writes of Antoinette's family, *Yes everybody hate them in Jamaica and also in this beautiful island where I hope your stay will be long and pleasant in spite of all.* . . . (p. 515, Rhys's italics).

Both Rochester and Daniel Cosway have become the things they hate in their fathers. Cosway says his father had no mercy and no love of women, both of which are true of Daniel Cosway himself. According to Rochester, his father was dishonest, unloving, and a man who betrayed his son, reserving the major portion of his wealth and his love for an older brother.

Both Rochester and Cosway translate their bitterness and hurt, their feeling of love denied, into a preoccupation. Certainly earlier when Rochester has discussed Antoinette's openness with money, he unconsciously reveals a niggardly quality in himself. Although he also says that no settlement had been made for Antoinette and that he wanted to make sure that was done, as the novel progresses he becomes more and more mercenary. Both Antoinette's Aunt Cora and Christophine have early seen his underlying interest in money. Cora, who is furious at Richard Mason for leaving Antoinette without a settlement, even gives Antoinette her remaining jewelry. Christophine says of Rochester: " 'Money have pretty face for everybody, but for that man money pretty like pretty self, he can't see nothing else' " (p. 526).

From the very beginning of his narrative, Rochester betrays his proclivity toward money and his view of human relations as something to be bought and sold in the marketplace. About his new wife he says, "And the woman is a stranger. Her pleading expression annoys me. I have not bought her, she has bought me, or so she thinks" (p. 498). This passage reveals many aspects of Rochester's character: his coldness and distance (he often refers to Antoinette as "the woman" or "the girl" or "my wife"); his attribution of his own interests and concerns to others (e.g., money and the possession of things and people); his paranoia; his spitefulness and meanness; his egocentrism (that Antoinette would want to buy or possess him); and finally and most importantly his lack of desire for and disavowal of the truth. Rochester knows that, in fact, it was Antoinette who wanted to withdraw from the marriage and that he convinced her with false promises. Furthermore, Antoinette, of all the characters in *Wide Sargasso Sea,* shows the least knowledge of the possible relationship between money and possession, between money and power.

In his last confrontation with Christophine, when she tries to convince him to have sympathy and understanding for Antoinette, Rochester listens to her impassively, even distractedly. Christophine convincingly rehearses her view of the story of Antoinette's and Rochester's marriage. Toward the conclusion of her request for love and mercy Rochester tells us that she says, " 'It's you beg her to marry. And she love you and she give you all she have. Now you say you don't love her and you break her up. What you do with her money, eh?' " (p. 556). Rochester adds, "Her voice was still quiet but with a hiss in it when she said 'money'. I thought, of course, that is what all the rigmarole is about. I no longer felt dazed, tired, half hypnotized, but alert and wary, ready to defend myself" (p. 556). And though he has no intention of giving anything, when Christophine suggests that he give a sum of money to Antoinette, he goes as far as asking the exact sum she has in mind, as if he cannot resist the possibility of bargaining.

Finally, in the penultimate paragraph of his narration, Rochester, as he leaves the island, thinks, "I'd sell the place for what it would fetch. I had meant to give it back to her. Now—what's the use?" (p. 565). Rochester has earlier half-heartedly contemplated a settlement for Antoinette and yet with every opportunity, every possibility of separation with Antoinette and restitution to her, he has an excuse for not doing either. Through marriage Rochester has gained both the mastery and the money; for him, one senses the two are equivalent.

I have said that Rochester at Granbois experiences what it is like to be a woman and that he circumspectly waits for an opportunity to seize his male prerogatives of power and control. But Rochester gets ample help from Antoinette. She innocently offers the kind of personal servitude to him that all of Rhys's women offer to their lovers. Even when they first arrive at Granbois and Rochester "crowns" himself with the frangipani wreath, her words to him, which constitute her first statement of obeisance, are: " 'You look like a king, an emperor' " (p. 500). Further on, we hear Antoinette telling Christophine not to put her usual perfume on her because Rochester doesn't like its scent. Antoinette has taken the first step in the cycle of descent of Rhys's women—the desire to please the man who will take that desire and use it as further reason to reject her.

But though Antoinette has already entered the female trap (in Rhys's fiction) of trying to please her lover, she is still, at this point, in control of her environment as, for example, when she gives Rochester warnings and advice about how to protect himself when he leaves to go to the bathing pool. And Rochester too is still partly under the spell of the place—a place which becomes momentarily less and less threatening and hostile to him. He says that the "fever weakness" has left him and "so did all misgiving" (p. 507). But that he is still maintaining his defenses, still views their relationship as a battle, is revealed in his words a little later, again the words of war and power. He says, "she had given way, but coldly, unwillingly, trying to protect herself with silence and a blank face. Poor weapons, and they had not served her well or lasted long" (p. 512). Rochester still shows very little love for Antoinette, and even less understanding of her, in assuming that her passivity and acquiescence are the equivalent of weapons. It is already clear that Antoinette has begun to give up everything for Rochester, and to make herself his doll or marionette, as he derisively calls her. It is, therefore, difficult to understand why Rochester perceives the need for continued "warfare." Already Antoinette has given him total control over her happiness and her life, as he demonstrates in a conversation between them: " 'Why did you make me want to live?' " Antoinette asks him. Rochester responds: " 'Because I wished it. Isn't that enough?' " and Antoinette agrees.

Further on, Antoinette says to him: " 'I am not used to happiness. . . . It makes me afraid.' " Rochester tells her, again espousing his own philosophy of self-defense, " 'Never be afraid. Or if you are tell no one' " (p. 512). Then, one night, Rochester tells us, apparently with neither guilt nor satisfaction, that Antoinette whispered to him, " 'If I could die. Now, when I am happy. Would you do that? You wouldn't have to kill me. Say die and I will die. You don't believe me? Then try, try, say die and watch me die' " (p. 513). Clearly Rochester has assumed the ascendancy. Antoinette, like Anna Morgan, has turned her life over to her lover. That this capitulation, like Anna's, is connected with the opening of her sexuality seems implicit from what Rochester says following his report of this conversation. He immediately and vituperatively says: "Die then! Die!" and adds that he "watched her die many times" (p. 513), but this time he uses the word in the sexual sense. He adds: "Very soon she was as eager for what's called loving as I was—more lost and drowned afterwards" (p. 513). That Rochester also seems to have, for the time, been drawn into this sexual and sensual world seems implicit. He says, "She said, 'Here I can do as I like,' not I, and then I said it too. It seemed right in that lonely place. 'Here I can do as I like' " (p. 513). But Rochester's statement has a far more ominous and menacing implication than Antoinette's.

Following his ascendancy over Antoinette, Rochester begins to control the servants too. While previously he has harbored criticisms of them and has indicated that it is Antoinette's prerogative to command and reprimand them, he assumes this right. When he sees an argument between Amelie and his wife, he not only sides with Amelie, who is clearly in the wrong, but orders her to fetch Christophine. Amelie senses immediately that he is now in control. She says: " 'Yes master, yes master' " (p. 518).

Following this, Rochester's attitude toward the place, Antoinette, and the servants is irrevocably altered—a fact punctuated by his sleeping with Amelie within hearing of the love-obsessed Antoinette. That he does this so that Antoinette may hear we only learn later when he silently acknowledges it to himself in a conversation with Christophine. Rochester approaches self-honesty only in his conversations with her.

Following the sexual episode with Amelie, Rochester becomes arrogant with the servants. He is less concerned with what they think of him—as if they have provided previously, through his fear that they suspect him, a check to his more malevolent ambitions. But his most important coup vis-à-vis the blacks is his letter of inquiry to the magistrate about Christophine. When he receives a response from the magistrate offering to prosecute her, Rochester reveals that he is ready to fight Christophine, the person by whom he has felt intimidated and sexually belittled. About the magistrate's promise that Christophine " 'won't get off lightly this time,' " Rochester smugly concludes: "So much for you, Josephine or Christophine. . . . So much for you, Pheena" (p. 546)—his words indicating the "personalness" of his vendetta as he uses Antoinette's familiar name for Christophine. At the same time his use of the law to fight Christophine fulfills her earlier prophesy about the "new ones" who come to the island with English law on their side. His access to the law demonstrates the ways in which the new colonialist, even in the post-Emancipation era, could use the letter of the law to satisfy personal whims regarding the blacks—and the way a man could use the law to satisfy his desires regarding his wife's wealth and liberty.

The struggle between Christophine and Rochester over Antoinette has the quality of a medieval argument between Good and Evil, between Light and Dark, though their skin colors reverse this usual dichotomy. Christophine achieves a kind of practical and unusual wisdom—indeed she is perhaps the only character in *Wide Sargasso Sea* who attains what might be an ideal of Christian love.

After Rochester receives the magistrate's promise of support, his attitude toward the blacks moves from surliness to provocation so that they, except of course for Christophine, appear frightened and intimidated.

Rochester's anger and hate degenerate into an overt desire to bully, to possess, and to destroy. But this desire for revenge is still connected to his feelings about his father, a fact that remains apparent to us even toward the end of his narrative. At one point, after a nostalgic evocation of the past time with Antoinette, he seems to consider reining in his fury and says: 'I knew what I would say. 'I have made a terrible mistake. Forgive me.' " But then he adds:

I said it, looking at her, seeing the hatred in her eyes—and feeling my own hate spring up to meet it. Again the giddy change, the remembering, the sickening swing back to hate. They bought me, *me* with your paltry money. You helped them to do it. You deceived me, betrayed me, and you'll do worse if you get the chance. . . . (p. 563, Rhys's ellipses)

Even at this point Rochester cannot separate his hate of Antoinette— her imagined betrayal of him through collusion with Richard Mason and his relatives—from his hatred of his father and brother. Rochester proclaims to himself that he is sane. ("All the mad and conflicting emotions had gone and left me wearied and empty, sane" [p. 564].) But, like Antoinette, he too reveals the symptoms of one who is out of touch with reality, unable to see the truth, and who is, finally, paranoic. When he sees Christophine comforting Antoinette he says: "But whatever they were singing or saying was dangerous. I must protect myself" (p. 550). And later, when Antoinette is truly mad, he says:

Very soon she'll join all the others who know the secret and will not tell it. Or cannot. Or try and fail becaue they do not know enough. They can be recognized. White faces, dazed eyes, aimless gestures, high-pitched laughter. The way they walk and talk and scream or try to kill (themselves or you) if you laugh back at them. Yes, they've got to be watched. For the time comes when they try to kill, then disappear. But others are waiting to take their places, it's a long, long line. She's one of them. (p. 565)

While Rochester anticipates the final outcome of *Wide Sargasso Sea,* that does not diminish the "mad" aspect of this diatribe. In fact, his speech reveals that what began as a perhaps justified hatred toward his father has now turned into a full-fledged and self-created persecution mania. That his fear becomes a reality does not diminish his own madness. Nor does it deny the more important truth that Rochester, in his own madness and mania, his own obsession, has created, by design, the very monster he now fears.

Like the picture of Dorian Gray, Antoinette, with her disheveled and frightening aspect (in *Jane Eyre* she is described as a monster) is perhaps the living embodiment of Rochester's own corruption and evil, his own more pernicious madness. If Antoinette is mad, it is a madness that turns inward and wounds the self, whereas Rochester's madness is connected to the impulse to control, to possess, and to destroy—the impulse of a warrior, and, in the world of *Wide Sargasso Sea,* a male impulse. In fact, in *Wide Sargasso Sea* there seem to be female and male versions of madness: Antoinette and her mother turn their madness inward and destroy the self, only passively and accidentally harming others. The males who are crazy or half-crazed, like Daniel Cosway and Rochester, turn their madness outward, expressly wounding the females.

Based on his false equation of his father's and brother's duplicity, Rochester makes Antoinette his scapegoat and swears his hate and damnation. Following that equation, he says:

. . . If I was bound for hell let it be hell. No more false heavens. No more damned magic. You hate me and I hate you. We'll see who hates best. But first, first I will destroy your hatred. Now. My hate is colder, stronger, and you'll have no hate to warm yourself. You will have nothing.

I did it too. I saw the hate go out of her eyes. I forced it out. And with the hate her beauty. She was only a ghost. A ghost in the grey daylight. Nothing left but hopelessness. *Say die and I will die. Say die and watch me die.* (pp. 563–64, Rhys's ellipses and italics)

Rochester believes that he has destroyed Antoinette's soul, her mind, and her spirit, and that she lingers without anger, bereft of hope. But later, in Section III while Antoinette is apparently insane, her madness allows her new insight. In detaching her from "reality," it allows her to make certain symbolic connections that let her hope the firing of Thornfield Hall will enable her to return to her lost Eden. While many critics view Antoinette's burning of Thornfield Hall as an act of rebellion and resistance (and Rhys herself also suggested this in letters), it is so passive, and literally suicidal, that even Antoinette is unaware of any revenge and rebellion attached to her act.

While it is difficult to know, by the end of Rochester's narrative, what

Antoinette is feeling and thinking, one senses that her hatred has not, could not, reach the proportions of Rochester's. Certainly, even if Antoinette does hate Rochester, as she says only once, it is not like his, a cold or calculating hate. And perhaps it is not personalized either. Ironically, when Rochester says she will have nothing to warm herself, his words anticipate the conclusion of Section III, in which Antoinette dreams of red, of warmth and heat; it is this dream that suggests to her the firing of Thornfield, a blind attempt to simulate and recover the heat and fire of her dream and of home and concomitantly to recapitulate the heat and fire that destroyed Coulibri. Rochester is right only in saying that it is not anger that will warm her, but for him that is the only warmth or fire left.

When Rochester takes Antoinette to Spanish Town prior to returning to England, he makes careful and cunning arrangements to protect himself: he arranges for servants who will not talk; he writes a surly letter to his father warning him to be discreet. While engaged in these conscious and careful manipulations, he still manages to deceive himself about his motives and his plans. Like the subject of a psychological test, he describes a drawing he made, "I drank some more rum and, drinking, I drew a house surrounded by trees. A large house. I divided the third floor into rooms and in one room I drew a standing woman—a child's scribble, a dot for a head, a larger one for the body, a triangle for the skirt, slanting lines for arms and feet. But it was an English house" (p. 559). Rochester prefigures his unconscious plans—which he *seems* to be engineering and materializing quite consciously—in the dehumanized and depersonalized stick-figure of a woman.

There is little doubt that this non-woman, a figure that he has created (both in the drawing and in Antoinette), represents his wife, incarcerated on the third floor of Thornfield Hall. Yet following the description of this drawing with the English House, now more real and specific than his wife, he says: "English trees. I wondered if I ever should see England again" (p. 559). Apparently Rochester cannot commit the crimes he does without disguising them and his part in them. His self-duplicity protects him from acknowledgment of guilt and responsibility.

Only Christophine is able to anticipate what Rochester might do. Her knowledge of his interior motives terrifies him and prompts his very personal struggle with her. Christophine's power vis-à-vis Rochester comes from many sources. Certainly it derives in part from the very honesty and sense of fairness with which she approaches the world. That Christophine understands Rochester's make-up better than Antoinette is clear. Part of her understanding of who he is comes from her very acute understanding of the social and cultural—even the political—realities of the West Indies in the post-Emancipation era. This understanding includes not only Rochester but the earlier interloper, Mason, and the entire new wave of colonialists. In fact, like Antoinette and her mother, Christophine too laments the passing of the old plantation owners, at least in comparison to the new ones. She says, " 'These new ones have Letter of the Law. Same thing. They got magistrate. They got fine. They got jail house and chain gang. They got tread machine to mash up people's feet. New ones worse than old ones—more cunning, that's all' " (p. 471).

While *Wide Sargasso Sea* is apparently about Antoinette rather than Rochester, one is tempted to comment on his character more—perhaps because his narrative is longer, perhaps because he is a more complicated character than Antoinette. Or perhaps because, as a character, he is less passive than she: his actions have determining effects, whereas Antoinette is always the receiver of action—from childhood, through her marriage, and up until her final burning of Rochester's home. And even though, in this last act, she does initiate important action, it is executed in a dream-like state, apparently without reason or rationalization. Even before her madness, when she goes to Christophine for help, what she asks for is black magic to sustain her white marriage. No action comes from the force of her character or her personality. She is identified by herself and by Rochester with the island. She is, like it, static, passive, accepting, sensual, trapped by time and history and by forces outside of herself— just as Rochester embodies the character of the colonizing English: aggressive, controlling, urban, a warrior who captures wealth, property, and people.

8

Women: Daughters and Mothers

Antoinette Cosway, like all of Rhys's heroines, is displaced from both culture and family. The first lines of her opening narrative define her problem. She says, "They say when trouble comes close ranks, and so the white people did. But we were not in their ranks" (p. 465). One might believe from this opening that the narrator is, in fact, not white. Antoinette is shut out by the white Jamaican women who would be her most identifiable allies. They exclude her and her mother because Antoinette's mother, like most of Rhys's victimized women, is pretty and therefore unacceptable to the British matrons. Second, her mother, a "Martinique girl" is resented by all the British Jamaicans because of her origins. Even the family's closest servant, Christophine, also from Martinique, "was not like the other women" (p. 467) who "would have nothing to do with her" (p. 467).

Antoinette describes growing up in complete isolation from the other families and also being despised by the recently freed blacks, who jeer at the Cosway's state of genteel poverty. Antoinette says: "I got used to a solitary life, but my mother still planned and hoped" (p. 465). Apparently her mother's marriage to Mason, which ultimately leads to her madness and incarceration, becomes part of this planning and hoping.

Antoinette, after her marriage to Rochester, like Anna Morgan after she meets Walter, also seems to renew her interest in planning and hoping—the lesson apparently being that both are fruitless. But until her marriage, Antoinette has little happiness, little faith or trust in anyone, except Christophine. She grows up feeling that there is a "them" and an "us." That "us" is sometimes understood to include no more than Antoinette and her mother, at other times women, and still other times, the

West Indians—both black and white. While Mason briefly provides the family of females with the security that both money and the presence of a male can supply, the sense of the "other" for Antoinette never disappears. At one point, when Mason criticizes Aunt Cora, Antoinette first tries to defend her aunt but finally says to herself: "'None of you understand about us'" (p. 474)—the "us," being Antoinette and her family, women, and finally West Indian Creoles.

Antoinette's differentness is both cultural and familial. Despised by both the whites and blacks, Antoinette is also alienated from the meager remains of her family itself, and most specifically from her mother's love. Antoinette's loss of her mother's affection is linked to her more general sense of loss, a loss to which she becomes resigned. Antoinette says of her mother, who at one point sends her away:

Once I would have gone back quietly to watch her asleep on the blue sofa—once I made excuses to be near her when she brushed her hair, a soft black cloak to cover me, hide me, keep me safe.

But not any longer. Not anymore. (p. 468)

That Antoinette suffers not only from this rejection by her mother but also from her mother's inability to protect her is never overtly stated, but that it occurred is a theme throughout *Wide Sargasso Sea*; it insures that Antoinette inevitably follows in her mother's footsteps. That is, in some sense, Antoinette finally retrieves her mother by becoming her. Antoinette's mother's coldness to her is described in terms remarkably similar to Rhys's description of her own mother. Antoinette says that her mother "pushed me away, not roughly but calmly, coldly, without a word, as if she had decided once and for all that I was useless to her" (p. 467).

Like Anna Morgan's mother's connection to Constance Estate in *Voyage in the Dark,* Antoinette's mother and Coulibri Estate are also linked. After the burning of Coulibri (which is based on the burning of Rhys's maternal grandfather's home), Antoinette learns that her mother is ill and has gone to the country. She says, "This did not seem strange to me for she was part of Coulibri, and if Coulibri had been destroyed and gone out of my life, it seemed natural that she should go too" (p. 539). Like Rhys herself, Antoinette tells us that she was "a little afraid of" her mother, who also preferred another sibling—this time not a sister but the idiot brother,

Pierre. Thus, like Anna Morgan, Antoinette seeks female love and mothering from other women: first in the kitchen with a black female servant and later in the kind sorority of a convent.

The world of *Wide Sargasso Sea* is the most complicated in Rhys's novels in terms of this alienation from the mother, for in *Wide Sargasso Sea* Antoinette's mother is presented at times sympathetically—indeed, she is a most horrible victim herself. Finally, in Part Three, the daughter attempts, albeit madly, to bridge the gap between them. In Part Three, when Antoinette, like her mother, is a mad and incarcerated woman, she has a vision of her mother, which appears in a tapestry hanging on the wall. She says, "I recognized my mother dressed in an evening gown but with bare feet" (pp. 567–68). This vision echoes Antoinette's last sight of her mother, locked up in the country with the two black warders, a memory she has described earlier, saying, "I remember the dress she was wearing—an evening dress cut very low, and she was barefooted" (p. 540). But though Antoinette's mother "haunts" her and though she apparently is reliving her mother's last years, the image Antoinette sees remains as unsympathetic and, if we remember the contrast of the convent nuns, as unsisterly as she had been to her daughter while alive. Antoinette says of the figure in the tapestry: "She looked away from me, over my head just as she used to do" (p. 568).

Like the daughter in *After Leaving Mr. Mackenzie* and Rhys herself in *Smile Please,* Antoinette also looks up to her mother, viewing her as a more perfect being—an adoration that presumably intensifies her fear. When Tia steals Antoinette's dress and Antoinette returns to her mother in Tia's, Antoinette is sure that her mother is ashamed of her. Antoinette's mother's concern about the stolen dress and the subsequent sacrifices she makes to replace it, however, reflect her own pride—which she maintains before blacks and whites. But Antoinette (like all of Rhys's heroines) finally adopts her mother's very symbolic involvement with clothes. In Part Three, the insane Antoinette is as obsessed with her red dress as her mother was with replacing the stolen one. In fact, it becomes the final symbolic link between the heat, the light, and the beauty of home, an evocative symbol of Antoinette's relationship to sensuality and nature and finally the only object imbued with meaning. She says:

Time has no meaning. But something you can touch and hold like my red dress, that has a meaning. . . .

. . . As soon as I turned the key I saw it hanging, the colour of fire and sunset. The colour of flamboyant flowers. . . . The scent that came from the dress was very faint at first, then it grew stronger. The smell of vetivert and frangipanni, of cinnamon and dust and lime trees when they are flowering. The smell of the sun and the smell of the rain. (p. 571)

While Antoinette's mother's involvement with the stolen dress reflected a prideful stance, that stance nevertheless reflected her own identity, her own connection with the world and with others. In that sense, though Antoinette's involvement with the red dress is linked to a childish sensuality, it also reflects, like her oft-changed name, her identity and her own fear of her self having been lost. As Grace Poole symbolically tries to cloak her in her "grey wrapper" provided by "them," Antoinette holds the red dress in her hand,

wondering if they had done the last and worst thing. If they had *changed* it when I wasn't looking. If they had changed it and it wasn't my dress at all—but how could they get the scent? . . . .

'If I had been wearing my red dress, Richard would have known me.' (p. 572)

Part of Antoinette's problem is that, on many levels, she is caught between different worlds—more so than her mother, who reached her maturity before Emancipation. Though Antoinette's mother suffers because of the Emancipation Act, her relation to the blacks is surer and more certain, even though, in some sense, she has changed position with the "free blacks" of the past. (Antoinette's mother refers to their being "marooned"—a reference to those West Indian blacks of the past who were first freed and then forced to hide in "exile" in the mountains.)[1] But Antoinette's mother is a Creole who understands her sociopolitical context. To that extent she is a person more sure of herself and more convinced of her own authority than Antoinette. That she goes mad—as does her daughter subsequently—has more to do with the impossibleness of her situation. But when it comes to understanding her own environment and her own impossible situation in it, Antoinette's mother and Aunt Cora are clear and sure and show a greater, perhaps a more realistic understanding, of the blacks.

Clearly, in her anticipation of the dangers inherent in the family's situation vis-à-vis the blacks, Antoinette's mother shows more understanding than the new white, Mason. What Antoinette's mother knows, and what Mason cannot, is the nature of Creole society. Edward Braithwaite discusses that society in his study of Creoles in Jamaica and points to the problem of the displacement of several differing cultures to a new land where they must inevitably have contact with one another, resulting in an unmixed and dual society. Braithwaite writes:

The single most important factor in the development of Jamaican society was . . . a cultural action—material, psychological and spiritual—based upon the stimulus/ response of individuals within the society to their environment and—as white/ black, culturally discrete groups—to each other. The scope and quality of this response and interaction were dictated by the circumstances of the society's foundation and composition—a 'new' construct, made up of newcomers to the landscape and cultural strangers each to the other; one group dominant, the other legally and subordinately slaves (p. 296)

Antoinette, who was born into the pre-Emancipation world but who was married to an Englishman after the Emancipation Act, is a living embodiment of this cultural dichotomy, a dichotomy that Braithwaite says could have been avoided had Creolization been able to happen more completely and had the two cultures merged to form a new and "residential" one. He says:

Cultural autonomy demands a norm and a residential correspondence between the 'great' and 'little' traditions within the society. Under slavery there were two 'great' traditions, one in Europe, the other in Africa, and so neither was residential. Normative value-references were made outside the society. Creolization . . . certainly mediated the development of authentically local institutions, and an Afro-creole 'little' tradition among the slave 'folk'. But it did not . . . provide a norm. (p. 309)

Braithwaite believes that the only ones who could have provided the impetus for the establishment of such a norm were the "Euro-creole elite." But he adds that they would have had to have been culturally "stronger," but that their "continuing social dependence merely created the pervasive dichotomy . . ." (p. 309). It is this dichotomy, based on black slavery and the white Creole's social slavery to the "mother" country, that makes Antoinette its victim.

Antoinette Cosway, unlike Anna Morgan, is seen and perhaps even faintly sees herself, as the direct victim of this mixed and yet not-mixed enough culture of the Creoles. Even Anna Morgan, a half century later, is still perhaps the victim of this society, though certainly Rhys presents Anna's confusions as far more personal and less cultural than Antoinette's. Perhaps Rhys, in her re-exploration of the effect of place on the psyche and lives of her heroines, has examined in *Wide Sargasso Sea* the full implications of place—that place is far more than topography and climate, that it is the summation of its own social and cultural history as well. And for that reason, she is also able to explore more fully not only the effects of place on her characters but also to see with more perspective the effects of family and personal history as they mingle with the culture, the topography, and the climate of place.

Secondly, Antoinette also represents perhaps a particular "type"—the nineteenth-century colonial planter's daughter—and the special problems that come to bear upon her. While as Braithwaite points out, there may have been no strong or clear "residential" West Indian culture, there certainly was a process of Creolization of both the whites and blacks, with often pernicious results for the whites who lived under the cloud of criticism from the mother country—in this case, England. He points to the blacks' effects on whites, especially in the areas of language, dress, and diet and includes in his study the reports of white female visitors from England on their observations of white Creole women. One observer wrote that "'the ladies who have not been educated in England . . . [speak] a sort of broken English, with an indolent drawling out of their words, that is very tiresome if not disgusting'" (p. 302). This observation by an English woman in 1839—the time Antoinette leaves her convent— echoes the same criticisms made of Anna Morgan sixty years later in *Voyage in the Dark.* Even a difference over food surfaces in *Wide Sargasso Sea* when Antoinette says that after her mother married Mr. Mason, "We ate English food too now." She adds that she "was glad to be like an English girl" but that she "missed the taste of Christophine's cooking" (p. 477). Later, Rochester, in describing the meals served by Christophine, ascribes the diet and schedule to Christophine's "whims" and "fancies" (p. 511), rather than recognizing the differences between West Indian and British customs. In fact, one senses that Rochester, at times, feels excluded from the Creole world with which Antoinette is so intimate and familiar.

Like Anna Morgan, Antoinette seeks succor and relief from her suffering and maternal rejection through the ministrations of women caretakers—first and foremost from Christophine, but also from her Aunt Cora, who provides for a time a center and a strength that her mother cannot. It is Aunt Cora, for example, who ministers to Antoinette with kisses, songs, and sustenance after the fire at Coulibri when her mother, always remote, is now no longer physically present. Antoinette's last experience with caretakers in Part I takes place in the all-female world of the convent. One might say that, like Part Two of *Voyage in the Dark,* the entire movement of Part I of *Wide Sargasso Sea* leads toward the illusion of safety and security, of nurture and warmth, that Antoinette finds there. The world of the convent is almost completely female (except for the intrusion of the Bishop and Mr. Mason) and it is a world in which the differences between black and white are apparently minimized.

Like Jane Eyre herself, Antoinette enters the convent school in a state of emotional destitution. There she is befriended and cared for both by the nuns—in particular the Mother Superior—and by the La Plana sisters whom she (as Jane Eyre does Helen Burns) looks up to as models. Both Jane Eyre and Antoinette find spiritual mothers in their boarding schools.

Rhys's depiction of the life of the convent is, like Anna Morgan's remembered ride to the female world of Constance Estate, crucial to an understanding of *Wide Sargasso Sea.* First, it is presented as a female cloister embodying love, peace, and harmony. It is a rarified and idealized environment where racial and class differences disappear and it stands in marked contrast to the more male world outside—both on the island and in England.

The convent (named Mother Mount Calvary, the name of the head of Rhys's own convent) is governed by an idealized Mother Superior—a type in Rhys who is rare but most usually a nun. She is wise, kind, and firm. While her office surrounds her with an apparent power, this nun (here and in her appearances in *Voyage in the Dark,* the Black Exercise Book and *Smile Please*) resorts to no magic, unlike the black priestesses; she makes no threats either in her words or demeanor and appeals to no higher authority. She is, quite simply, to paraphrase Chaucer, a very perfect Christian gentlewoman. In *Wide Sargasso Sea,* as long as the convent and the Mother Superior remain undisturbed by the outside (male) world, it remains a place of peace, harmony, and love.

This disturbing intrusion of the male into the clearly defined female world of the convent was apparently true in Rhys's own experience of convent life. In a story in *Sleep It Off, Lady,* "The Bishop's Feast," which is based on an incident that occurred when Rhys returned to Dominica, she writes about the convent.[2] In the story, the bishop is a stern, unloving, and patriarchal figure who takes as his adversary the Mother Superior whom Rhys loved. This entrance of the male governor into the female school in both the story and in *Wide Sargasso Sea* is reminiscent of the entrance of Mr. Brocklehurst into the world of Lowood and suggests that part of Rhys's interest in *Jane Eyre* lay in the exploration of a "woman's world." Both books examine the intrusion of the male governor and his disturbance of the peaceful female serenity and, in particular, his attacks on the female teachers who are legally powerless before him.

In *Wide Sargasso Sea,* the convent is the only place that provides Antoinette with security, safety, and trust. Rhys felt similarly about her own convent which she calls, in *Smile Please,* a "safe place." She writes, "there I could live happily (but not for too long), the bride of Christ, my place in heaven secure. If I got anxious or doubtful there would always be Mother Mount Calvary to comfort me" (p. 79). Rhys's ideal mothers— the nuns and black obeah women—are never attached to a man; they are outside sexuality and outside the continual triangles that occur and reoccur in Rhys's work, triangles in which the second female, whether she be mother, stepmother, or wife, becomes the heroine's enemy. In Rhys's work, the appearance of sexuality between male and female inevitably leads to destruction and to enmity between women; the nurture that all of her heroines seek, both from males and from females, cannot occur in a world in which sexuality also exists.

While the Mother Superior rules the convent perfectly, the other, lesser nuns are treated with a gentle irony. They remain pedestrian literalists, unlike the Mother Superior, who symbolizes a "true" and ideal mother. One might say that the Mother Superior serves as a stark counterpart to the "queen bee" natural mothers and stepmothers in Rhys, women who are central and powerful figures in the house but whose message is not love and Christian kindness, but rather, rejection and indifference.

While the Mother Superior suggests the model of a mother for whom all of Rhys's heroines are searching, the convent—as it did in the young Rhys's life when her family left for an extended visit to England—provides the family. When Antoinette enters the convent, she is without family of any kind: Christophine has gone to live with her son; her stepfather has gone away for months; her aunt has gone to England; and her mother, insane, is being attended in the country. Antoinette says: "This convent was my refuge. . ." (p. 490).

The convent is a place where right and wrong are clearly distinguished, where rules are obeyed and the explanations for those rules, which Rhys presents with a charming simplicity and irony, are clear and accepted. The world of the convent is presented in nostalgic and visual terms; it is a world of childlike simplicity where good and evil are reduced to ritual and order—like dressing with modesty or washing under cotton chemises without exposing one's body. The convent contains a synthesis or merging of the opposites that seem so often at war in the rest of *Wide Sargasso Sea*. In a voice that is perhaps somewhat too ironic for her, Antoinette describes the attractions of the convent: the simplicity and clarity; the sure knowledge of what is right and wrong and the apparent lack of the latter; and the peace and the illusion of the reconciliation of opposites. She says:

Everything was brightness, or dark. The walls, the blazing colours of the flowers in the garden, the nuns' habits were bright, but their veils, the Crucifix hanging from their waists, the shadow of the trees, were black. That was how it was, light and dark, sun and shadow, Heaven and Hell, for one of the nuns knew all about Hell and who does not? But another one knew about Heaven and the attributes of the blessed, of which the least is transcendent beauty. The very least. I could hardly wait for all this ecstasy and once I prayed for a long time to be dead. (p. 491)

The girls are also filled with stories of the lives of the saints—all young women who rejected sexuality and sex, earthly love, and marriage for a life—as well as a premature death—devoted to Christ. Though Antoinette only mentions their names in passing, the saints she names, except for the patron saint of the Americas, St. Rosa, are the subjects of tales of female innocence and chastity sacrificed to male power and lust, emblems for Antoinette herself.

Antoinette's sense of security at the convent is interrupted by three things: the first comes from within her, the second two from visits from men. In a passage that echoes Rhys's own accounting of her religious experience in the Black Exercise Book, Antoinette says that she began to doubt and that she "did not pray so often after that and soon, hardly at all. I felt bolder, happier, more free. But not so safe" (p. 492). While the convent provides a refuge, it is not one that Antoinette can use. It is a world for little girls, a world without sex and without risk. In fact, when Mason removes Antoinette from the convent, she criticizes the nuns for the first time saying: "They are safe. How can they know what it can be like *outside*" (p. 493, Rhys's italics). Clearly, at this juncture, the "outside" contains the world of men, sexuality, and marriage.

The insularity of the female world of the convent is also interrupted by two male figures: one is Mr. Mason, who visits Antoinette there and finally removes her; the other is the Bishop who visits the convent once a year. The Bishop, like the bishop in "The Bishop's Feast" and like Mr. Brocklehurst in *Jane Eyre,* criticizes the laxity of the nuns and teachers. But the Mother Superior courageously stands up to him.

Mr. Mason also expresses implied criticisms of the convent world, though his criticisms are the opposite of the Bishop's. His visits bring in an air of worldliness and materialism. He encourages Antoinette to be more worldly and brings her presents of "sweets, a locket, a bracelet, once a very pretty dress which, of course, I could not wear" (p. 492)—all items of courtship and female decoration. Antoinette is caught between the values of these two men who visit the convent, both of whom try to impose those values on the girls and the nuns. But Mason's visit, especially his final visit which signifies the end of Antoinette's stay at the convent, is the most dangerous threat, for he brings the advent of sexuality and marriage into Antoinette's life. When he removes her from the convent at the age of 17 (the age Rhys left Dominica) we understand that it is for the precise reason of arranged matrimony. His supercilious and lascivious response to her question as to whether the English friends he has invited to stay with them will really come makes Antoinette uneasy. She says: "It may have been the way he smiled, but again, a feeling of dismay, sadness, loss, almost choked me" (p. 493). Certainly Antoinette is right to feel this way, as her departure from the convent and her subsequent marriage signify the beginning of her end.

Although all three sections of *Wide Sargasso Sea* reflect a series of female caretakers, none is as idealized or compelling as the world of the nuns of Section I. In Section II, almost as an adversary to Rochester, Christophine attempts to care for Antoinette; in Section III, Rhys makes use of the Grace Poole of Brontë's novel as the final and least sympathetic of Antoinette's mother substitutes. However, in *Wide Sargasso Sea,* even

Grace Poole who, in Brontë's novel, is a rather unsympathetic character, is presented sympathetically. It would seem that in her last novel, Rhys does several things that she has done in none of her other works. For the first time she explores, on a more conscious level, areas that are suggested in her earlier work; the Grace Poole episode is an interesting example.

In Rhys's earlier works the males are all rather shallow representatives of a patriarchal governance. Females, other than the rather fragile and victimized heroines, are either matronly keepers of the patriarchy or unattractive working women, like Ethel Mathews in *Voyage in the Dark*. But in *Wide Sargasso Sea,* Grace Poole, perhaps a type similar to Ethel, attains a purity and humanitarianism not evident either in *Jane Eyre* or in Rhys's other fiction. Though Rhys's Grace Poole is coarse, "unattractive," and tough, and though her services as caretaker are clearly given for money, nevertheless she shows a sympathy and concern for her charge. In fact, she shows far more sympathy and concern for Antoinette than does Rochester or any other male in the novel. It would seem that in *Wide Sargasso Sea,* the male and female worlds are more completely and consciously polarized than in any of Rhys's other fiction—though the opposition has been an undercurrent in all the previous work. In her last novel, there are no female "villains" or unsympathetic characters. The male/female dichotomy or struggle has been crystallized—which may account for Rhys's use of two separate narrators or voices, one male, one female, to present the opposing points of view.

Grace Poole hesitates to take on the job of caring for Antoinette. She is appalled by her physical condition, though she says she is also afraid that she would be blamed should Antoinette die on her hands. Mrs. Eff, the Mrs. Fairfax of *Jane Eyre,* comes perhaps the closest to those women who, in Rhys, support the rights and privileges of men. Mrs. Eff still sees herself as the protector and server of Mr. Rochester, whom she recalls as ""*"gentle, generous, brave"*"" and whose stay in the West Indies has ""*"changed him out of all knowledge"*"" (p. 566; Rhys's italics). And she adds to Grace Poole: ""*"Don't ask me to pity anyone who had a hand in that"*"" (p. 566; Rhys's italics). Even in this detail, Rhys seems to be consistent in what amounts to a total recasting of the characters in *Jane Eyre.* In that novel, Mrs. Fairfax is presented as a "good" character, a woman of kindly, perhaps wise disposition, certainly more sympathetic than Grace Poole. But Rhys's Grace Poole, though not the idealized caretaker we see in the Mother Superior, nor the passionate spokesperson for the good we see in Christophine, reveals a humanity and understanding of a sisterhood of working women that one does not see in any other Rhys character.

In *Wide Sargasso Sea,* Rhys apparently reveals a deeper understanding of the motivations that govern single women and her own sympathy for their plight has expanded from the time of the writing of *Voyage in the Dark.* For example, in a monologue to her fellow servant Leah, Grace Poole talks about her reasons for accepting the job at Thornfield. She suggests that those reasons have less to do with money than with the conditions of being single and female in England. She says, "*'After all the house is big and safe, a shelter from the world outside which, say what you like, can be a black and cruel world to a woman. Maybe that's why I stayed on'*" (p. 566; Rhys's italics). Rhys not only retrieves the doomed Bertha of *Jane Eyre* but humanizes, gives grace, so to speak, to Mrs. Rochester's brutish warder. Though the quality of Antoinette's caretaking has diminished from the cloister of Part I, still, as long as she is under the care of women, there is some concern for her well-being, something that none of the men in *Wide Sargasso Sea* provide, except perhaps Mason, whose attempt to provide for Antoinette places her under Rochester's control.

Whereas the convent was a refuge, the last cloister is a prison; whereas the nuns were idealized caretakers, Grace Poole is a warder and guard. But even this woman shows an empathy for the spirit of the imprisoned Antoinette. She says:

Past the lodge gate a long avenue of trees and inside the house, the blazing fires and the crimson and white rooms. But above all, the thick walls, keeping away all the things that you have fought till you can fight no more. Yes, maybe that's why we all stay—Mrs. Eff and Leah and me. All of us except that girl who lives in her own darkness. I'll say one thing for her, she hasn't lost her spirit. She's still fierce. I don't turn my back on her when her eyes have that look. I know it. (pp. 566–67; Rhys's italics)

Clearly Grace Poole recognizes something kindred in Antoinette and also knows that unlike what Rochester thinks (that Antoinette is a dead ghost with no spirit left), there is still fire left in Antoinette. Grace properly, or at least at times, keeps her guard.

This sympathy for the working-class woman who is outside the world of the demi-mondaine, who is not similar to the flower women of her earlier works, is rare in Rhys. Certainly Rhys's range of sympathy has expanded to include perhaps all women alone. In fact, there is a strange communication in Part III between Grace Poole and Antoinette. One wonders, in fact, if Grace Poole's falling asleep, leaving Antoinette free to wander about, her insistence later that Antoinette should be allowed to go outside which Antoinette uses as an opportunity to purchase a knife, make Grace—especially after she has said that she should not let her guard down—an unwitting or even unconscious accomplice to Antoinette's final act of firing Thornfield Hall and maiming Rochester. Grace Poole, like Christophine, has also associated Rochester with the devil saying: " " '*I don't serve the devil for no money*' " " (p. 566; Rhys's italics).

What has led to Antoinette's downward move from the idealized and kindly Christian mothering she finds in the convent in Section I to her degradation and wardship under Grace Poole in Section III? First, part of the cause is the essential nature of Antoinette who, like so many of Rhys's women and Rhys herself, prefers the risk of the "outside world" to the safety and security of the cloister. In Rhys's work that risk and danger is male and sexual. Perhaps the first hint of this danger occurs to Antoinette in the first dream she has while still living with her mother, who has not yet remarried. The dream occurs the night Antoinette's mother has visitors for the first time, among whom probably is her future husband. This dream is interesting first, for what it contains and second, for what it reveals about her relationship with her mother. In describing her nightmare, Antoinette says, "I dreamed I was walking in the forest. Not alone. Someone who hated me was with me, out of sight. I could hear heavy footsteps coming closer and though I struggled and screamed I could not move. I woke crying. The covering sheet was on the floor and my mother was looking down at me" (p. 471). Antoinette's mother covers her up, sighs and says, " 'You were making such a noise. I must go to Pierre, you've frightened him' " (p. 27). Even the rough Grace Poole attempts to provide more comfort than Antoinette's mother.

This dream of Antoinette's becomes one to which she returns later in greater detail and contains, I think, the essential danger posited by the "outside world"—a danger connected to men and to sex; a danger from which her mother cannot protect her and about which she offers no comfort or sisterly alliance as do the nuns, Christophine, and even Grace Poole. What is important here in this first abbreviated representation of

Antoinette's dream are the mother's response, the content of the dream itself, which follows the first visit of the courting male, and Antoinette's words following her mother's departure from the room. She says, "I lay thinking, 'I am safe. There is the corner of the bedroom door and the friendly furniture. There is the tree of life in the garden and the wall green with moss. The barrier of the cliffs and the high mountains. And the barrier of the sea. I am safe. I am safe from strangers'" (p. 471).

Ironically, it is the sea that the child Antoinette counts on as her barrier, as her shield against strangers. But this very barrier has been crossed, as evidenced that day by her mother's new English visitors. Furthermore, at the end of the novel, it is Antoinette herself who is forced to cross that barrier, to live surrounded by strangers who are her captors and warders, representatives of the stranger who has married her and who hates her, who has declared himself her enemy. After her dream, Antoinette wakes the next morning with the premonition that her imagined safety is an illusion. She says: "I woke next morning knowing that nothing would be the same. It would change and go on changing" (p. 472).

The second time Antoinette has her dream, she is at the convent and when she awakens in fear, she is for the first and last time offered real comfort. I present the dream in its entirety because I think it, like the dream Anna Morgan has of the child bishop and "the different trees" in *Voyage in the Dark,* contains much of the conflict essential to *Wide Sargasso Sea.* It is crucial to an understanding of the nature of the "evil" that Rhys explores in her novel. This particular dream apparently had tremendous significance for Rhys herself. It contains much of the unresolved problems of sexual initiation that Rhys experienced in the unfortunate episode with the elderly Mr. Howard. The dream, as it appears in *Wide Sargasso Sea,* is taken almost verbatim from a passage in the Black Exercise Book, which predates Rhys's last novel by about 30 years.

That Antoinette's dream seems to encapsulate the dangers of the "outside" world seems implicit in that she reports the dream immediately after she knows she will be leaving the convent and for the first time resents "the nuns' cheerful faces." She asks, "How can they know what it can be like *outside?*" Following that question she says, "This was the second time I had my dream." Then she relates it as follows:

Again I have left the house at Coulibri. It is still night and I am walking towards the forest. I am wearing a long dress and thin slippers, so I walk with difficulty, following the man who is with me and holding up the skirt of my dress. It is white and beautiful and I don't wish to get it soiled. I follow him, sick with fear but I make no effort to save myself; if anyone were to try to save me, I would refuse. This must happen. Now we have reached the forest. We are under the tall dark trees and there is no wind. 'Here?' He turns and looks at me, his face black with hatred, and when I see this I begin to cry. He smiles slyly. 'Not here, not yet,' he says, and I follow him, weeping. Now I do not try to hold up my dress, it trails in the dirt, my beautiful dress. We are no longer in the forest but in an enclosed garden surrounded by a stone wall and the trees are different trees. I do not know them. There are steps leading upwards. It is too dark to see the wall or the steps, but I know they are there and I think, 'It will be when I go up these steps. At the top.' I stumble over my dress and cannot get up. I touch a tree and my arms hold on to it. 'Here, here.' But I think I will not go any further. The tree sways and jerks as if it is trying to throw me off. Still I cling and the seconds pass and each one is a thousand years. 'Here, in here,' a strange voice said, and the tree stopped swaying and jerking. (p. 493)

This time after the dream Antoinette wakes to the ministration of Sister Marie Augustine, who tells her not to disturb the others. But, unlike Antoinette's mother, the nun does not forsake her. She attends to Antoinette, giving her hot chocolate. That the dream is in part bound up with Antoinette's mother, who affected white dresses, seems clear. Antoinette tells Sister Marie Augustine, "'I dreamed I was in Hell'" (p. 493). The nun tells her the dream is evil and not to think of it again. She continues to comfort Antoinette, but when she tells the girl to drink her chocolate, it reminds Antoinette of the drink after her mother's funeral. She says: "Now the thought of her is mixed up with my dream" (p. 494). The memory of her mother makes Antoinette cry. She asks Sister Marie Augustine why "such terrible things happen," to which the nun replies: "'You must not concern yourself with that mystery,'" and, echoing the earlier words of the servant Godfrey, adds, "'We do not know why the devil must have his little day. Not yet'" (p. 494).

This is the last scene in Section I and ends with the nun's gentle counsel: "'Think of calm, peaceful things and try to sleep. . . . Soon it will be tomorrow morning'" (p. 494). But if one remembers the false sense of security with which Antoinette fell asleep after the first time she had the dream and her sad recognition the following morning that everything changes and "will go on changing," the solace the nun offers rings hollow, especially as we know that Antoinette is to leave the convent shortly, to be thrust into that "outside."

What is outside for Antoinette is contained in her dream—a dream which like Anna Morgan's is about male power, the patriarchy, and women's masochistic relationship to men and to sex. The dream itself prefigures Antoinette's immediate future—her wedding (hence the white dress) which Mason is planning and to which, in the dream, she is being led like a sacrificial lamb. But, like all Rhys's women, she masochistically and insistently lays herself on this sexual altar. ("If anyone were to try to save me I would refuse. This must happen.") Antoinette, like Rhys herself, insists on her fate. The dream also suggests her future husband Rochester—her "enemy" whose face is "black with hatred." But though the man hates her, she continues to ask him where something will occur, apparently the sexual act itself in which the dream seems to culminate.

That the dream is finally mixed up in Antoinette's mind with her mother and with her mother's death Antoinette makes clear. And since the dream is about "I," Antoinette, there is no doubt that Antoinette has already begun a confounding of herself and her mother—a confusion which culminates in the final section, where Antoinette mirrors both her mother's madness and the burning of Coulibri in the burning of Thornfield.

Both Antoinette and her mother are eventually driven mad and destroyed by their marriages to "strangers" from England. And both she and her mother are exploited by men—her mother by her caretaker, whose face is literally "black," and Antoinette by her husband, who is prefigured by the man of her dream. If we recall the words of Sister Marie Augustine, and Antoinette's statement that she dreamed she was in Hell, the strange man, the enemy who appears to be a sexual partner, becomes linked to the devil. For Antoinette and for women like her, those women who court risk and who are sensual and sexual by nature, sex and risk are the same. Men become evil partners, the devil incarnate.

As in Anna Morgan's dream, there is in Antoinette's a confusion of sex and male power and their connection to her own "rape" across the ocean to England, almost as if all three are equated. Perhaps both for Anna and Antoinette female sexual masochism and separation are inseparable. To leave the convent, to leave the island, even to lose the mother—all are connected to sex and sex to the devil and evil, and ultimately to male power.

To remain in the convent is to remain innocent of what is outside—sex. Innocence, as illustrated in all the saints' lives Antoinette refers to, is sexual innocence, indeed is rejection of sex all together. Both *Voyage in the Dark* and *Wide Sargasso Sea* are about innocence and the loss or destruction of innocents like Anna and Antoinette. For Rhys, innocence is, I think, primarily sexual innocence. Sex itself is tainted and unclean like Antoinette's white dress which she can't keep out of the dirt.

This view of the convent innocence as counterposed to sexual initiation and female masochism is borne out in Rhys's short stories, especially those connected to Mr. Howard. For example, in the story "Goodbye Marcus, Goodbye Rose,"[3] Phoebe learns from Captain Cardew "that love was not kind and gentle as she had imagined, but violent. Violence, even cruelty was an essential part of it" (p. 28). In that story, after Captain Cardew leaves the island, Phoebe lies in bed and thinks of the girls in the convent and the words of the nuns—the latter's talk of chastity and the girls' talk of marriage. But Phoebe, who is saddened by "the thought of some vague irreparable loss" (p. 30), is suddenly outside of and banished forever from either sorority—the nuns who remain perpetually virginal or the girls who will safely marry. She has become a "wicked girl" (p. 29). Although Phoebe believes she has participated in her own "seduction," and therefore is wicked, the consequences for her are similar to those for Antoinette, who is removed from the convent still in an unwicked state—unless one counts her dream, which presages her slavery to sexuality. For Phoebe and Antoinette, the initiation into sex and marriage removes them forever from the safe insularity of the convent which is, above all, a sexless, even an antisexual, world.

In Rhys's work, and specifically in *Voyage in the Dark* and *Wide Sargasso Sea,* there is a polarity about sex. Her heroines, for reasons of their own psychology, cannot be excluded from knowledge of sex, and perhaps even welcome their initiation into it—even with the knowledge that in Rhys's world it is a violent and humiliating affair for women. But counterposed to the destructive magnet of sex, there remains in Rhys's work the world of the convent as a recurring ideal of the haven it offers from sex, men, and male domination. Even a woman like Sasha Jansen in *Good Morning, Midnight,* who otherwise ostensibly has no historical link with a convent school, at one moment recalls the words of a nun who comforted her once, a nun whose name is also Sister Marie Augustine. Given the choice between the most insular island of all—the convent—and the world of humiliating sex, Rhys's women still choose the latter. Phoebe's last thought on her exclusion from the world of chastity and proper marriage sums it up: "The prospect before her might be difficult and uncertain but it was far more exciting" (p. 30). That there might be irony intended here is quite possible, but there does seem to be a very strong conviction in Rhys's fiction and in her private writing that the lives of her heroines, unfortunate and unhappy as they are, are preferable to the dull and repetitive life of the conventionally married woman. It is a difficult and puzzling choice though, especially if we remember that in *Wide Sargasso Sea* and in Rhys's intended conclusion for *Voyage in the Dark* the price a woman pays for sensuality and sexuality—for freedom—is death.

Rhys's heroines often accord their lovers a godlike superiority, power, and position, though there is certainly irony in that accord because the men never reveal or exhibit godlike behavior. Rhys even reduces Rochester, in Brontë a "master" and Byronic character, to a mediocre and petty man. Rhys's reversal of the character and function of Rochester in terms of women goes even further. For Jane Eyre, it is her cousin St. John who represents a cold and bitter sternness. She describes him in words that are similar to those that several characters use for Rochester, saying that he is "hard and cold like a rock."[4] Eventually, for Jane, Rochester is the one who appeals to her passionate nature and who gives her the possibility of a moderate autonomy. In fact, as St. John's arguments begin to weaken Jane, she uses an image stark in its connection to the image of enclosure used by Anna Morgan in *Voyage in the Dark*. She says, "My iron shroud contracted round me" (p. 45). Rhys's reversal of the master-slave function of Rochester suggests, given especially her very careful reading of *Jane Eyre,* that the sexual enslavement of her heroines is perhaps as much a function of their own characters, dispositions and cultural backgrounds as it is of the men's characters or the existence of a patriarchal tradition. Even Jane Eyre's and Antoinette's "education" are reversed in *Wide Sargasso Sea*. As many critics have pointed out, part of Jane's education is learning to control passion. In fact, we might say that her career follows an opposite curve to Antoinette's: that she moves from expressed passion and rage to controlled passion, while Antoinette moves from an apparently affectless behavior to the "mad" expression of passion and rage.

As soon as Rhys's heroines give themselves sexually—and that is the crucial rite—they enslave themselves. Even little Phoebe in "The Birthday," an unpublished version of the Mr. Howard story, says, in her final thoughts of Mr. Howard, that his "Greek profile" was "clear cut, benevolent and relentless as that of some aged—and ageless—god."⁵ Once launched into the world of love and sex, Rhys's women, and girls, become immersed in that world to the exclusion of the possibility of consideration of a life without these men. Such responses in young women are not unusual. In *My Mother/My Self,* a personal exploration of the relationship between women and their mothers, Nancy Friday discusses the need of some women to "elevate" a man with whom they have sex into the men of their dreams as a way of justifying their involvement with sex.⁶ For Antoinette, of course, Rochester literally becomes the man of her dream.

Anna and Antoinette, Rhys's Caribbean heroines, say that they wanted to be black and envied the black women's more autonomous relationships to men. Both women actualize this fantasy as they become slaves to lovers who become their masters—unlike Jane Eyre, who *calls* Rochester her master but remains her own mistress. It may be that the sexual fantasy is related to or precedes the desire to be black, that the desire to be black is, in part, a symptom or symbol of their relationship to the opposite sex. As the black slave was to her master, Rhys's heroines are to their lovers—with the difference that theirs is a voluntary enslavement, probably connected to a self-doubt and a self-hate engendered by the antipathy of their mothers and family and by their being outside white society and the safe enclaves of white women.

Antoinette makes it clear that Rochester and the advent of her own sexuality have changed her entire feeling about life. She says to him, "'I never wished to live before I knew you. I always thought it would be better if I died'" (p. 512). Antoinette adds that she has never told anyone of her wish to die; in her blindness about Rochester and her misapprehension of their supposed closeness she adds, "'There was no one to tell, no one to listen'" (p. 512). Antoinette regains her will to live only after becoming sexually involved with Rochester. Like Anna Morgan, she imbues her lover with the power over her life; but like Anna, this awakening of the desire to live is itself short-lived and culminates in its complete opposite—the desire for death.

Unlike Rhys's previous male characters, Rochester reveals a male response to Rhys's women and expresses his indifference and antipathy. Of Antoinette he says, "I did not love her. I was thirsty for her, but that is not love. I felt very little tenderness for her, she was a stranger to me, a stranger who did not think or feel as I did" (p. 513).

The maintenance of this dichotomy between sex and love is not possible for Rhys's women. Once having made love to a man, outside of the pure acts of prostitution that Anna Morgan later engages in, they are pledged to him. Sex and sensuality are for Anna and Antoinette, and Marya in *Quartet,* traps from which they can only be extricated by abandonment and/or death. In fact, the abandonment precipitates a desire for death. For Rochester, that Antoinette is a "stranger," an "alien," cuts off the possibility of love. But for Antoinette and Anna Morgan, masochistically bound to their first lovers, the aspect of the lover *must* have the aspect of the stranger, the enemy, and ultimately, in Rhys's iconography and most clearly developed in *Wide Sargasso Sea,* the aspect of the devil himself. It is for this Antoinette "thirsts" and, unlike Rochester's stated position, for her, to "thirst for someone" is to be obsessively in love and obsessively fixated on sexual union with the object of that love.

Rhys's heroines, except perhaps for Sasha Jansen at the end of *Good Morning, Midnight,* have scant and naive understanding of men and of the relationship between the sexes. Men continuously remain strangers. But that Rhys also intended a comment on her heroines' confusion of sex and love I think is apparent in *Wide Sargasso Sea.* The voice of Christophine, which articulates a friendly opposition to Antoinette's point of view about men and sex, is continually logical, coherent, and sympathetic. For example, when Antoinette goes to Christophine for obeah help, the argument between the two reveals the naiveté and limitedness of Antoinette's thinking. Antoinette, in making her request, says to Christophine that Christophine has the power to "'make people love or hate . . . or die'" (p. 526).

Ironically, the untutored woman of magic and black religion has more practical and pragmatic understanding of social relationships and a more logical connection to the world than her white suppliant. She insists that even if she could make Rochester come again to Antoinette's bed, she could not make him love her and insists furthermore that afterward, he would indeed hate her. In her talk with Christophine, Antoinette also reveals, I think, that her dilemma stems in part from the opening up of her sexuality; she reveals that it is primarily for love-making that she wants him to return. She says to Christophine that she wouldn't care if Rochester hated her after if only he were to come to her for just one night. It is only at this point, in the face of Christophine's repeated refusal to involve Antoinette with obeah, that Antoinette forces herself to *act* calm and to try to convince Christophine with logic. But Antoinette has already revealed that the basis of her wish is not logical or reasonable but rather consists of an overwhelming desire to resume sexual relations with her husband.

Antoinette and Anna Morgan become sexually obsessed, tormented by their desire for lovers who have abandoned them. In Rhys this constitutes a strong element of female sexuality. However, in her depiction of Rochester, and perhaps Heidler and Stefan Zelli in *Quartet,* Rhys also suggests an opposite undercurrent in male sexuality: the desire for sexual dominance and possession even in the absence of love, infatuation, or sexual desire. In Section Two, Rochester concludes by damning Antoinette, by driving her mad, by gaining full possession and control of her. He says of her: "Made for loving? Yes, but she'll have no lover, for I don't want her and she'll see no other" (p. 560). Rochester's diatribe, within the context of his narrative, seems overwrought and overly vindictive. One wonders why he has such a desire for destruction and revenge. However, in Section Three, in her "insane" monologue, Antoinette reveals that, unless one supposes—and there seems to be no evidence to suggest it— that she is fabricating, she has been sexually involved with her "cousin" Sandi after she married Rochester. She says:

Sandi often came to see me when that man [presumably Rochester] was away and when I went out driving I would meet him. I could go out driving then. The servants knew, but none of them told.

Now there was no time left so we kissed each other in that stupid room. . . . We had often kissed before but not like that. That was the life and death kiss and you only know a long time afterwards what it is, the life and death kiss. The white ship whistled three times, once gaily, once calling, once to say good-bye.

I took the red dress down and put it against myself. 'Does it make me look intemperate and unchaste?' I said. That man told me so. He had found out that Sandi had been to the house and that I went to see him. I never knew who told. 'Infamous daughter of an infamous mother,' he said to me. (p. 571)

If "that man" is Rochester—and that is the only possible conclusion— then we can assume that Rochester has left out a crucial piece of information in his narrative, a fact that "explains" his terrible possessiveness of Antoinette toward the end of Section II. Like Heidler and Stefan Zelli in *Quartet,* even though he no longer wants the woman sexually, he cannot abide others having her. In fact, the addition of this information by Antoinette further reveals Rochester's need to dissemble and his rather traditional male response—the wrath of a "jealous husband." In terms of the sexual responses and the relationships between men and women, Rhys's last novel bears a remarkable similarity to her first. Even Antoinette's relationship to Sandi resembles Marya's relationship to Cairn, a sympathetic male who tries to offer comfort and helpful advice to Marya, advice she is no longer free to accept. Like Sandi, he suggests a kindly alternative to the sadomasochistic relationship she has with her lover, an alternative of which Rhys's heroines can never take advantage.

Antoinette's allusion to the affair with the warm and kindly Sandi also serves another function in terms of Rhys's literary dialogue with *Jane Eyre.* That is, in *Jane Eyre,* Rochester tells Jane that his monstrous Caribbean wife was mad, lascivious, and unchaste. Rhys reinterprets this as the understandable search by a rejected and mistreated young girl for a companion and sympathetic lover and Rochester's response to that as the spiteful and possessive calumny of the "cheated" male. Furthermore, his own sexual foray with the black Amelie reveals his own trading in sex and his own deceitfulness concerning his British views on slavery. This theme—of the Briton who is opposed to slavery and yet less understanding or loving toward blacks—recurs in Rhys's Caribbean fiction and in her private writings. Antoinette herself speaks for the Creole point of view when she points out the disparity between Rochester's statements about justice and his own actions. She says, "'You abused the planters and made up stories about them, but you do the same thing. You send the girl away quicker, and with no money or less money, and that's the difference'" (p. 548).

In short, Antoinette accuses Rochester of the very crime of which Daniel Cosway has accused her father—exploitation of black women—and of the crime of which he has accused Antoinette—sex between black and white. And yet in *Wide Sargasso Sea* Rochester's crime is far worse than Antoinette's planter father's, primarily because he has acted out of malice and hypocrisy. Even Amelie, after the sexual encounter with Rochester and after, one presumes, that she sees him as he is, expresses sympathy for her "enemy" Antoinette. In fact, Rochester compounds the severity of his transgression by his response to the passionate Antoinette. He responds with British coldness, saying that "slavery was not a matter of liking or disliking. . . . It was a question of justice" (p. 548). One recalls his earlier abhorrence of touching blacks: after he sees Antoinette embrace

Christophine he says: "'*I* wouldn't hug and kiss them . . . I couldn't'" (p. 512; Rhys's italics).

Antoinette's responses to Rochester's view of justice completes the circle of her identification of herself with her mother and of Rochester with the devil, and of sex as the compound that ties them all together. She says:

'Justice . . . I've heard that word. It's a cold word. I tried it out . . . I wrote it down. I wrote it down several times and always it looked like a damn cold lie to me. There is no justice. . . . My mother whom you all talk about, what justice did she have? My mother sitting in the rocking-chair speaking about dead horses and dead grooms and a black devil kissing her sad mouth. Like you kissed mine. . . .' (p. 548)

The devil in *Wide Sargasso Sea,* whether he be white or black, is always male and almost always seen in his sexual aspect. Both Antoinette and her mother relinquish themselves to the devil—as do Marya Zelli, Anna Morgan, Sasha Jansen, and Julia Martin. But it is only in *Wide Sargasso Sea* that the females' cooperation is clearly seen not only as the destruction of innocence but as self-destruction by innocents. Furthermore, for the first time in Rhys, that impulse is clearly a form or an expression of madness.

Antoinette is, like her island, "colonized," her independence and autonomy subsumed to British culture and to British law. Her marriage to Rochester simply completes that analogy. While Brontë's *Jane Eyre* presents the long-suffering Rochester as the victim of nineteenth-century British marriage laws, as a man forever manacled to a mad and monstrous wife, *Wide Sargasso Sea* reverses that picture so that it is Antoinette who is trapped, indeed imprisoned by those laws and customs—her property stolen, her freedom denied, her sanity forfeited.

That these marriage laws further exacerbated the schism between the sexes and that they benefited the male to the detriment of the female is a fact of which the two strong maternal figures in *Wide Sargasso Sea,* Aunt Cora and Christophine, are aware and which the men, less aware perhaps, take for granted. For example, not only does Aunt Cora secretly give jewels to Antoinette as insurance but Antoinette herself recalls, but with no comment, a conversation between her aunt and Richard Mason in which the aunt insists that Richard have some settlement arranged for Antoinette so that she is protected legally. But Mason, reflecting the male attitude that a female—like a colony—is a thing to be bartered and bought, says that they were lucky that they could get anyone to marry Antoinette; true to nineteenth-century colonial and male attitudes, he adds that Rochester is "'an honourable gentleman'" (p. 527) with whom he would trust his life. Aunt Cora, well aware that this "gentleman's agreement" has few repercussions for Richard Mason, reminds him that it is with Antoinette's life that he is trusting Rochester, not his own.

Christophine's reaction to the economic and personal realities of British marriage law is far more outspoken. When Antoinette says finally that she cannot leave Rochester because he is her husband, the discussion both of marriage and women that ensues reveals how Antoinette, caught in the binds of those laws and furthermore as a colonial heiress, is the victim of a patriarchal system which is ultimately more injurious to her than is the system of primogeniture that has left Rochester bereft of his inheritance and his father's love. When Christophine points out that her three children were fathered by three different men and that she has not been constrained by the bonds of marriage nor forced to give her money to "'no worthless man'" (p. 524), she reflects a commonplace in Rhys's work (i.e., the black women's freedom from the constraints of marriage). In this sense, for Rhys, the white Creole woman is at the bottom of the scale in terms of personal freedom. She is perhaps the emblem of the colony itself.

Though Antoinette has entered her marriage reluctantly, its very existence disallows her quitting it. And while her own character complements the anonymity and powerlessness enforced on her by the marriage laws, and while she expresses no conscious anger at or resentment of those laws, and indeed explains them quite patiently to Christophine, her subterranean rage about it is expressed in the last episode with Richard Mason in Section III. In that part we learn through Grace Poole, though Antoinette does not remember it, that she has attacked her stepbrother when he visits her in her room at Thornfield. Grace says that Antoinette attacked him with a knife when he told her that "'"I cannot interfere legally between yourself and your husband."'" Grace adds: "'It was when he said "legally" that you flew at him . . .'" (p. 570). On a less than conscious level Antoinette is aware that her present situation of enclosure and powerlessness has been brought to its present circumstances in part by legal marriage custom and law. Not only may her husband assume her possessions and property but he may lock her up as his own property.

Like Anna Morgan, and almost all of Rhys's heroines, Antoinette winds up enclosed in a cold and unsympathetic room in England, her only solace alcohol and memories of the past. Like those other women, she is attended by a remote female—this time Grace Poole rather than the constant stream of landladies and hotel keepers; like those other women, her world has contracted to an interior of "cardboard," to a bare and colorless room whose artifacts are at once deadening and yet compose the only catalogue of her days. When the room is all that one of Rhys's heroines has, one knows that she has reached the limit of destitution, isolation, and hopelessness. However, in *Wide Sargasso Sea,* more than in any of Rhys's other novels, the causes for that finale are not simply the results of a passive and self-destructive personality. They are social and historical as well. Unlike her predecessors, Antoinette has not locked herself up.

Wide Sargasso Sea brings to the surface many of the underlying causes in Rhys's earlier works. Ironically, it is Grace Poole, the equivalent perhaps of those earlier landladies, who best articulates those causes: a woman alone in England is a sorry thing. Certainly the British interior in *Wide Sargasso Sea* is the most claustrophobic of all of Rhys's English rooms, unrelieved by glimpses of the outside world except for one brief sojourn sympathetically arranged by Grace Poole. There is no place for growth, no place for a natural expansion.

That marriage subsumes the female, deprives her of liberty and autonomy, is implicit in *Wide Sargasso Sea.* Indeed, in the two marriages presented, it contributes to the destruction of the female. Perhaps that loss of self and identity is best represented in the loss of name the married woman undergoes, a motif that is present in all three sections of *Wide Sargasso Sea*—and very different from *Jane Eyre,* whose title itself suggests the consistency of name and character.

In Section One, Antoinette is already dimly aware of the subsuming of herself to imposed names. When she enters the convent a nun asks her name and she responds with her only "true name," and, in fact, a variant of her mother's name. "'Antoinette,'" she says. The nun responds: "'I know. You are Antoinette Cosway, that is to say Antoinette Mason'" (p. 488). Later, Antoinette describes the embroidery she is doing and says: "Underneath, I will write my name in fire red, Antoinette Mason, Cosway, Mount Calvary Convent, Spanish Town, Jamaica, 1839" (p. 489), noting the already changed nature of her name and the desire, unconscious as it may be, to hold on to her self as well as the unconscious association of herself with fire.

By Part Two, Antoinette has recapitulated the experience of the blacks brought from Africa: she lives in a foreign land without liberty, cloaked in three false names: Bertha Mason Rochester. That Antoinette herself has grown increasingly aware of the power of the change of name becomes clear when she tells Rochester in Part Two that his desire to call her by a name other than her own is "'obeah too'" (p. 548). And obeah, of course, is a form of spiritual possession. Rochester, in his insatiable desire for control, power, and possession, is not content simply with the imposition of his surname. That he uses the imposition of a first name on Antoinette as a weapon and as a form of control is apparent in Section Two when, in his own interior monologue, as opposed to his more controlled narrative, he refers to her neither as "my wife" nor "Bertha" but as "Antoinetta" and "Antoinette."

Antoinette herself, in Section Three, recognizes the power of the deprivation of name when she comments on Grace Poole's given name, remarking on its inappropriateness. She says, "Names matter, like when he wouldn't call me Antoinette, and I saw Antoinette drifting out of the window with her scents, her pretty clothes and her looking-glass" (p. 568). Antoinette's words indicate her understanding that the change of name equals the loss of self and identity, and hence the loss of autonomy and power—the very thing that Christophine represents and fights for when she insists that Rochester refer to his wife by name. That Antoinette's name is so often and so easily changed by new names imposed on her by British colonial men suggests her own identification with the black Creoles and with the colony itself. An outsider, without a clear place in an already pluralistic society, Antoinette is easy prey to whoever lays claim upon her.

9

Race and Betrayal

And what does anyone know about traitors,
or why Judas did what he did?
                                    from *Wide Sargasso Sea*

In *Wide Sargasso Sea,* the flawed relationships between parent and child are microcosmic mirrors of the failure of culture and history to provide for succeeding generations of British and succeeding generations of white and black West Indians. The novel examines the intersections of those interrelated betrayals. In Rhys's novel, betrayal leads to madness, madness to betrayal; the two are barely separable. All the principal characters are, in some way, mad. While Antoinette and her mother ultimately become insane and detached from ordinary reality, Daniel Cosway and Rochester are consumed by idées fixes and the need to destroy; even the anonymous blacks, both in the mob at Coulibri and in the persons of Antoinette's mother's caretakers, have lost their reason, or at least their charity. For the females the madness turns inward; for the males it is directed toward women. Whether the man is black or white, his "victim" is always female even though, in the case of Cosway and Rochester, that desire to wound the woman contains their rage at their fathers.

All the characters, early in their lives, have incorporated a sense of betrayal from the past: Antoinette by her mother; Antoinette's mother by the blacks; Daniel Cosway by his father and Rochester by his. Only Christophine, who perhaps encompasses a "reality principle" in a world in which most of the characters express difficulty in determining what is real, manages to escape the madness of hating and the problem of distinguishing what is real and what is right. She is, excluding the idealized Mother Superior, the only character who does not betray. That there is an underlying breakdown of trust, charity (Christian and otherwise), and love in *Wide Sargasso Sea* is apparent; but there is a hierarchy amongst those who have broken these principles of human community. Clearly, the two males, Rochester and Daniel Cosway, are the greatest transgressors.

The levels of betrayal range from the cultural and historical implicit in the relationships between blacks and whites to the familial and filial levels, which reflect the larger social destruction of the values of the New Testament. The breakdown of trust spans the continents, the races, and the family and spans the "time" of *Wide Sargasso Sea.*

The relationship of the Creole blacks to the Creole whites is different and separate from that of all the Creoles to the recently arrived second wave of colonial British represented by Mason and Rochester. The complicated relationships among the Creoles in post-Emancipation Jamaica is perhaps characterized by reversals. From the white point of view, those reversals are negative as, for example, in the "marooned" condition of Antoinette and her mother who have become hostages and outcasts. The culmination of their reversal is pictured in the sexual exploitation of Antoinette's mother by her black caretaker—a tableau that transposes the elements of Daniel Cosway's accusations against the white planters.

In her exposition of the relationship between Antoinette and Tia, Rhys explores the complexity and confusion of the post-Emancipation Creole experience. That experience is both economic and sexual. While Antoinette's betrayal by her mother is perhaps the primary and central "fault" in her life, her betrayal by her black friend Tia is emblematic of the problem that exists between the races. The breakdown of their friendship serves as a symbol of the breakdown of the relationship between whites and blacks following the abolition of slavery.

First, we must remember that Antoinette forms her friendship with Tia after being taunted and called a "white cockroach" by another black girl. Following that incident, it is not to her white mother that she turns, but first to the black servant Christophine and then to Tia, the daughter of Christophine's Martinique friend. Antoinette's confusion has been further confounded. While she is prey to taunts by blacks, it is only from them that she receives comfort, love, or friendship. Again Antoinette is caught in the middle, ultimately feeling inferior both to her white mother and to her black friends. Antoinette describes the black Tia in terms that are familiar in Rhys: Tia has a more intimate relationship to the natural world and hence to the island. She says: "Fires always lit for her, sharp stones did not hurt her bare feet" (p. 469). And like many of the black females in Rhys's work, she is apparently able to bear pain stoically. "I never saw her cry" (p. 469), Antoinette adds.

But unlike the blacks in *Voyage in the Dark* or Rhys's other works, both private and public, we learn that Tia is also envious of Antoinette. That envy is clearly connected to Antoinette's meager economic superiority. When Tia sees the new pennies that "shine like gold," pennies given to Antoinette ironically by the black Christophine, she bets Antoinette that she cannot turn a somersault in the water. This particular episode is also referred to briefly by Rhys in the Black Exercise Book and seems to be based on an incident in Rhys's own life. When Antoinette is successful, Tia denies it and takes the money. Tia's corruption by the "false gold" releases in both girls the social and economic realities underlying their lives. Antoinette, in retaliation for Tia's theft, calls her a " 'cheating nigger' " (p. 470), reminding one of the vituperation she hurls at her friend Christophine later when she calls her a " ' "damned black devil from Hell" ' " (p. 540). In both cases, the underlying racial and economic situation perverts human affection and friendship just as Anna Morgan's sudden realization of her whiteness severs her from intimacy with Francine.

Tia's response to Antoinette repeats the calumnies that she has heard about Antoinette's family. She calls to Antoinette: "Old time white people nothing but white niggers now, and black nigger better than white nigger" (p. 470). Tia's retort places the family at the very bottom of the socioeconomic scale in Jamaica just as Antoinette's legal relationship to white men places her at the lowest level of the sexual hierarchy. That the situation in post-Emancipation Jamaica has been turned topsy-turvy is further illustrated when Tia takes Antoinette's dress, forcing the child to return home in the black child's garments which makes her "dirtier than usual" (p. 470) but, ironically, forces for the moment her mother's attention upon her. While Antoinette surmises that her mother is ashamed of her in Tia's dress, it extracts from the mother one of the few, if only caring acts she performs for her daughter: she makes certain that new fabric is procured for another dress for Antoinette.

Tia's betrayal is permanently impressed on the young white Creole girl's mind. That betrayal, accompanied by Antoinette's own identification and confounding of herself with Tia, becomes the final focus for Antoinette while Coulibri burns. As she turns from the sight of her burning home, she says:

Then, not so far off, I saw Tia and her mother and I ran to her, for she was all that was left of my life as it had been. We had eaten the same food, slept side by side, bathed in the same river. As I ran, I thought, I will live with Tia and I will be like her. Not to leave Coulibri. Not to go. Not. When I was close I saw the jagged stone in her hand but I did not see her throw it. I did not feel it either, only something wet, running down my face. I looked at her and I saw her face crumple up as she began to cry. We stared at each other, blood on my face, tears on hers. It was as if I saw myself. Like in a looking-glass. (p. 483)

In this scene, so strongly reminiscent of the crucified Christ and the tearful Mary Magdalene—and of Magdalene's own reversal—the white Creole child and the black Creole child become reflections of each other. Despite what their desires might be, they are determined to act and to be participants in situations which are determined by circumstances outside of themselves. They are the same and the complete opposites of each other—mirrors in which everything is both reflected and reversed. Antoinette's racial confusion, her desire to seek comfort and identify with one who has, probably because of race, already spurned her, reminds one of her later flight to Christophine after her betrayal by her husband. In the presence of Christophine, in Christophine's house, she is flooded by past memories of Christophine and then says: "The sky was dark blue through the dark green mango leaves, and I thought, 'This is my place and this is where I belong and this is where I wish to stay' " (p. 523).

That Antoinette's mother and Aunt Cora—both pre-Emancipation white Creole women—do not share this confusion is also made pointedly clear at the burning of Coulibri by two incidents. First, when Antoinette's mother desperately tries to return to the burning house for her parrot, it is only Aunt Cora's words that get her to leave. Cora says that the blacks are laughing at her, and warns, " 'Do not allow them to laugh at you' " (p. 481). Though crazed, Antoinette's mother still feels obliged to maintain the separation between herself and the blacks, to maintain a distance and dignity before them. Secondly, in front of the burning house, as the family attempts to escape, they are blocked by a belligerent black. It is Aunt Cora's sureness and her knowledge of them that saves the family. She threatens the blacks with a white "obeah"—the threat of burning in hell. Her tactic is very similar to Christophine's, who threatens Amelie with a "bellyache" and death if she does not behave. While the black man who has been threatening the family with a machete calls Aunt Cora an "old white jumby" and threatens to "throw her on the fire" (p. 483), his own present and real equivalent of burning in hell, he lets her go.

Both Cora and Antoinette's mother reveal an understanding of the behavior of the blacks, as the blacks do of them, that Antoinette does not have. Certainly the two incidents at Coulibri involving the two older women reveal that prior to Emancipation, there was a clearer understanding between the blacks and the whites. I do not mean to imply that in *Wide Sargasso Sea* there is a harking back to the "good old days" of slavery but rather that those caught in the middle of this historical and social change, unable to redefine themselves, unable to deal with the reversals, without an old order and yet with a new order that seems to suddenly involve "strangers," are at a loss. Hence, the breakdown of Tia's and Antoinette's friendship and the burning of Coulibri. Certainly Emancipation exacerbated the sense of loss and alienation with which Antoinette lives. She is not only isolated culturally but historically too.

In the persons of Tia, Christophine, and Sandi, all of them black, Antoinette receives or yearns for the only solace she gets in the world outside the convent. Spurned by her white mother she turns to them. But Tia betrays her, as she must. That betrayal, and her own confusion about it, has made a permanent mark on Antoinette—the scar that Antoinette says " 'did spoil me for my wedding day and all the other days and nights' " (p. 539). It emerges again in her last dream, the dream that suggests to the now-mad Antoinette the firing of Thornfield. Furthermore, at the end of that dream, Tia and Rochester become confounded in Antoinette's mind. In her dream, as Thornfield burns, Antoinette runs up to the battlements and sits quietly. She says:

Then I turned round and saw the sky. It was red and all my life was in it. I saw the grandfather clock and Aunt Cora's patchwork, all colours, I saw the orchids and the stephanotis and the jasmine and the tree of life in flames. I saw the chandelier and the red carpet downstairs and the bamboos and the tree ferns, the gold ferns and the silver, and the soft green velvet of the moss on the garden wall. I saw my doll's house and the books and the picture of the Miller's Daughter. I heard the parrot call as he did when he saw a stranger, *Qui est là? Qui est là?* And the man who hated me was calling too, Bertha! Bertha! The wind caught my hair and it streamed out like wings. It might bear me up, I thought, if I jumped to those hard stones. But when I looked over the edge I saw the pool at Coulibri. Tia was there. She beckoned to me and when I hesitated, she laughed. I heard her say, You frightened? And I heard the man's voice, Bertha! Bertha! All this I saw and heard in a fraction of a second. And the sky so red. Someone screamed and I thought, *Why did I scream?* I called 'Tia!' and jumped and woke. (p. 514)

While at the end of this dream Antoinette rehearses much of her life prior to her marriage, it is on Tia that the last call and focus rests. It is Tia's betrayals that have prefigured Rochester's.

The small black girl, caught, like all of the characters in *Wide Sargasso Sea,* in the devastating and destructive effects of colonialism and racial exploitation, is the first to rob Antoinette, as Rochester does later, and the first to betray a trust of love and friendship. Furthermore, her initial violation (taking the money and the dress) leads Antoinette to confirm her mother's indifference. " 'She is ashamed of me,' " Antoinette thinks to herself (p. 471). Tia's second violation (casting the stone) leaves the scar on Antoinette—a reminder of the burning of Coulibri and its after-effects—which does, despite Aunt Cora's words, spoil her. Though Tia is Antoinette's first intimate to show overt hate and the first to wound her, in her final call to Tia, one senses that Antoinette wishes for a synthesis: to return and to become whole with her other—the mirror of herself who sheds tears while Antoinette, Christlike, stands before her, reflecting her tears in blood. Later, when Antoinette asks: "And what does any one know about traitors, or why Judas did what he did?" (p. 529), her question, made apparently in reference to herself, recalls Tia at Coulibri.

While both black and white Creoles suffer because of the pre-existing and existing inequalities, with all of the resultant ramifications that Braithwaite describes,[1] they also suffer from the intervention of " 'these new ones,' " as Christophine calls the new wave of British colonialists represented in the extremes of Mason and Rochester. Mason, whose attitude toward the blacks reflects a benevolent paternalism, still cannot see them as functioning human beings, as capable of malice as they are of having a good time. It is Antoinette's mother, the widow of a slaveowner and the daughter of a slaveowner, as Mason himself points out, who expresses the existence of a subtle understanding between the Creole blacks and whites—an understanding which is based both on economics and on history. She says:

'The people here [meaning the blacks] hate us. They certainly hate me. . . .

'We were so poor then [prior to Mason's support] . . . we were something to laugh at. But we are not poor now. . . . You are not a poor man. Do you suppose that they don't know all about your estate in Trinidad? And the Antigua property? They talk about us without stopping. They invent stories about you, and lies about me. They try to find out what we eat every day.' (p. 475)

But when Mason interrupts to remind her that it was she who reprimanded him for using the epithet "nigger," she says, " 'You don't like, or even recognize, the good in them . . . and you won't believe in the other side' " (p. 475).

Mason's unwitting reply, apparently on the eve of the burning of Coulibri, is that the blacks are " 'too damn lazy to be dangerous' " (p. 475). But again, in her answer to him, Antoinette's mother refers to an understanding based on a long coexistence, an understanding unavailable to an interloper like Mason—or later, like Rochester. She says, " 'They are more alive than you are, lazy or not, and they can be dangerous and cruel for reasons you wouldn't understand' " (p. 475). Antoinette herself sums up the difference between her family and Mason. She says, "Then I looked . . . at Mr. Mason, so sure of himself, so without a doubt English. And at my mother, so without a doubt not English, but no white nigger either" (p. 477). It is Mason's stubborn ignorance which results in the first half of the Cosway tragedy—the burning of Coulibri, the death of Pierre and Antoinette's mother's resultant madness, which ultimately places her firmly in the hands of those whom she has defined as hating her.

While Mason finally believes that the blacks " 'are children' " who "wouldn't hurt a fly" (p. 477), Rochester's point of view is the complete opposite. He sees the blacks as savage, intimidating, too perceptive about his own behavior. Of his own wedding he says, "I played the part I was expected to play. . . . But I must have given a flawless performance. If I saw an expression of doubt or curiosity it was on a black face not a white one" (p. 502). Furthermore, Rochester is appalled by Antoinette's physical propinquity to them and apparently concerned with the possibility and probability of past miscegenation. Of his wife he says, "Creole of pure English descent she may be, but they [her eyes] are not English or European either" (p. 496). Later, more succinctly, when he notices a resemblance between his wife and Amelie, he entertains the thought that they might possibly be related and then adds: "It's even probable in this damned place" (p. 535).

While Mason's and Rochester's attitudes toward the blacks represent two polar views, they apparently share an equal abhorrence of miscegenation. When Antoinette mentions her rescue by her cousin Sandi from the torments of the two black children as she goes to the convent, she comments, "Once I would have said 'my cousin Sandi' but Mr. Mason's lectures had made me shy about my coloured relatives" (p. 487). This fear and disgust of miscegenation appears in Rhys most often in the newly arrived English. The Creole whites in Rhys are generally more relaxed about the subject—a further cause of friction between the two groups of whites. Whether the new colonialist is of Mason's ilk or of Rochester's, in *Wide Sargasso Sea* it makes no difference. In either case, his presence exacerbates the already precarious relationship among the Creoles.

None of the principals in *Wide Sargasso Sea* remain unaffected and unharmed by the underlying racial situation. Daniel Cosway, though, is the one most maddened by it. He owes his obsession and malevolence directly to his being racially "in-between," just as Antoinette is culturally and historically. He is at once a comic and pathetic character in his Iago-like role.

Edward Braithwaite points out that it was not only the white Creole who suffered from the West Indian cultural ambivalence. He notes that the field blacks on the plantations at least had the opportunity to pursue their African customs, unmonitored by the whites. But those blacks who Braithwaite refers to as "elite blacks" and the free colored "conceived of visibility through the lenses of their masters' already uncertain vision as a form of 'greyness'—an imitation of an imitation. Whenever the opportunity made it possible, they and their descendents rejected or disowned their own culture, becoming, like their masters, 'mimic-men' " (p. 308). Certainly the force and comedy of Daniel Cosway's letter to Rochester and his language and posture come from this "mimic-man" pose. He, perhaps more than Antoinette, serves as both the victim and symbol of the cultural dichotomy in the West Indies. Neither black nor white, neither really free nor slave, he suffers the same cultural perdition as does Antoinette. His response however, unlike Antoinette's masochistic passivity, is an active malevolence, similar in fact to Rochester's. He becomes, through the accident and fault of his parents, as much a devil as Rochester. In fact, Daniel Cosway serves as a "colored" mirror for Rochester in much the same way that Tia does for Antoinette.

When Rochester visits him, Cosway begins his diatribe with reference to " 'that damn devil my father' " (p. 532), and reveals that he is as obsessed with the question of not receiving love from his father as is Rochester. Like Rochester, he curses and rejects his father and like Rochester, he cannot let him go. In describing old Cosway's burial tablet he says " 'I can still see that tablet before my eyes because I go to look at it often' " (p. 532). And, like Rochester, Cosway accuses his father of crimes (e.g., pride and lack of mercy) that he eventually himself commits. While despising him, he becomes him.

As Cosway continues to talk about his father, he reveals that his own love-hate for him is confounded with his own confused feelings about being part black. He also reveals that like Rochester, the hurt caused by the paternal rejection comes to be translated into an interest in money and envy of a more beloved, and more richly bestowed upon, brother. In his talk with Rochester, he describes his last visit to his father:

'Sixteen years old I was and anxious. I start very early. I walk all the way to Coulibri—five six hours it take. He don't refuse to see me; he receive me very cool and calm and first thing he tell me is I'm always pestering him for money. This because sometimes I ask help to buy a pair of shoes and such. Not to go barefoot like a nigger. Which I am not. He look at me like I was dirt and I get angry too. "I have my rights after all," I tell him and you know what he do? He laugh in my face. When he finished laughing he call me what's-your-name. "I can't remember all their names . . ." he says . . . "It's you yourself call me Daniel," I tell him. "I'm no slave like my mother was." ' (pp. 532–533)

That description is immediately followed by Cosway's reference to his brother. He says, " 'Then there is my half brother Alexander, coloured like me but not unlucky like me, he will want to tell you all sorts of lies. He was the old man's favourite and he prosper right from the start. Yes, Alexander is a rich man now but he keep quiet about it. Because he prosper he is two-faced. He won't speak against white people' " (p. 533). Like Esau, which Daniel says is his real name, he feels tricked out of his birthright and cursed by his father. Daniel ends his diatribe of hatred of and hurt by his father by attacking Antoinette, an abbreviated version of Rochester's action. His parting words to Rochester also suggest a kindred fixation with miscegenation. He says, " 'Give my love to your wife—my sister. . . . You are not the first to kiss her pretty face. Pretty face, soft skin, pretty colour—not yellow like me. But my sister just the same . . .' " (p. 534, Rhys's ellipses). In some ways, Daniel Cosway gives voice to the darkest and meanest feelings that Rochester harbors. He functions as a kind of comic devil, externalizing and venting a parody of Rochester's feelings. But whereas Rochester's vengeance finally rests solely on Antoinette, Cosway's feelings about women include the entire sex; " 'demons incarnate' " he calls them (p. 534).

In *Wide Sargasso Sea,* the past has betrayed the present through the institution of slavery and the inequality of the races; blacks betray whites; whites betray blacks; coloreds betray both blacks and whites; and the Europeans betray the white Creoles. Mirroring this cultural and historical failure is the betrayal of the child by the parent—a failure that is as pernicious as the larger cultural and historical one, a failure that the child can neither forgive nor forget. Just as Cosway cannot leave the memory of the hurt done to him by his father, so does Rochester perpetually return to his similar wound. Even toward the end, when Rochester is making plans to return to England, he fantasizes about writing a letter to his father that reads " 'I know now that you planned this because you wanted to be rid of me. You had no love at all for me. Nor had my brother' " (p. 558).

Whereas *Voyage in the Dark* is concerned with a particular failure of a step-parent to a child, in *Wide Sargasso Sea* all the major characters, except Christophine, suffer from a parent's failure and, like Rhys herself, from the pain of seeing another sibling preferred. The failures of the parents lead to irreparable schisms between them and their children and the destruction or the moral corruption of those offspring.

Furthermore, in one way or another, the children all repeat their parents' failings: Antoinette in her repetition of her mother's madness, Daniel Cosway in the repetition of his father's crimes and Rochester in his victimization of and denial of love to Antoinette. These spurned children become either passive victims like Antoinette and her mother or victimizers, like Rochester and Cosway. Perhaps the difference is one of gender. Certainly the men equate the lack of love from their fathers with a concomitant monetary deprivation; they turn to money as a perverted symbol or substitute for love.

Wide Sargasso Sea is comprised of personal and cultural failures and betrayals. In the world of Rhys's novel, the personal betrayal mirrors the failure of history, the failure of a society and culture that creates parents unable to save their children from repeating their errors. And in *Wide Sargasso Sea*, those failures seem peculiarly tied to the institutions of slavery and racial exploitation, to colonization, and to patriarchal systems and sexual exploitation.

10

The Dialogue between Good and Evil

The only character in *Wide Sargasso Sea* who is not guilty of betrayal of others is Christophine. Indeed, her only act of betrayal is toward herself and her own principles when she relents to Antoinette's demand for obeah medicine—an act of love that results in her own persecution by Rochester. She is the most sympathetic and unflawed character in the novel and probably reflects its point of view most accurately.

Like the women she serves, Christophine too is an outsider, but one of a different order. The two Cosway women, mother and daughter, incorporate a hopeless and passive colonial past with their passive personalities. But Christophine represents female power and mystery, wisdom and autonomy, strengths she vainly attempts to encourage in Antoinette.

That Christophine's gifts and her separateness are important, both to Antoinette and to *Wide Sargasso Sea* as a whole, is apparent in the strong focus Antoinette gives to her description of Christophine in the opening pages of her narrative, a description that focuses on Christophine's specialness and which acts as a counterpoint to Antoinette's description of her mother. She says:

Her songs were not like Jamaican songs, and she was not like the other women.

She was much blacker—blue-black with a thin face and straight features. She wore a black dress, heavy gold earrings and a yellow handkerchief—carefully tied with the two high points in front. No other negro woman wore black, or tied her handkerchief Martinique fashion. . . .

The girls from the bayside who sometimes helped with the washing and cleaning were terrified of her. That, I soon discovered, was why they came at all—for she never paid them. Yet they brought presents of fruit and vegetables and after dark I often heard low voices from the kitchen. (pp. 467–68)

Christophine, in her blackness, is linked to an older and purer African past; her link to Africa is part of her power as an obeah priestess. Even her garments suggest a solemnity and importance befitting her role as priestess.

Christophine, like most household blacks in nineteenth-century Jamaica, maintains a veneer of Christianity but her links to black African religion remain strong and she is as much the object of "talk" as is Antoinette's mother. When Antoinette's family returns to the newly repaired Coulibri after her mother's marriage to Mason, Antoinette says, "But it didn't feel the same. . . . It was their talk about Christophine that changed Coulibri, not the repairs or the new furniture or the strange faces. Their talk about Christophine and obeah changed it" (p. 474). Antoinette has also overheard a white woman attribute her mother's wealthy marriage to Christophine's obeah powers. Antoinette says that this woman said it "mockingly" but adds that "other people were saying it—and meaning it" (p. 473). It may be this memory that prompts Antoinette, as a reflection of her mother, to approach Christophine later for help in keeping Rochester.

Antoinette's early description of Christophine's room indicates both her attraction to and terror of the black woman's power of obeah. In the first part of her description she depicts the Christian and Europeanized veneer of Christophine's possessions. She says, "I knew her room so well—the pictures of the Holy Family and the prayer for a happy death. She had a bright patchwork counterpane, a broken-down press for her clothes, and my mother had given her an old rocking-chair" (p. 474). But then she adds:

Yet one day when I was waiting there I was suddenly very much afraid. The door was open to the sunlight, someone was whistling near the stables, but I was afraid. I was certain that hidden in the room (behind the old black press?) there was a dead man's dried hand, white chicken feathers, a cock with its throat cut, dying slowly, slowly. Drop by drop the blood was falling into a red basin and I imagined I could hear it. No one had ever spoken to me about obeah—but I knew what I would find if I dared to look. (p. 474)

Antoinette, like many white Creoles, knows that beneath the Christianized surface lies another culture, another religion, the memory of another continent, one that is cloaked in mystery and power. It is this same mystery and power that Rochester himself recognizes and which he seeks to control and conquer, much like the earlier white colonizers and missionaries themselves.

Edward Braithwaite points out that perhaps the greatest conflict between the black and white Creoles arose over religion, an easily recognizable symbol of control and black autonomy overtly represented in the person of the obeah man or woman. Braithwaite writes:

Equally significant were the black and/or slave preachers, doctors and obeah-men. . . . [They] were almost entirely independent of white control and contributed enormously to the physical and psychological well-being of the slave population and therefore to the health of the society as a whole. Slave doctors usually confined their work to their own particular plantation. A good obeah-man would have influence throughout the district. These obeah-men (and women) received a great deal of attention from the white legislators of the island. . . .[1]

Braithwaite also discusses Clause X of the Acts of Assembly of 1769.[2] Its details are reminiscent of Antoinette's recollection of Christophine's room and its imagined artifacts and reinforce the sense that the obeah person had contact with, and control over, the devil and evil. The purpose of Clause X was " 'to prevent the many Mischiefs that may hereafter arise from the wicked Art of Negroes, going under the Appellation of Obeah Men and Women.' " To that purpose, Clause X provided that:

'any Negro or other Slave, who shall pretend to any supernatural Power, and be detected making use of any Blood, Feathers, Parrots Beaks, Dogs Teeth, Alligators Teeth, broken Bottles, Grave Dirt, Rum, Egg-shells or any other Materials relative to the practice of Obeah or Witchcraft, in order to delude and impose on the Minds of others, shall upon Condition thereof, before two Magistrates and three Freeholders, suffer Death or Transportation. . . .' (Braithwaite, p. 162)

That whites also used obeah at times, either because of their own belief in it or because it offered an easy way to control the blacks, seems to have been the case and provides another example of the ways in which black and white Creole cultures intermixed.

Part of the job of the European missionaries and priests in the West Indies was to convert the blacks to Christianity without raising questions about the rightness of slavery or apartheid. The greatest religious obstacle to this conversion was the obeah man or woman. Braithwaite writes:

To achieve this [the conversion of the blacks], it was necessary for the missionaries to pluck out, root and branch, all vestiges of heathen (i.e., African) practices from those over whom they had acquired influence. The drum had to go. The dance had to go. A plurality of wives or women had to be put out of mind. Above all, obeah had to be confronted and defeated. (pp. 255–256)

In *Wide Sargasso Sea,* the conflict between Rochester and Christophine becomes more than a conflict of personality or personal interests. It includes the conflict between the underlying principles and aspects of their two societies, represented by their respective religions. Certainly, Christophine, who has already been persecuted for obeah under English law, must be well aware of this. It is through English law against obeah that Christophine is finally controlled by Rochester. And in their final and long confrontation, they actually argue about religion and the differences between Rochester's god and Christophine's "spirits."

This religious and political conflict is integral to the struggle between Rochester and Christophine. It is implicit in the episode in which Rochester becomes lost in the forest. Rochester goes out after Christophine has said she will leave and after Antoinette declares her own alien position in the West Indies (" 'Between you [the Creole black and the white English] I often wonder who I am and where is my country and where do I belong . . . ,' " she says. p. 519) Rochester goes for a walk and discovers in the forest the ruins of a French pavé road and the remains of a stone house overgrown with wild orange and rose trees. Most significant are the "little bunches of flowers tied with grass" that he notices under the orange tree. Later, Baptiste begrudgingly tells Rochester, who has asked him if the spot is inhabited by a ghost or zombie, that a priest " 'lived here a long time ago' " (p. 521).

That evening Rochester looks up obeah in a book on the West Indies; the passage he reads recapitulates what he has seen in the woods. The passage also suggests the conflict between whites and blacks over obeah and the reluctance of blacks to give information about obeah to whites who are " *'sometimes credulous'* " (p. 522; Rhys's italics).

If the conflict between white and black in the Indies is symbolized by the differing religions, then the sight of the ruined priest's house, an obvious defeat in this contest, is terrifying to Rochester. The very ruins of the priest's place have become "obeahized" by the blacks and the site itself turned back once more to tropical forest, the power of which Rochester recognizes later, toward the end of his narrative, when he recalls the vision of the honeymoon house on the island. He says:

But the sadness I felt looking at the shabby white house—I wasn't prepared for that. More than ever before it strained away from the black snake-like forest. Louder and more desperately it called: Save me from destruction, ruin and desolation. Save me from the long slow death by ants. But what are you doing here you folly? So near the forest. Don't you know that this is a dangerous place? And that the dark forest always wins? Always. If you don't, you soon will, and I can do nothing to help. (p. 561)

Despite Antoinette's overt fears about obeah and Rochester's less articulated ones, ironically, it is Christophine who most personifies Christian virtues—a gentle humanism and pragmatism, and a practicality about economic and emotional survival. She has early provided Antoinette with a wise and liberal mothering, often documented by Antoinette in memories of her childhood. She has even provided protection for Antoinette's mother, who declares that without Christophine they would not have lived. Furthermore, Christophine is the only character who is able to recognize the humanity of both black and white, Creole and non-Creole. Even of Rochester she says, when counselling Antoinette about how to deal with him: " 'Ask him pretty for some of your own money, the man not bad-hearted, he give it' " (p. 524) and " 'The man not a bad man, even if he love money . . .' " (p. 527).

In her advice to Antoinette, Christophine articulates her belief in her own authority and the principles by which she lives. She reveals herself to be self-supporting, independent of men, and a believer in the truth—which is what she advises Antoinette to tell Rochester in place of using obeah. She also expresses the need for courage, especially for women.

Ultimately Christophine's advice to Antoinette supposes a lack of passivity, an autonomy and courage, and a commitment to the truth. Not only does Christophine give Antoinette direction but her behavior itself exhibits a code of decency that no other character, save the Mother Superior, manifests. As long as Christophine maintains power over Antoinette, Antoinette is able to maintain power over herself and to stay within the realm of sanity. It is only as Christophine's hold on her wanes and hence her own hold on herself and reality, that Antoinette lapses into madness.

Christophine, whose name suggests St. Christopher—the bearer of the infant Christ, sees the care and survival of Antoinette as her own mission. Rochester's struggle with Christophine becomes a struggle over who will have power over Antoinette. This becomes apparent in their last confrontation, a scene which is one of the most climactic in *Wide Sargasso Sea* because it offers Rochester his last chance to change the doomed nature of his relationship with his wife and offers him the last chance to stay within the community of Christian faith, love, and harmony.

Christophine pleads for Antoinette, but Rochester shows no mercy. In her plea, Christophine shows an intimate understanding of Antoinette and of her Creole nature. "She is Creole girl, and she have the sun in her," Christophine says (p. 555). Furthermore, she reviews what she has been doing to nurse Antoinette back to health, ministrations that she says are destroyed when Rochester tells Antoinette that he does not love her.

Christophine's argument is an impassioned statement of love and for love; but Rochester interprets it as malicious, motivated by a desire for Antoinette's money and property, which he coolly asserts " 'belongs to me now' " (p. 556). Finally, Rochester gains the mastery with his threat of the police and his assertion that " 'there must be some law and order even in this God-forsaken island' " (p. 556). But when he reveals his plan to consult the Spanish Town doctors because Antoinette is " 'not well' " (p. 557), Christophine identifies him with the Devil and Antoinette with her mother. She says, " 'The doctors say what you tell them to say . . . She will be like her mother. You do that for money? But you wicked like Satan self' " (p. 557). In Antoinette's earlier indirect identification of Rochester with the devil of her dreams, he is a devil connected to sex and to male power. Christophine's identification of Rochester with Satan is connected to money and theft and to an abnegation of love and mercy; Grace Poole's later identification of Rochester and the devil suggests his basic violation of the concept of Christian charity.

To Christophine, Rochester's triumph and the suffering of Antoinette and her mother suggest a Godless universe, a view that Antoinette herself has expressed earlier. When Rochester questions her about her belief in God, Antoinette asserts that " 'it doesn't matter . . . what I believe or you believe, because we can do nothing about it, we are like these' " (p. 535), and she flicks a dead moth from the table.

In his dialogue with Christophine, Rochester identifies his own goals and self-righteous plans with his God. And he also identifies that God with his own British and male values. Christophine's assertion that " 'This is free country and I am free woman' " (p. 557), is a brave and spirited gesture that reveals her personal courage and strength but which, pitted against Rochester's God and British law, simply is not true, at least not in any political sense.

The contest between Rochester and Christophine dramatizes the essentially Manichean world of *Wide Sargasso Sea,* a world in which the forces of light, like Christophine, battle courageously and helplessly against the evil of self-interested and self-righteous enforcers of law like Rochester. There is no explanation or reason known, as Sister Marie Augustine has told the young Antoinette, for the ascendency of the devil and the forces of evil.

There is a strong dichotomy in *Wide Sargasso Sea* between good and evil, more so than in Rhys's other novels. But the "evil" is far more complexly represented as is the "good." Even Christophine has more depth and psychological complexity than, say, Francine in *Voyage in the Dark.* Francine serves a function in the mind of Anna Morgan but she has very little "reality" outside that function. But Christophine has a reality and existence outside of Antoinette's need for her.

Before he leaves for England, Rochester is the apparent "winner." He has gained legal and economic ascendency even though he has driven his wife mad; he maintains legal possession of her. However, there is in the concluding section of his narrative the suggestion that he is not the spiritual winner. He is a man forever bereft of what is important and essential for human existence. In a nostalgic and poetic interlude, a stream of consciousness toward the end of his narrative, Rochester creates a pastiche in his mind of the past events, including some of Christophine's words to him and some of the incidents shared with Antoinette. While Rochester appears to be cool and capable of severing all ties with the past and his wife, one sees that he cannot escape the memory and implications of his argument with Christophine, a dialogue which he continues in her absence. Her voice has become so internalized that he continues to remonstrate with it.

He recalls Christophine's last words to him when she says that Antoinette loves him terribly and that she is " 'thirsty for him' " (p. 560). In this later interior monologue, Rochester says that Antoinette is thirsty for anyone, although he has witnessed her love for him and her desire to please him. He needs to believe that she does not love him and only him. As his monologue continues, he reveals that his earlier ambivalence toward Antoinette has turned to malicious hatred. He vows to break her and deny her all sources of sensual pleasure—the sun, clothes, love. And he vows that though Antoinette has declared her love for her island, "this is the last she'll see of it" (p. 560). Clearly Rochester's desire, as Christophine has divined, is to "break" Antoinette.

While Antoinette has withdrawn into a madness that protects her from Rochester, Rochester turns to an egoistic mania for possession—like the devil desiring souls. He says:

I'll watch for one tear, one human tear. Not that blank hating moonstruck face. I'll listen. . . . [Rhys's ellipses] If she says good-bye, perhaps adieu. . . . If she too says it, or weeps, I'll take her in my arms, my lunatic. She's mad but *mine, mine*. What will I care for gods or devils or for Fate itself. If she smiles or weeps or both. *For me*.

Antoinetta—I can be gentle too. Hide your face. Hide yourself but in my arms. You'll soon see how gentle. My lunatic. My mad girl. (pp. 560–61)

As Rochester leaves the island, he is again reminded of Christophine and this time, confirming the depth and opposition inherent in their "argument," it is he who calls her devil. He says, "I could feel his [Baptiste's] dislike and contempt. The same contempt as that devil's when she said, 'Taste my bull's blood.' Meaning that will make you a man. Perhaps" (p. 562). In his only reference to the devil, Rochester, like Antoinette, makes an association of the devil with a negative "sexual" experience: Christophine's possible contempt for his manhood and sexual prowess.

Rochester then says of Antoinette that "I'd forgotten her for the moment" (p. 562). But that he cannot forget her or the sense of loss and isolation that is now his permanent possession is indicated when he follows that statement with a declaration of his own confusion and loss. He says, "So I shall never understand why, suddenly bewilderingly, I was certain that everything I had imagined to be truth was false. False. Only the magic and the dream are true—all the rest's a lie. Let it go. Here is the secret. Here" (p. 562). Rochester then hears a voice that tells him the secret "is lost" and that *"Those who know it cannot tell it"* (p. 562, Rhys's italics). And again expressing his need to possess and his self-delusion, he answers, "Not lost. I had found it in a hidden place and I'd keep it, hold it fast. As I'd hold her" (p. 562).

While Rochester attempts to free himself of the influence of the West Indies, an influence contained in the persons of the two Creole women, one black and one white, it becomes clear that he cannot. He attempts to obliterate them and their influence by possessing them—a form of obeah too. But instead, he is left with a permanent sense of loss and a lasting incomprehension of the mystery: in personal terms, the mystery of passion, feeling, and truth; in political terms, of the West Indies and the colonized; and in sexual terms, of women.

Rochester's desire for possession, unlike Antoinette's, is not motivated by inordinate love but rather, as in obeah, the desire to possess the soul and spirit, the desire to destroy the supposed enemy. Rochester believes that by driving Antoinette mad, he has gained permanent possession of her. Instead, he is only able to control her physically. Her madness has placed her and all that she represents permanently beyond his reach. Antoinette's retreat into madness and Rochester's mad retreat into his male prerogatives of possession of his wife and her property has clarified the fact that the distance between them cannot be resolved. That Antoinette too has not known the ways to repair the breach does not signify that she has not tried. On the other hand, the very nature of a man like Rochester and the world he represents insures that the connection between the two is impossible, despite the valiant attempts of Christophine.

That Christophine is finally thwarted in her attempt to save Antoinette by the English law aligns that law with the cold and male person of Rochester. That the essentially "Christian" Christophine should lose in the contest with Rochester verifies the earlier words of Godfrey: " 'The devil prince of this world.' "

The struggle represented by Rochester and Christophine is present in all of Rhys's work as a subterranean motif. Underlying all the paralyses, the "personal" problems and dilemmas of her heroines, there is always in Rhys this conflict or struggle between those with power and those without it, between the aggressive and sadistic male and the passive and masochistic female. But in *Wide Sargasso Sea*, the struggle is played out on a more overt philosophical and political level. The defeat of Christophine is therefore more devastating than say, the collapse of Marya Zelli, Anna

Morgan, Julia Martin or Sasha Jansen, simply because, in Christophine, Rhys has created a full character who is wise, intelligent, kind, and courageous, a woman who is willing to fight for a code of decency. That she fails presumes that there is no room for such a person to succeed, at least not in the world controlled and represented by the English male colonialists and their laws—both the marriage laws that obliterate women and the laws governing the colonized, a group with which the women become identified.

In *Wide Sargasso Sea,* the woman is no more and no less than a colony, to be caught and possessed, enclosed and controlled by the male governor—a conclusion that leaves a void, empty of love and meaning. That Rochester and those like him are blind to these consequences is expressed ironically, in the closing words of his narrative: Rochester watches the young boy accompanying Baptiste cry because he wants to go with Rochester to England. When he is told that the boy loves him, Rochester says in words that echo King Lear: "Who would have thought that any boy would cry like that. For nothing. Nothing. . . ." (p. 565, Rhys's ellipses).

One may agree with Christophine that it is preferable to tell the truth and to try to make the other understand, that it is better to resist and to have courage; but in Rhys's picture of the world in *Wide Sargasso Sea,* it is the passive Antoinette who is more accurate in her assessment of the lack of power of the weak. She thinks, as she argues with Christophine, that "it is always too late for truth" (p. 528). And later, when nevertheless she does try to make Rochester know and understand the truth of her own history, as she has promised Christophine she will do, she concludes hopelessly:

'I have said all I want to say. I have tried to make you understand. But nothing has changed. . . .

I will tell you anything you wish to know, but in a few words because words are no use, I know that now.' (p. 540)

Christophine's point of view encompasses what is right and good and what is necessary for personal survival, if not victory. Antoinette's declaration reflects the hopelessness and impossibility of communication with the other and the irreconcilable nature of the differences delineated in *Wide Sargasso Sea* and suggested in its progenitor, *Voyage in the Dark.*

Though she was 90 when she died, the past remained vivid for Jean Rhys. Her letters and private notebooks reveal that, as with many good writers, it was often easily available to her. Associations seemed to come with a certain ease and randomness. One sees in the Black Exercise Book how an image triggers the desire to recapitulate, and how recorded memories became the stuff of her fiction. One sees how a common phrase turns into atmosphere, how a cliché becomes a choric voice of fate and inevitability, and how the remembered detail, once retrieved, actualizes the suffering of her heroines.

Both of Jean Rhys's West Indian novels were written and published while she lived in England. The first, *Voyage in the Dark,* representing her own voyage out, was originally drafted when the young Ella Williams had only recently left home to become a stranger in a country that had figured as the elevated myth of the Motherland of her youth. The second, *Wide Sargasso Sea,* representing perhaps her "return," was written more than half a century later, after the writer Jean Rhys had lived most of her life in the harsh reality of England and more than a quarter of a century since she'd last seen home.

Only in its opposite, England, with its distance from and its contrast to her island, could Dominica assume its own mythological function for Rhys. Being in England allowed her to encapsulate it and define it, and finally, in her art, to redeem it for herself. The revivifying image of the island came to represent, for Rhys, writing itself. The contemplation of her youth there recalled her to the act of writing and its restorative powers.

Though Christophine's voice may represent the philosophical point of view of *Wide Sargasso Sea,* the dual voices of Antoinette and Rochester represent the whole and considered experience of Jean Rhys herself, an experience that includes the life of a post-Victorian colonial woman and the inevitable emotional upheaval suffered by the immigrant who dreams of home. If, in *Wide Sargasso Sea,* Antoinette's voice is hopeless about the reconciliation of the opposites presented in the novel, the very existence of her counterparted voice, the voice of Rochester, indicates the reconciliation of those opposites in Rhys herself and the recognition of the myth and the reality of both her homes.

Notes

INTRODUCTION

1. "Black Exercise Book," fol. 14, Jean Rhys Collection, McFarlin Library, University of Tulsa. All further references to this notebook are included in the text.

The Black Exercise Book, some 30 folio pages in length, was kept by Rhys in pencil. It is at times most difficult to read—often disjointed and with virtually no punctuation. In most quotations from the Black Exercise Book, I have tried to stay as close as possible to Rhys's punctuation. However, I have inserted periods where she clearly intended them, replaced the ampersand with "and," and added a few commas and quotation marks only where the text becomes too difficult to follow without them; I have added apostrophes to contractions and included obvious omissions in brackets.

2. Elizabeth Vreeland, "Jean Rhys: The Art of Fiction LXIV" (an interview), *Paris Review,* 21, no. 76 (Fall 1979): 218–237.

3. David Plante, *Difficult Women: A Memoir of Three* (New York: Atheneum, 1983), p. 37.

4. *Voyage in the Dark* appears though, to be a different case. It was apparently published before Rhys kept the Black Exercise Book (see note 6 below) and, compared to the other works listed, only small phrases are repeated in the notebook, suggesting that Rhys may have internalized some of the lines in her earlier fiction—a suggestion that is borne out by Rhys's habit, both in interviews and within the Black Exercise Book itself, of repeating herself and using certain phrases again and again.

5. Mary Lou Emery, in "Modernism and the Marginal Woman: A Sociocritical Approach to the Novels of Jean Rhys" (Ph.D. diss., Stanford University, 1951), comments on the connections between the young Rhys's experience with Mr. Howard, the short story "Goodbye Marcus, Goodbye Rose," and an unpublished story, "The Birthday Party" (also in the McFarlin Library). Emery does not discuss Rhys's extensive use of material in the Black Exercise Book.

6. Until recently, the University of Tulsa's description of the Jean Rhys holdings dated the Black Exercise Book: "Uncertain, though early—i.e., 1920–1930." In answer to my initial queries and doubts about their dating, Caroline Swinson, Curator of Literary Manuscripts and Art, contacted Dr. Thomas Staley, who was highly instrumental in acquiring the collection for the University of Tulsa. Ms. Swinson informed me that the collection description was done by a graduate student of Dr. Staley's and that Dr. Staley was unable at that time to comment on the accuracy of the dating. In August 1985 the McFarlin Library issued a new

"Guide to the Jean Rhys Collection" which corrects some of the dating and organizes the material more coherently. In this later version of the holdings description, the Black Exercise Book is dated, "Late 1930's"; the guide acknowledges the help of readers' notes in making some of the emendations that appear in it.

However, within the Black Exercise Book, as I discovered, there are several references which place at least sections of the manuscript within a time frame that is certainly later than 1929 and almost certainly within the year 1938. Some of those references are explained below:

Rhys refers in one passage to the Mother Superior of the convent school she attended and apparently refers to a visit she paid to the Mother Superior on her return trip to Dominica in 1936. She writes: "I saw her again two years and realised at once how right I'd been to love her." (fol. 18) If we assume that Rhys meant "two years *ago*," as seems more than likely, then the Black exercise Book was kept after 1936, about 1938.

There is only one problem with this assumption. Further on, Rhys writes in the notebook:

Then she [the Mother Superior] said I hear you've written a book. Will you send it to me as I wish to read it. You wouldn't like it I said. I will judge that for myself she said. No no you wouldn't like it. I wrote some stories I'll send you those.

But I couldn't get a copy of the stories. She died in a few months as she said and I was sorry then that I hadn't sent her the book she wanted to see. (fol. 19)

In 1938 Rhys had already published three novels plus a book of short stories, which makes her reference to "a" book confusing, although the last line in which Rhys refers to "the book she wanted to see" suggests that Rhys had written others. (In the new McFarlin guide, the reader's notes of Françoise Chartier are included. She also notes this reference to the meeting with the Mother Superior as indicating a post–1936 date.)

There are, however, some other inclusions within the notebook that point to its dating. Rhys mentions her daughter Maryvonne (fol. 35) who was born in 1922. Other entries in the notebook suggest that Rhys was living at the time of its composition with her second husband, Leslie Tilden Smith. For example, there is a dialogue with "L" (Leslie?) and a seeming "story" about a Mr. Smith. However, in her reader's note Françoise Chartier questions whether "L" might not be Jean Lenglet, Rhys's first husband. Chartier makes note of a dialogue that follows a description by Rhys of an experience that happened to her on the Côte d'Azur. Of the experience, Chartier says, it "might have occurred after JR separated from Ford but may, of course, have been written later." Following Rhys's description of the experience, there is, as Chartier describes it, "a dialogue between the narrator and L. (Lenglet?)."

My own feeling is that "L" most probably refers to Rhys's second husband, Leslie Tilden Smith. The description of the Côte d'Azur experience is written in a language and style that suggests a distance of time between the experience and the present. The language is evocative, charged, and nostalgic. Following that, the tone changes and Rhys writes about wanting to "write a story about the English attitude to women writers." She recalls a volume of short stories, written by a woman, that she read after she "got back to England" (fol. 49) and then reports a dialogue between herself and "L" in which they discuss that female author and a critic who dislikes women writers. The dialogue almost certainly occurs in England and "L's" familiarity with English critics (Tilden Smith was a publisher's reader) and the fact that Rhys never lived in England with Lenglet, nor ever based characters on him with such an "English" quality to their speech, suggests that "L" is more likely Tilden Smith. According to most sources, Rhys and Tilden Smith had begun living together by about 1929.

Rhys also makes mention of her reading of Richard Hughes's novel, *A High Wind in Jamaica* (originally published with the title *The Innocent Voyage*), identifying herself with the sexually abused child Margaret. Hughes's novel was published in 1929; since Rhys appears to be writing about the novel from some distance of time, this conclusively marks the Black Exercise Book as later than 1929.

Rhys used both covers as front covers of the Black Exercise Book. In other words, she initiated writing from both the front and the back. The shorter section constitutes a long description which appears almost verbatim in a flashback in *Good Morning, Midnight* which was published in 1939. Chartier also comments about the use of this material in *Good Morning, Midnight*. In addition, in the longer section Rhys refers to a novel in progress "about Paris" which may very well have been *Good Morning, Midnight*.

In sum, we can say that the notebook was definitely kept after 1929, and, if we rely on the reference to the Mother Superior, in 1938, two years after Rhys's return from Dominica.

Aside from the problems in dating the Black Exercise Book, there is the problem of its disjointedness and difficult decipherability. As I worked with the notebook, it became clear to me that several sections had been placed in incorrect sequence, an error that would not be immediately apparent because of the sketchy quality of the entire book. My work in rearranging the notebook into its proper sequence was done with the generous help of Caroline Swinson, Curator of Art and Manuscripts of the McFarlin Library. Her understanding of the physical construction of the notebook, as well as her perceptive deciphering of Jean Rhys's handwriting, were invaluable to me in ascertaining the notebook's correct sequence. Since the notebook pages are un-numbered, all further references in the text are to folio pages.

7. Telephone interview with David Plante, 21 May 1983.

8. Jean Rhys, *Smile Please* (London: André Deutsch, 1979), p. 11. All further references appear in the text.

9. Letter from M.R. Bateman, Perse School for Girls, 17 May 1983. Concerning the discrepancy about Rhys's age, David Plante said he wondered why no one had ever contacted the Perse School; it was at his suggestion that I did so.

10. Letter from Richard O'Donoghue, Administrator-Registrar, Royal Academy of Dramatic Art, 14 June 1983.

11. Letter from Dr. M.K. Kappers-den Hollander, Universiteit van Amsterdam, 14 June 1983. Dr. Kappers-den Hollander confirmed the 1890 birthdate in a phone conversation with Jean Rhys's daughter, who lives in the Netherlands.

12. This line is, however, confusing because Rhys's birthday, according to Francis Wyndham and Diana Melly in their edition of her selected letters, was August 24. See *Jean Rhys Letters, 1931–1966* (London: Andre Deutsch, 1984),

p. 13. In one letter to Wyndham, she says she was born in August (p. 183). In answer to my inquiry, Francis Wyndham writes that Rhys "always gave August 24th as her birthday . . . and that it also appears on earlier forms, visas, passports etc. that have survived." He further writes that he knows of no reason why Rhys might have implied a July 9th birthdate. (Letter, 11 October 1985.)

Wyndham and Melly's long-awaited collection was published when this study was virtually completed. While many of the letters referred to here were studied in manuscript form, if the letter appears in Wyndham and Melly's collection, the note refers to the published edition and appears in the text with the abbreviation *JRL*. Wyndham and Melly have at times normalized Rhys's punctuation. When the letters were used in manuscript form, I have kept Rhys's original punctuation. Differences in my transcription and theirs are described in the notes.

Jean Rhys Letters, 1931–1966, is particularly rich in letters from Rhys while she was writing *Wide Sargasso Sea.* Her letters to her daughter, Maryvonne Moerman and to her friend Peggy Kirkaldy, as well as letters to Francis Wyndham, Diana Athill and Selma Vaz Dias, illuminate her life during the time between the appearance of *Good Morning, Midnight* and *Wide Sargasso Sea.*

13. Francis Wyndham, "Introduction," in *Wide Sargasso Sea* (New York: W.W. Norton, 1966), p. 10.

14. A. Alvarez, "The Best Living English Novelist," *New York Times Book Review,* 17 March 1974: 6–7.

15. Louis James, *Jean Rhys* (London: Longman Group, 1978).

16. Thomas F. Staley, *Jean Rhys: A Critical Study* (Austin: University of Texas Press, 1979).

CHAPTER 1

1. Joseph Sturge and Thomas Harvey, *The West Indies in 1837: Being the Journal of a Visit to Antigua, Montserrat, Dominica, St. Lucia, Barbados, and Jamaica* (London: Hamilton, Adams, 1838), p. 10.

2. *Voyage in the Dark* in *Jean Rhys: The Complete Novels* (New York: W.W. Norton, 1985), p. 9. All further references to this book are from this edition and are included in the text.

3. "The Day They Burned The Books" in *Tigers Are Better Looking* (André Deutsch, 1968; rpt. Middlesex: Penguin Books, 1972), p. 41. All further references to this story are from this edition and are included in the text.

4. James Froude, *The English in the West Indies* (London: Longmans, Green, 1888), pp. 140–141. All further references to this volume are included in the text.

5. "Temps Perdi" in *Penguin Modern Stories I* (Middlesex: Penguin Books, 1969).

6. Letter received from Jean Rhys, 5 December 1975.

7. There appear to be some inaccuracies in Rhys's account of her family history. In his book, published before Rhys's autobiography, Louis James indicates in his footnotes that he consulted the Dominica National Archives for some of the family history that he mentions in his text. James identifies the great grandfather as a "John Potter Lockhart of Old Jewry, London" who acquired the 'several plantations and estates in Dominica . . . now known by the name of Genever Plantation,' some 1213 acres and 258 souls" (p. 45, James's ellipses). In his notes, James says: "The negotiations began in 1813 when Lockhart was evi-

dently at least visiting the island. They continued until the agreement found its final form in 1837." (p. 63) James also states that James Lockhart died on October 2, 1837 (which would be after the Emancipation Act), leaving his widow to continue running the estate through her overseer. James states that the estate house was burned down in 1844 when there were "rumors spread that it [a census taken] was the preliminary to a return to slavery. The black population rioted and the Genever estate was looted and burned." He adds that "in 1932 the blacks burnt down the new house" (p. 47).

It would seem that on certain details (events before and after Emancipation, dates, names) Rhys is not entirely accurate and we can assume that she relied on memory and family stories, indicating that the family history had assumed the role of myth and legend in her own mind.

8. Kenneth Ramchand, *The West Indian Novel and Its Background* (London: Faber and Faber, 1980), p. 32. All further references to this volume are included in the text.

9. Mary Cantwell, "A Conversation with Jean Rhys," *Mademoiselle*, Oct. 1974): 71.

10. *After Leaving Mr. Mackenzie* in *Jean Rhys: The Complete Novels* (New York: W.W. Norton, 1985), pp. 294–95. Rhys's ellipses. All further references to this book are from this edition and are included in the text.

11. *Wide Sargasso Sea* in *Jean Rhys: The Complete Novels* (New York: W.W. Norton, 1985), p. 467. All further references are to this edition and are included in the text.

12. Letter received from Diana Athill, 27 May 1983.

13. Telephone interview with David Plante, 21 May 1983.

14. In *Tigers Are Better Looking*.

15. David Plante, "Jean Rhys: A Remembrance," *Paris Review* 21, no. 76 (Fall 1979): 238–284. All further references appear in the text.

16. Thomas Staley, *Jean Rhys: A Critical Study* (Austin: University of Texas Press, 1979), p. 4. All further references to this work are included in the text.

17. This passage appears in a very similar form in the Black Exercise Book and the line, "The hills like clouds and the clouds like fantastic hills," also occurs in *Good Morning, Midnight*.

CHAPTER 2

1. "Overtures and Beginners Please" in *Sleep If Off, Lady* (New York: Harper & Row, 1976), p. 77. All subsequent quotes are from this edition and are included in the text.

2. In *Tigers Are Better Looking*, p. 76.

CHAPTER 3

1. As Martien Kappers-den Hollander has noted, Rhys's pen-name is a combination of her first husband's nickname and her father's name. Martien Kappers-den Hollander, "Jean Rhys and the Dutch Connection," *Maatstaf* 4 (1982): 30–40. This article, in slightly different form, was originally presented at a Jean Rhys Commemorative Colloquium at the MLA Convention, New York, 28 Dec. 1981.

2. My information about Lenglet is based on many sources but most useful

is Martien Kappers-den Hollander's article, cited above. Kappers-den Hollander, a Dutch scholar who has been most helpful to me, has done a lot of work on what she calls the "Dutch connection" of Jean Rhys. Her information is based on interviews with relatives of Lenglet, on the work of the Dutch historian Prof. L. de Jong, who is writing a work on the history of the Netherlands during the German occupation, on the 1973 autobiography *Dierbare Welrel (Dear World)* written by Lenglet's second wife, the Dutch writer Henriëtte van Eyck, who also knew Rhys, and on unpublished interviews with Rhys's and Lenglet's daughter, Maryvonne Moerman, who lives in Holland.

3. Telephone interview with David Plante, 21 May 1983. In "Jean Rhys: A Remembrance" in the *Paris Review* (21, no. 76 (Fall 1979): 238–284), Plante describes Rhys, their work together and conversations between them. In his book, *Difficult Women,* a description of his relationships with three women, among them Rhys, Plante includes a much-revised version of the *Paris Review* article. (David Plante, *Difficult Women: A Memoir of Three* (New York: Atheneum, 1983). I have relied on both pieces. The second differs in important areas from the original, although both essays follow the same shape and contain a great deal of the same material and passages.

In *Difficult Women* Plante has added some new stories and anecdotes, some of which are similar to those that later appeared in Rhys's posthumous autobiography, though the information they contain is at times abbreviated and at times expanded; some interesting discussions with her about writing; some new anecdotes that do not appear elsewhere or in the autobiography; some physical descriptions of Rhys—several quite unflattering; the name of Sonia Orwell, previously identified as a "friend," and a few stylistic changes.

He has cut some small introspections and a great deal of a rather haphazard chronology that he attempted to assemble with Rhys. Great sections of this chronology, however, had to do with Rhys's rendition to him of her affair with Ford Madox Ford, of her relationship and perception of Stella Bowen, of her work in the south of France as a ghostwriter, her later time with her first husband, Jean Lenglet, his involvement with the Ford affair, some information about her daughter by Lenglet and her eventual breakup with her husband and remarriage to Leslie Tilden Smith. Much of this information does not appear in any other source and I have used parts that seem reliable.

In addition, Plante has rearranged some of his text so that some of the material in the *Paris Review* piece is reorganized and apparently included as snatches of other conversations with Rhys—especially some of the material originally included in the chronology.

While these two essays are perhaps essentially the same, the changes described above lead one to question the possible accuracy of some of the renditions of the conversations between Plante and Rhys and also some of the information Plante reports as coming from Rhys. David Plante has told me his intention was not to do "something academic," but rather to write a "very personal" account (telephone interview, 21 March 1983).

4. Mary Cantwell, "A Conversation with Jean Rhys," *Mademoiselle,* Oct. 1974: p. 208.

5. Mary Cantwell, p. 208.

6. Jean Rhys, "Vienne," *Transatlantic Review,* No. 6 (Jan. 1925), p. 639.

7. Stella Bowen, *Drawn from Life: Reminiscences* (London: Collins, 1941),

p. 166. All further references to this memoir are from this edition and are included in the text.

8. Elgin W. Mellown, "Characters and Themes in the Novels of Jean Rhys," *Contemporary Literature* 13 (Autumn, 1972): pp. 458–475, 459–460. Further references to this article appear in the text.

9. Marcelle Bernstein, "The Inscrutable Miss Jean Rhys," *Observer,* 1 June 1969: 40–42; 49–50.

10. Letter from Jean Rhys, 22 July 1975.

11. John Hall, "Jean Rhys," *Arts Guardian,* 10 Jan. 1972: 8.

12. Nan Robertson, "Jean Rhys: Voyage of a Writer," *New York Times,* 25 January 1978.

13. Letter from Diana Athill, 19 October 1984.

14. Edouard de Nève, *Barred* (London: Desmond Harmsworth, 1932).

15. *Good Morning, Midnight* in *Jean Rhys: The Complete Novels* (New York: W.W. Norton, 1985), p. 423. All further references to this novel are from this edition and are included in the text.

16. Paul Delaney, "Jean Rhys and Ford Madox Ford: What 'Really' Happened," presented as a paper at a Jean Rhys Commemorative Colloquium at the MLA Convention, New York, 28 Dec. 1981. All page references below refer to an expanded version given to me by Mr. Delaney and appear in the text. Page references within quotations from Delaney's unpublished article refer to pages in *Barred*. Delaney notes that a comparison of the two texts finds the following omissions and changes:

1. Deletion of "passages that gave a moral or ideological analysis of the social hierarchy." Delaney adds that "Rhys may be only speeding up the narrative, but she also seems to be impatient with *any* theoretical explanation for the misuse of power by society's rulers. Her viewpoint is not that of the underclass, but of the underdog" (p. 8).

2. Delaney claims that Rhys "cut and revised" *Barred* "to produce a much more direct, rapid, and sensuous work, whose flavor is much closer to her own novels than Lenglet's somewhat ponderous and moralistic original" (p. 13).

3. Rhys cut "every mention of Hubner's (Ford's/Hueffer's) wife, and even of such passages as a casual reference to the frequency of 'ménages à trois" in Bohemian Paris (p. 161)" (p. 13).

4. "Rhys also toned down Lenglet's bitter criticism of Hubner, omitting passages ranging from innuendo about his sexual tastes to a jeer at his false teeth [pp. 94, 192]. But much more important is her move to effectively absolve Bowen of any guilt for what happened—presumably because Bowen had now herself been added to the list of victims of Ford's caprice" (p. 13).

5. Rhys omitted "some explicit sexual complaints against the hero's wife, Stania" (p. 6).

In a comparison of all three texts, Martien Kappers-den Hollander notes that the difference between the English and French version "is far from minimal" (p. 124). She points out that Rhys "scrapped . . . about twenty-five pages of text, or one-tenth of the entire manuscript" (p. 124) and that if one examines "any page taken at random from the English and French editions hardly a paragraph has remained unchanged" (p. 124). Furthermore she says that when Lenglet translated his original French manuscript into Dutch he used "with few exceptions" Rhys's English version (p. 124). Kappers-den Hollander concludes, "Reading the three versions of Edward de Nève's counterpart of *Quartet* one hears Jean Rhys and Jean Lenglet engaged in a long conversation about events still painful to them both, with *Barred* answering the charges made by *Sous les verrous,* and *In de Strik* offering the final gesture of reconciliation" (p. 129). Martien Kappers-den Hollander, "A Gloomy Child and Its Devoted Godmother: Jean Rhys, *Barred, Sous les Verrous* and *In de Strik*" in *Autobiographical and Biographical Writing in the Commonwealth,* ed. Doireann MacDermott (Departamento de Lengua y Literatura Inglesa, Universidad de Barcelona, 1984), pp. 123–130.

17. In *Sleep It Off, Lady,* p. 111. The University of Tulsa has a typescript copy of "The Chevalier of the Place Blanche" and at least one other story ("Vengeance"), both of which reflect collaboration with de Nève and both probably done in the 1920s.

18. Letter from Diana Athill, 19 October 1984.

19. Letter from Jean Rhys, 22 July 1975.

20. *Quartet* in *Jean Rhys: The Complete Novels* (New York: W.W. Norton, 1985), p. 220. All further references to this novel are from this edition and are included in the text.

21. Samuel Putnam, *Paris Was Our Mistress: Memoirs of the Lost and Found Generation* (New York: Viking, 1947), p. 127.

22. *The Left Bank and Other Stories,* with a preface by Ford Madox Ford (London: Jonathan Cape, 1927; reprint ed., New York: Books for Libraries Press, 1970), pp. 23–24. This is the only one of Rhys's books not to have been reprinted, except for the above photocopy, in its entirety. Some of the stories from *The Left Bank* do appear, however, in the second section of *Tigers Are Better Looking.* All further references to this book are included in the text.

23. Francis Carco, *Perversity* (Chicago: Covici, 1928).

24. Ford Madox Ford, *Letters,* ed. Richard M. Ludwig (Princeton: Princeton University Press, 1965), p. 177.

25. Letter from Jean Rhys, 5 Dec. 1975.

26. The Humanities Research Center possesses nine letters from Rhys to her friend Evelyn Scott, four of which include the date, 1936; all letters to Evelyn Scott referred to here are in this collection.

27. Selma Vaz Dias, "In Quest of a Missing Author," *Radio Times,* 3 May 1957, p. 25. All further references appear in the text.

28. Francis Wyndham, "Introduction" to *Wide Sargasso Sea* (New York: W.W. Norton, 1966), p. 11. This introduction appeared first in a more abbreviated form in *London Magazine* (Jan. 1960: 15–16), a draft of which Wyndham sent to Rhys. She corrected at least one fact that was mistaken in Vaz Dias's *Radio Times* article: the correction of her father's background from Scottish to Welsh (JRL, p. 172). However, in his *London Magazine* piece Wyndham is less specific about the "facts" of Rhys's discovery by Selma Vaz Dias than he is in the introduction to *Wide Sargasso Sea.*

29. Letter from Diana Athill, 19 Oct. 1984.

30. The first letter of this six-month contact with Vaz Dias has an envelope clipped to it by Vaz Dias in which she noted, "After a silence of 2 or 3 years from a London hotel or boarding house.—Her idea of 'Postures' for a play—ballads—letters. After these a second disappearance till 2nd Statesman advert by BBC which I told them to do." (McFarlin Library, "Guide to the Jean Rhys Collection," p. 16.)

31. Elgin W. Mellown, ed., *Jean Rhys: A Descriptive and Annotated Bibliography of Works and Criticism* (New York: Garland Publishing, 1984), p. xii.

32. Letter from Diana Athill, 20 Sept. 1983.

33. Letter from Diana Athill, 19 Oct. 1984.

CHAPTER 4

1. But some of the echoes in *Voyage in the Dark* of *A Portrait of the Artist as a Young Man* suggest that Rhys's book might have been influenced by Joyce's. In particular, Mother St. Anthony's talk of the Four Last Things and Anna's repetition in the cinema of the words, "never, not ever, never," (p. 67), suggest the Hellfire sermon in Part III of *A Portrait of the Artist*. The conclusion of *Voyage in the Dark,* ending as it does in April suggests an ironic commentary on Stephen's more optimistic vision in April at the end of Joyce's novel.

2. Simone de Beauvoir, *The Second Sex,* trans. H.M. Parshley (New York: Knopf, 1953), pp. 354–355. All references are to this edition and are included in the text.

3. William Mudford (1792–1848) was a journalist who also wrote short stories. "The Iron Shroud" is the most well-known and, according to *The Bedside Book of Famous British Stories,* ed. Bennett Cerf and Henry Moriarty (New York: Random House, 1940), pp. 57–69, first appeared in *Blackwood's Magazine.* The story also appears in *Gothic Tales of Terror,* ed. Peter Haining (New York: Taplinger, 1972), pp. 453–466.

Haining lists the author as anonymous but adds that "it has been established that the author was William Mudford" (p. 453). Haining also states that the story first appeared in *Blackwood's Magazine* in autumn, 1832, but I have been unable to locate it. There are differences between the two above texts and, when not otherwise noted, references are from Cerf and Moriarty's edition.

4. Colette, *The Vagabond,* trans. Enid McLeod (London: Secker & Warburg, 1954), p. 9. (All further references are from this edition and appear in the text.)

5. Frederick R. Karl, "Doris Lessing in the Sixties: The New Anatomy of Melancholy," *Contemporary Literature* 13, no. 1 (winter 1972): 15–33.

6. Wyndham's and Melly's transcription of this letter is slightly different from my own. The phrase, "(downward career of girl)" was inserted by Rhys above the already written line. Wyndham and Melly locate it *after* the word "dreamlike." The physical placement of the phrase by Rhys allows for either interpretation, but mine seems to me to be more in keeping with the pattern of the sentence.

7. Annis Pratt, "Archetypal Theory and Women's Fiction: 1688–1975," presented at a panel, "The Theory of Feminist Literary Critics," MLA Convention, San Francisco, 27 Dec. 1975. All further references to this paper appear in the text.

8. Annis Pratt, "Women and Nature in Modern Fiction," *Contemporary Literature* 13, no. 4 (Autumn 1972): 477. All further references to this article appear in the text.

9. Johann Wolfgang von Goethe, *Selected Poems,* ed. Christopher Middleton, "Mignon" trans. by Christopher Middleton (Boston: Suhrkamp/Insel Publishers, 1983), pp. 132–133. In the first line of "Mignon" ("Kenst du das Land, wo die Zitronen blühn,") "Zitronen" is often translated as citrus tree or orange tree, as in the song in *Voyage in the Dark.*

10. Letter from Richard O'Donoghue, Administrator-Registrar, Royal Academy of Dramatic Art, 14 June 1983.

11. Original ending to *Voyage in the Dark,* McFarlin Library, TS, Item #1:11, p. 15. Though my work made use of the manuscript version, Nancy Hemond Brown has recently published Rhys's preferred ending in *London Magazine* 25, nos. 1 and 2 (April/May 1985): 40–59. This line is on p. 52 in *London Magazine.* All further references appear in the text with the abbreviation *LM* when Brown's transcription of the ms and mine do not disagree.

12. V.S. Naipaul, "Without a Dog's Chance," *New York Review of Books,* 18 (18 May 1972): 29.

13. Walter Allen, *The Modern Novel in Britain and the United States* (New York: E.P. Dutton, 1964), p. 1.

14. Original ending to *Voyage in the Dark,* McFarlin Library, TS, Item #1:11, p. 20. Brown's transcription (*LM,* p. 56) omits a comma after the first occurrence of the phrase "so still" and normalizes the extended periods after the last word into an ellipsis.

15. Joan Givner, "Charlotte Brontë, Emily Brontë and Jean Rhys: What Rhys's Letters Show about that Relationship," presented at Jean Rhys Commemorative Colloquium, MLA Convention, New York, 28 Dec. 1981. All further references to this paper appear in the text.

CHAPTER 5

1. *Gothic Tales of Terror,* ed. Peter Haining (New York: Taplinger, 1972), p. 463.

2. Florence L. Barclay, *The Rosary* (New York and London: Knickerbocker Press, 1909).

3. Wayne Booth, *The Rhetoric of Fiction* (Chicago: University of Chicago Press, 1961).

CHAPTER 6

1. Elizabeth Vreeland, "Jean Rhys: The Art of Fiction LXIV," *Paris Review* 21, no. 76 (fall, 1979): p. 235.

2. Coulibri is the actual name of a Dominican estate that existed in St. Marks Parish at the tip of the island on the Martinique Canal. It existed as early as *1817* as indicated in Appendix XVI of *The West Indies in 1837* by Sturge and Harvey. In this detail, Rhys, as she does in *Voyage in the Dark,* includes "clues" that indicate that the heroine's home replicates the island of Dominica.

In a letter to Francis Wyndham, Rhys also mentions Coulibri. She writes: "The place I have called Coulibri existed, and still does. . . . It was this Part II [of *Wide Sargasso Sea*] which was so impossibly difficult. I had no facts at all. Or rather I had one—the place. Again a real place. It was a small "estate" my father bought. "Coulibri" was, for Dominica, an "old" estate. . . . (May 14, 1964; JRL, pp. 276–77). It is difficult to tell from Rhys's letter whether the actual estate named Coulibri was the one owned by her father or whether she uses the characteristics of his estate and the name of another owned by someone else.

3. *Paradise Lost,* Book I, ll. 254–255.

CHAPTER 8

1. The parallels between the plight of the pre-Emancipation Maroons and the post-Emancipation Cosway women are obvious. Of the Maroons, Edward Braithwaite writes: "The Maroon War was the result of white 'apartheid' policy. This small body of mountain-dwelling ex-slaves had won their independence in 1740, after a ten-year struggle against British/Jamaicans, but they had been relegated and confined to the area of their high and rather barren reservations." Edward Braithwaite, *The Development of Creole Society in Jamaica: 1770–1820* (Oxford: Clarendon Press, 1971), p. 248. All further references are included in the text.

2. The convent of "The Bishop's Feast" and *Wide Sargasso Sea* is apparently the same, peopled by the same nuns and Mother Superior. For example, "a young nun from Ireland" whom Antoinette sees "looking at herself in a cask of water, smiling to see if her dimples were still there" (p. 490), appears again in "The Bishop's Feast," now older. The narrator of that story says upon seeing a nun she recognizes from her childhood: "She was the little Irish nun, I had once seen smiling at her reflection in a barrel of water. There were no dimples now. She was a frightened old lady" (p. 34).

3. In *Sleep It Off, Lady*, pp. 23–30. All further references are included in the text.

4. Charlotte Brontë, *Jane Eyre* (New York: Dell, 1961), p. 456. All further references are included in the text.

5. "The Birthday," TS, Item 1:5 in the Jean Rhys Collection of the McFarlin Library, University of Tulsa, p. 8.

6. Nancy Friday, *My Mother/My Self: The Daughter's Search for Identity* (New York: Delacorte Press, 1977).

CHAPTER 9

1. Edward Braithwaite, *The Development of Creole Society in Jamaica: 1770–1820* (Oxford: Clarendon Press, 1971).

CHAPTER 10

1. Edward Braithwaite, *The Development of Creole Society in Jamaica* (Oxford: Clarendon Press, 1971), p. 162.

2. I Geo. III, c. 22; Act 24 of 1760, Clause X, *Acts of Assembly* (1769), vol. I, p. 55.

Selected Bibliography

PRIMARY SOURCES

A. Books by Jean Rhys.

The Left Bank and Other Stories, with a preface by Ford Madox Ford. London: Jonathan Cape, 1927; photo reprint ed. New York: Books for Libraries Press, 1970.

Jean Rhys: *The Complete Novels,* with an introduction by Diana Athill. New York: W.W. Norton, 1985. This collection contains all of Jean Rhys's novels but does not include the introduction by Francis Wyndham to *Wide Sargasso Sea.*

Wide Sargasso Sea, with an introduction by Francis Wyndham. New York: W.W. Norton, 1966.

Tigers Are Better Looking, with a selection from *The Left Bank.* London: André Deutsch, 1968; paperback, Middlesex: Penguin Books, 1972.

My Day: Three Pieces by Jean Rhys. New York: Frank Hallman, 1975.

Sleep It Off, Lady. New York: Harper & Row, 1976.

Smile Please: An Unfinished Autobiography. London: André Deutsch, 1979.

Jean Rhys Letters, 1931–1966. Francis Wyndham and Diana Melly, eds. London: André Deutsch, 1984.

B. Uncollected pieces by Jean Rhys, arranged by date of publication.

"Vienne." *Transatlantic Review,* Jan. 1925: 639–45. (This story appears in an expanded version in *The Left Bank.*)

"I Spy A Stranger." *Art and Literature,* winter 1966: 41–53.

"Temps Perdi." *Art and Literature,* winter 1967: 121–38.

"Making Bricks Without Straw." *Harper's,* July 1978: 70–71.

"The Whistling Bird." *New Yorker,* 11 Sept. 1978: 38–39.

C. Translations by Jean Rhys, arranged by date of publication.

Carco, Francis. *Perversity.* Chicago: Covici, 1928. This translation is credited to Ford Madox Ford but Ford, in several letters, attributed the translation to Jean Rhys; Rhys has acknowledged the work as hers.

Nève, Edouard de. *Barred.* London: Desmond Harmsworth, 1932.

D. Collections of unpublished manuscripts and letters by Jean Rhys.

Jean Rhys Collection. McFarlin Library, the University of Tulsa. Among its items, this collection contains manuscripts of unpublished stories, drafts and notes by Rhys, as well as letters both to and from her. In particular it contains the Black Exercise Book, the

unpublished conclusion of *Voyage in the Dark,* and "fictionalized" drafts of the
Mr. Howard episode. See "Guide to the Jean Rhys Collection," McFarlin Library, 1985.
Evelyn Scott Collection. Humanities Research Center, University of Texas at Austin. This
collection contains 42 letters by Rhys, in particular, 9 to Evelyn Scott dating from the
1930s.

E. Posthumously published manuscripts.

"Jean Rhys and *Voyage in the Dark,*" ed. and with an introduction by Nancy Hemond
Brown. *London Magazine,* 25, Nos. 1 & 2 (April/May, 1985): 40–59.

F. Personal letters and interviews.

Athill, Diana. Letter to author, 27 May 1983.
——. Letter to author, 29 September 1983.
——. Letter to author, 19 October 1984.
——. Letter to author, 21 November 1984.
Bateman, M.R., Headmistress, Perse School for Girls. Letter to author, 27 May 1983.
O'Donoghue, Richard, Administrator, Royal Academy of Dramatic Art. Letter to author,
14 June 1983.
Plante, David. Telephone interview. 21 May 1983.
Rhys, Jean. Letter to author, 5 September 1974.
——. Letter to author, 5 December 1975.
——. Letter to author, 22 July 1975.
Wyndham, Francis. Letter to author, 11 October 1985.

G. Published interviews with Jean Rhys.

Bernstein, Marcelle. "The Inscrutable Miss Jean Rhys." *Observer,* 1 June 1969: 40–42.
Cantwell, Mary. "A Conversation with Jean Rhys." *Mademoiselle* (Oct. 1974): 71.
Hall, John. "Jean Rhys." *Arts Guardian,* 10 Jan. 1972: 8.
Robertson, Nan. "Jean Rhys: Voyage of a Writer." *New York Times,* 25 Jan. 1978, pp. C1,
C11.
Vreeland, Elizabeth. "Jean Rhys: The Art of Fiction LXIV." *Paris Review* 21, no. 76 (Fall,
1979): 218–237.

H. Other.

Stang, Sondia J., ed. *The Presence of Ford Madox Ford: A Memorial Volume of Essays,
Poems and Memoirs.* Philadelphia: University of Pennsylvania Press, 1981, p. 214. This
collection contains a brief statement of a few lines by Jean Rhys about Ford Madox Ford.

SECONDARY SOURCES

A. Selected reviews of Jean Rhys's books, arranged according to original publication dates of her books.

The Left Bank and Other Stories:
New Republic, 16 Nov. 1927, p. 345.
New Statesman, 30 April 1927, p. 90.
New York Herald Tribune, 10 Feb. 1929, p. 8.

New York Times, 11 Dec. 1927, p. 28.
Saturday Review of Literature, 5 Nov. 1927, p. 287.
Times Literary Supplement, 5 May 1927, p. 320.

Quartet (Postures):

Bookman, April 1929, p. 193.
Gorman, Herbert. *New York Herald Tribune,* 10 Feb. 1929, p. 7.
Hazzard, Shirley. *New York Times Book Review,* 11 April 1971, p. 6.
Matthews, T. S. *New Republic,* 17 April, 1929, p. 258.
New York Times, 10 Feb. 1929, p. 8.
Saturday Review of Literature, 4 Oct. 1928, p. 936.
Times Literary Supplement, 4 Oct. 1928, p. 706.

After Leaving Mr. MacKenzie:

Clemons, Walter. *Newsweek,* 6 Mar. 1972, p. 77.
Cooke, Michael. *Yale Review,* Summer 1972, p. 599.
Graham, Gladys. *Saturday Review of Literature,* 25 July 1931.
Levin, Martin. *New York Times Book Review,* 27 Feb. 1972, p. 52.
Naipaul, V.S. "Without A Dog's Chance." *New York Review of Books,* 18 May 1972, p. 29.
New Republic, 16 Sept. 1931, p. 134.
New York Times, 28 June 1931, p. 6.
New Yorker, 8 April 1972, p. 130.
Orr, Leonard, "Two by Jean Rhys." *Village Voice,* 6 June 1974, p. 35.
Stone, Geoffrey, *Bookman,* Sept. 1931, p. 84.

Voyage in the Dark:

A.R. "Jean Rhys: la fille de Londres." *L'Express,* 6–12 May 1974, p. 5. (This is a review
    of a French translation, *Voyage dans les tenebres.*)
Britten, Florence H. *New York Herald Tribune,* 17 Mar. 1935, p. 34.
Frazer, Elizabeth. *Library Journal,* May 1968, p. 1919.
New Yorker, 24 August 1968, p. 119.
Publishers Weekly, 8 Jan. 1968, p. 65.

Good Morning, Midnight:

Broyard, Anatole. "A Difficult Year for Hats." *New York Times,* 26 Mar. 1974, p. 39.
Orr, Leonard. "Two by Jean Rhys." *Village Voice,* 6 June 1974, p. 35.
Ricks, Christopher. "Female and Other Impersonators." *New York Review of Books,* 23 July
    1970, p. 8.

Wide Sargasso Sea:

Allen, Walter. "Bertha the Doomed." *New York Times Book Review,* 18 June 1967, p. 5.
Braybrooke, Neville. *Spectator,* 28 Oct. 1966, p. 560.
Cook, Hillary. *Listener,* 19 Jan. 1967, p. 103.
Hearne, John. *Cornhill,* Summer 1974, pp. 323–33.

Hope, Francis. "The First Mrs. Rochester." *New Statesman,* 28 Oct. 1966, p. 638.
Kersh, Gerald. *Saturday Review of Literature,* 1 July 1967, p. 23.
Nation, 2 Oct. 1967, p. 638.
Publishers Weekly, 13 Feb. 1967, p. 75.
"A Fairy-Tale Neurotic." *Times Literary Supplement,* 17 Nov. 1966, p. 1039.

Tigers Are Better Looking:

Byatt, A.S. *New Statesman,* 29 Mar. 1968, p. 421.
Stade, George. *New York Times Book Review,* 20 Oct. 1974, p. 5.
Sullivan, Mary. *Listener,* 25 April 1968, p. 549.
Times Literary Supplement, 2 May 1968, p. 466.

Sleep It Off, Lady:

Bailey, Paul. "True Romance." *Times Literary Supplement,* 22 Oct. 1976, p. 1321.
Macauley, Robbie. "Things Unsaid and Said Too Often." *New York Times Book Review,*
    21 Nov. 1976, p. 7.
Wood, Michael. "Endangered Species." *New York Review of Books,* Nov. 1976, p. 30.

Smile Please: An Unfinished Autobiography:

Annan, Gabriele. "Turned Away by the Tropics." *Times Literary Supplement,* 21 Dec.
    1979, p. 154.
Time, 7 July 1980, p. T5.
Trilling, Diana. "The Odd Career of Jean Rhys." *New York Times Book Review,* 25 May
    1980, p. 1.

B. Books and Articles with Reference to Jean Rhys.

Alvarez, A. "The Best Living English Novelist." *New York Times Book Review,* 17 Mar.
    1974, pp. 6–7.
Ashcom, Jane N. "The Novels of Jean Rhys: Two Kinds of Modernism." Ph.D. disserta-
    tion, Temple University, 1981.
"A Woman's Lot" Review of BBC "Omnibus" program on Rhys which included an interview
    with her. *Times Literary Supplement,* 29 Nov. 1974, p. 1342.
Babakhanian, Grace S. "Expatriation and Exile as Themes in the Fiction of Jean Rhys."
    Ph.D. dissertation, University of Illinois at Urbana-Champaign, 1976.
Baer, Elizabeth Roberts. "The Pilgrimage Inward: The Quest Motif in the Fiction of Mar-
    garet Atwood, Doris Lessing, and Jean Rhys." Ph.D. dissertation, Indiana University,
    1981.
Bowen, Stella. *Drawn from Life: Reminiscences.* London: Collins, 1941.
Braybrooke, Neville. "Between Dog and Wolf." *Spectator,* 21 July 1967, pp. 77–78.
———. "Jean Rhys." In *Contemporary Novelists.* New York: St. Martins, 1972, pp. 1061–
    64.
Carter, Hannah. "Fated to Be Sad." *Guardian,* 8 Aug. 1968, p. 5.
Cummins, Marsha Z. "Point of View in the Novels of Jean Rhys: The Effect of a Double
    Focus." Paper presented at Jean Rhys Commemorative Colloquium, MLA Convention,
    New York, 28 Dec. 1981.

Delaney, Paul. "Jean Rhys and Ford Madox Ford: What 'Really' Happened." Paper presented at Jean Rhys Commemorative Colloquium, MLA Convention, New York, 28 Dec. 1981. (An expanded version of this paper was given to me by the author.)

Emery, Mary Lou. "Modernism and the Marginal Woman: A Sociocritical Approach to the Novels of Jean Rhys." Ph.D. dissertation, Stanford University, 1951.

Ford, Ford Madox. *Letters.* ed. Richard M. Ludwig. Princeton: Princeton University Press, 1965.

Froshaug, Judy. "The Book-Makers." *Nova,* Sept. 1967, pp. 4–5.

Givner, Joan. "Charlotte Brontë, Emily Brontë and Jean Rhys: What Rhys's Letters Show about That Relationship." Paper presented at Jean Rhys Commemorative Colloquium, MLA Convention, New York, 28 Dec. 1981.

Gordon, Eleanor, "Female Archetype and Myth in Jean Rhys's *Wide Sargasso Sea."* Paper presented at Jean Rhys Commemorative Colloquium, MLA Convention, New York, 28 Dec. 1981.

Hall, John. "Jean Rhys." *Guardian,* 10 Jan. 1972, p. 8.

Houts, Jan van. "Het gaatje in het gordjin" (with an introduction by Martien Kappers-den Hollander). *De Revisor,* 1982/2, pp. 16–25. This is a story based on van Houts' visits with Jean Rhys, which are also referred to by Rhys in her story "Who Knows What's Up in the Attic" in *Sleep It Off, Lady.*

James, Louis. *Jean Rhys.* London: Longman Group, 1978.

Kappers-den Hollander, Martien. "Jean Rhys and the Dutch Connection." *Maatstaf,* 4 (1982), pp. 30–40. This article was reprinted in *Journal of Modern Literature,* 11, No. 1 (March, 1984).

——. "A Gloomy Child and Its Devoted Godmother: Jean Rhys, *Barred, Sous les Verrous* and *In de Strik,"* in *Autobiographical Writing in the Commonwealth,* ed. Doireann MacDermott (Departamento de Lengua y Literatura Inglesa. Universidad de Barcelona, 1984), pp. 123–130. This is a compilation of papers presented at the European Association of Commonwealth Literature and Language Studies held in Sitges, Spain, April 1984.

Lane, Miriam. "Jean Rhys: The Work and the Cultural Background." Ph.D. dissertation, Tufts University, 1978.

Mellown, Elgin W. "Characters and Themes in the Novels of Jean Rhys." *Contemporary Literature* 13 (Autumn 1972), pp. 458–75.

——. *Jean Rhys: A Descriptive and Annotated Bibliography of Works and Criticism,* New York & London: Garland Publishing, 1984.

Mizener, Arthur. *The Saddest Story: A Biography of Ford Madox Ford.* New York: World Publishing, 1971.

Moss, Howard. "Going to Pieces." *New Yorker,* 16 Dec. 1974, p. 161.

Nebeker, Helen. *Jean Rhys: Woman in Passage.* Montreal: Eden Press, 1981.

Parkin, Molly. "Everything Makes You Want Pretty Clothes." *The Sunday Times,* 25 February 1973, p. 33.

Piazza, Paul. "The World of Jean Rhys." *The Chronicle of Higher Education,* 7 March 1977, p. 19.

Plante, David. *Difficult Women: A Memoir of Three.* New York: Atheneum, 1983.

——. "Jean Rhys: A Remembrance." *Paris Review* 21, No. 76 (Fall 1979), pp. 238–284.

Porter, Dennis. "Of Heroines and Victims: Jean Rhys and Jane Eyre." *The Massachusetts Review* 17, No. 3 (Autumn, 1976), pp. 540–541.

Ramchand, Kenneth. *The West Indian Novel and Its Background.* London: Faber and Faber, 1970.

Staley, Thomas F. *Jean Rhys: A Critical Study.* Austin: University of Texas Press, 1979.

Turner, Alice K. "Jean Rhys Rediscovered: How It Happened." *Publishers Weekly,* July 1, 1974, pp. 57–58.

Thurman, Judith. "The Mistress and the Mask: Jean Rhys's Fiction." *Ms.,* January 1976, p. 50.

Trilling, Diana. "The Liberated Heroine." *Times Literary Supplement,* 13 October 1978, pp. 1163–66.

"Twice Widowed." *Evening Standard,* June 12, 1967, p. 6.

Vaz Dias, Selma. "In Quest of a Missing Author." *Radio Times,* 3 May 1957, p. 25.

Wahlstrom, Ruth Margaret. "The Fiction of Jean Rhys." Ph.D. dissertation, University of Kentucky, 1977.

Webb, W.L. "Lately Prized." *Guardian,* 14 Dec. 1967, p. 7.

Wolfe, Peter. *Jean Rhys.* Twayne Publishers, 1980.

Wyndham, Francis. "Introduction to Jean Rhys." *London Magazine,* Jan. 1960, pp. 15–18. This is an earlier version of the same introduction that appears in every edition of *Wide Sargasso Sea* except *Jean Rhys: The Complete Novels.*)

C. General background.

Allen, Walter. *The Modern Novel in Britain and the United States.* New York: E.P. Dutton, 1964.

Barclay, Florence L. *The Rosary.* New York & London: The Knickerbocker Press, 1911.

Beauvoir, Simone de. *The Second Sex.* Trans. H.M. Parshley. New York: Knopf, 1953; paperback, New York: Vintage Books, 1974.

Booth, Wayne. *The Rhetoric of Fiction.* Chicago: University of Chicago Press, 1961.

Brontë, Charlotte. *Jane Eyre.* New York: Dell, 1961.

Carco, François. *Perversité.* Paris: Firenczi, 1925.

Colette. *The Vagabond.* Trans. Enid McLeod. Secker & Warburg: 1954; paperback, Middlesex: Penguin Books, 1960.

Dunning, R.C. "Twelve Poems." *Transatlantic Review,* April 1924, pp. 450ff. Contains the poem from which Rhys takes her epigraph for *Quartet.*

Flanner, Janet. *Paris Was Yesterday: 1925–1939.* Ed. Irving Drutman. New York: Viking, 1972.

Ford, Ford Madox. *Critical Writings of Ford Madox Ford.* Ed. Frank MacShane. Lincoln: University of Nebraska Press, 1964.

——. *The Good Soldier.* New York: Boni, 1927.

Friday, Nancy. *My Mother/My Self: The Daughter's Search for Identity.* New York: Delacorte Press, 1977.

Gilbert, Sandra M. and Susan Gubar. *The Madwoman in the Attic: The Woman Writer and the Nineteenth Century Imagination.* New Haven: Yale University Press, 1979.

Goethe, Johann Wolfgang von. *Selected Poems.* Ed. Christopher Middleton. Boston: Suhrkamp/Insel Publishers, 1983.

Gorman, Herbert. "Ford Madox Ford: A Portrait in Impressions." *Bookman,* Mar. 1928, pp. 56–57.

Hamnett, Nina. *Laughing Torso.* London: Constable, 1932.

Hemingway, Ernest. *A Moveable Feast.* New York: Scribner's, 1964.

Huddleston, Sisley. *Paris Salons, Cafés, Studios.* New York: Lippincott, 1928.

Hughes, Richard. *The Innocent Voyage (A High Wind in Jamaica.)* New York: Haynes & Brothers, 1929.

Karl, Frederick. "Doris Lessing in the Sixties: The New Anatomy of Melancholy." *Contemporary Literature* 13, No. 1 (Winter 1972), pp. 15–33.

Maupassant, Guy de. *Fort comme la Mort.* London: M. Walter Dunne, 1903.

Mudford, William. "The Iron Shroud." In *The Bedside Book of Famous British Stories.* Eds. Bennett Cerf and Henry Moriarty. New York: Random House, 1940. A slightly different version in *Gothic Tales of Terror.* Ed. Peter Haining. New York: Taplinger, 1972.

Pratt, Annis. "Archetypal Theory and Women's Fiction: 1688–1975." Paper presented at a panel, "The Theory of Feminist Literary Critics," MLA Convention, San Francisco, 27 Dec. 1975.

——. "Women and Nature in Modern Fiction." *Contemporary Literaature* 13, no. 4 (Autumn 1972), pp. 476–90.

Putnam, Samuel. *Paris Was Our Mistress.* New York: Viking, 1947.

Weiner, Seymour. *Francis Carco: the Career of a Literary Bohemian.* New York: Columbia University Press, 1952.

Young, Filson. *The Sands of Pleasure.* Boston: D. Estes & Co., 1905.

Zola, Emile. *Nana.* New York: Modern Library, 1928.

D. Background to Dominica and the West Indies.

Atwood, Thomas. *The History of the Island of Dominica: Containing a Description of Its Situation, Extent, Climate, Mountains, Rivers, Natural Production.* London: J. Johnson, 1791; reprint edition, London: Frank Cass, 1971.

Braithwaite, Edward. *The Development of Creole Society in Jamaica: 1770–1820.* Oxford: Clarendon Press, 1971.

Coleridge, Henry. *Six Months in the West Indies in 1825.* 1825; reprint edition, New York: Negro Universities Press, 1970.

Davy, John. *The West Indies, Before and Since Slave Emancipation.* London: W. and G. Cash, 1854.

Day, Susan De Forest. *The Cruise of the Scythian in the West Indies.* London: F. Tennyson Neely, 1899.

"Dominica." *West Indies and Caribbean Yearbook: 1976–77.* Ed. Colin Richards. Caribook, Ltd., n.d., pp. 386–403.

"Dominica." *Fact Sheets on the Commonwealth.* Issued by Reference Division, British Information Services, Oct. 1967.

Fermor, Patrick Leigh. *The Traveller's Tree: A Journey through the Caribbean Islands.* New York: Harper & Brothers, 1950.

Froude, James. *The English in the West Indies.* London: Longmans, Green, 1888.

Gurney, John Joseph. *A Winter in the West Indies.* London: John Murray, 1840; reprint edition, New York: Negro Universities Press, 1969.

Lewis, Gordon K. *The Growth of the Modern West Indies.* New York: Monthly Review Press, [1968].

Ober, F.A. *A Guide to the West Indies and Panama.* New York: Dodd, Mead, 1908.

Rodman, Seldon. *The Caribbean.* New York: Hawthorne Books, 1968.

Salmon, C.S. *The Caribbean Confederation: A Plan for the Union of the Fifteen British West Indian Colonies.* London: Cassell, 1888; reprint edition, n.p.: Frank Cass, 1971. Contains an argument against Froude.

Smith, Michael. *The Plural Society in the British West Indies,* Berkeley: University of California Press, 1965.

Sturge, Joseph and Thomas Harvey. *The West Indies in 1837 being the Journal of a Visit to Antigua, Montserrat, Dominica, St. Lucia, Barbados and Jamaica* London: Hamilton, Adams, 1838.

Ullman, James and Al Dinhofer. *The Official Caribbean Guide Book.* New York: Macmillan, 1968.

Wiseman, H.V. *A Short History of the British West Indies.* London: University of London Press, n.d.

Index

Sex (*continued*)
by heroines, 189; and evil, 186; as humiliation for heroines, 187–88; and love, 189–90; and men, 183–84; and men, in relation to devil, 193; in *Wide Sargasso Sea* compared to *Jane Eyre* (Charlotte Brontë), 192

Sex roles, in *Wide Sargasso Sea*, 149, 164

Sexes, the: and money, 96–97; power struggle between, 119; in *Wide Sargasso Sea* compared to *Quartet*, 191–92. *See also* Men; Women

Sexual imagery, female, and landscape of island in *Voyage in the Dark*, 113

Sexual initiation, of Phoebe (character) in "Goodbye Marcus, Goodbye Rose," 187

Sexual triangle, theme of, 26–27

Sexuality, 165; and father, 93–94; female, and abandonment, 191; ideal mother and, 178; male, and desire for possession, 191

Slaveowner, grandfather as, in Black Exercise Book and *Smile Please*, 20

Slavery: British views on, in *Wide Sargasso Sea*, 192; in *Voyage in the Dark*, 20. *See also* Enslavement

Sleep, desire for, in *Voyage in the Dark*, 102–4

Sleep It Off, Lady, 77

Smile Please: decision to become actress in, 44; envy of blacks in, 30–31; attitude toward books in, 137–38; convent in, 178; death of son, and Catholicism in, 52–53; family in, 38; father in, 22, 42; grandfather as slaveowner in, 20; London in, 41; money and first love affair in, 46; mother in, 27, 30–31; theme of outcast in, 26; religion in, 16–17; theme of rooms in, 104; and unpublished ending of *Voyage in the Dark*, 131; treatment of writing in, 47

Son, death of, and Catholicism in *Smile Please*, 52–53

Songs, used in *Voyage in the Dark*, 117. *See also* Music

Sous les verrous (Edouard de Nève). *See Barred* (Edouard de Nève)

Staley, Thomas, 9, 34–36, 37, 45, 55–56, 66, 68, 70, 72, 75; compared to David Plante, 67

Stepmother, in *Voyage in the Dark*, 93, 95, 96

Sturge, Joseph, and Thomas Harvey: *The West Indies in 1837*, 13–14

Sunday, image of, in *Voyage in the Dark*, 91, 109–10

"Temps Perdi," Carib Indians in, 15

Thomas, Dylan: "Fern Hill," 109

Tia (character), betrayal of Antoinette Cosway (character) by, 198–200, 201–2

"Tigers Are Better Looking," 45

Tigers Are Better Looking, and *The Left Bank and Other Stories*, 226n22

Tilden Smith, Leslie, 67, 68, 70, 220n6

Time, in *Voyage in the Dark*, 127; and *Wide Sargasso Sea*, 79–80. *See also* Dates; Past, the

Trees, English, dreaming about, in *Voyage in the Dark*, 120

Triangle, sexual. *See* Sexual triangle

Triple Sec, 54, 55, 56

The Vagabond (Colette), theme of rooms in *Voyage in the Dark* compared to, 105

Vaz Dias, Selma, 74–76, 226n28, 226n30; radio adaptation of *Good Morning, Midnight* by, 2, 72–74; and dramatization of *Voyage in the Dark*, 128–29

"Vengeance," and "The Chevalier of the Place Blanche," 226n17

"Vienne," 53, 56

Vivenzio (character) ("The Iron Shroud"), compared to Anna Morgan (character), 132–35

Voice: authorial versus narrative, in *Voyage in the Dark*, 138–39; in *Wide Sargasso Sea*, 143, 144, 158, 218

Voyage in the Dark, 1, 7–8, 83–140; and Black Exercise Book, 219n4; Carib Indians in, 15; ending of, in published versus unpublished versions, 128–31; ending of, compared to *Wide Sargasso Sea*, 130; unpublished ending of, and *Smile Please*, 131; father in, 23; home in, 49; and "Fern Hill" (Dylan Thomas), 109; intertextuality in, 135; reference to "The Iron Shroud" (William Mudford) in, 104, 106, 132–35; reference to "Kubla Khan"

(Samuel Taylor Coleridge) in, 101–2, 113; Jean Lenglet and Henriette van Eyck as translators of, 59; use of literary reference in, 132–39; reference to "Mignon" (Johann Wolfgang von Goethe) in, 117; reference to *Nana* (Emile Zola) in, 92, 113, 135–36, 139; Part One, 85–98; Part Two, 98–110; Part Three, 110–22; Part Four, 122–31; *A Portrait of the Artist as a Young Man* (James Joyce) as source for, 227n1; publishing history of, 56–57; theme of rooms in, compared to *The Vagabond* (Colette), 105; reference to *The Rosary* (Florence Barclay) in, 137, 139; slavery in, 20; structure of, 84–85; structure of, and doxology, 92; unpublished version of, 97; reference to *The West Indies in 1837* (Joseph Sturge and Thomas Harvey) in, 13–14; compared to *Wide Sargasso Sea,* 2–3, 79–80, 143; and act of writing, 139–40
Vreeland, Elizabeth, 44–45

West Indian novels. *See* Novels, West Indian
West Indies: mulattoes in, 204; as Paradise, 1–2; as setting, 80; white Creoles in, 21. *See also* Dominica; Island
West Indies in 1837, The (Joseph Sturge and Thomas Harvey), reference to, in *Voyage in the Dark,* 13–14
White Creoles. *See* Creoles, white
Wide Sargasso Sea, 76, 143–218; blacks in, 35, 124, 158–59; convent in "The Bishop's Feast" compared to, 229n2; death of

Max Hamer and writing of, 72; and *Jane Eyre,* 2, 145, 181, 188, 192, 193; men in, 158–70; mother in, 28; race relations in, 32; sexual relationships in, compared to *Quartet,* 191–92; structure of, 144; compared to *Voyage in the Dark,* 2–3, 79–80, 130, 143; women in, 171–96
Williams, Edward Rees (brother), 28
Williams, Ella. *See* Rhys, Jean
Williams, Minna Lockhart (mother), 20
Williams, Rhys (father), 22–23
Women, animal metaphors used to describe, 100–101; as caretakers, 177; attitude of Englishmen toward, 96; food served by, 102–3, 110; as outcasts, 100; single, attitude toward, 182; in *Voyage in the Dark,* 98–101; in *Wide Sargasso Sea,* 171–96. *See also* Sexes, the
Women, black. *See* Black women
Women, Creole. *See* Creole women
Women, English. *See* English women
Women writers, in Black Exercise Book, 136
Writing, act of, 70–71, 77, 78; in relation to autobiography, 1, 3–4; and relationships with men, 6; of nonfiction, 5; versus passivity, 140; treatment of, in *Smile Please,* 47; and *Voyage in the Dark,* 139–40
Wyndham, Francis, 9, 29, 74, 76, 221n12, 226n28, 227n6

Zelli, Marya (character), in *Quartet,* 63; and money, 53
Zola, Emile: *Nana,* 92, 113, 135–36, 139
Zombis, image of, in *Wide Sargasso Sea,* 156–57